Date: 4/16/14

320.540956 SAS
Sasson, Theodore,
The new American Zionism /

THE NEW AMERICAN ZIONISM

The New American Zionism

Theodore Sasson

NEW YORK UNIVERSITY PRESS

New York and London

NEW YORK UNIVERSITY PRESS
New York and London
www.nyupress.org

References to Internet websites (URLs) were accurate at the time of writing.
Neither the author nor New York University Press is responsible for URLs that
may have expired or changed since the manuscript was prepared.

LIBRARY OF CONGRESS CATALOGING-IN-PUBLICATION DATA
Sasson, Theodore, 1965- author.
The new American Zionism / Theodore Sasson.
pages cm
Includes bibliographical references and index.
ISBN 978-0-8147-6086-4 (cl : alk. paper)
 1. Zionism—United States—History. 2. Jews—United States—Politics and government. 3.
United States—Ethnic relations. I. Title.
DS149.5.U6S33 2013
320.54095694—dc23
                    2013023710

New York University Press books are printed on acid-free paper,
and their binding materials are chosen for strength and durability.
We strive to use environmentally responsible suppliers and materials
to the greatest extent possible in publishing our books.

Manufactured in the United States of America
10 9 8 7 6 5 4 3 2 1

Also available as an ebook

For Deborah,
Now . . . and always

CONTENTS

ACKNOWLEDGMENTS

This book emerged from my work at Brandeis University's Cohen Center for Modern Jewish Studies. I owe a special debt to the center's Director, Leonard Saxe, and Distinguished Scholar, Charles Kadushin. Len and Charles supported the project throughout its various stages, as co-investigators on studies of Jewish opinion, educational tourism, and philanthropy, as partners to numerous conversations that helped me formulate the book's argument, and as careful reviewers of the final manuscript. I also owe a debt to the rest of the Cohen Center team, for discussion of the book's ideas, for practical assistance with data, analysis, and figures, and for serving as coauthors of many of the studies cited in the book. Thanks especially to Shahar Hecht, Michelle Shain, Mathew Boxer, Graham Wright, Deborah Grant, Masha Sud Lokshin, Annette Koren, and Fern Chertok.

Nearly a decade ago, during my sabbatical in Israel, Ezra Kopelowitz and Steven M. Cohen invited me to join a faculty seminar at Hebrew University's Institute for Advanced Studies. The seminar enabled me to make the professional transition from criminology to the study of contemporary Jewry and Israel. Over the years, Ezra became a good friend and supportive colleague and Steven a generous supporter of my work, even when it challenged some of his own. During the sabbatical, I also met Shaul Kelner and Ephraim Tabory. Both became good friends, coauthors, and intellectual sounding boards. Thanks to Ezra, Steven, Shaul, and Ephraim—and to Mala Tabory as well—for reading and commenting on the book manuscript.

I had the help of several very talented research assistants. Special recognition is due to Hillel Buechler and Yael Kletter, who contributed greatly to the research on American Jewish giving to causes in Israel; Hillel also led the research on media coverage of Israel advocacy organizations. I am also grateful for the research assistance of Emily Baum, Yana Bushmelov, Benjamin Briscer, and Monica Pevzner. As a Brandeis doctoral student and research fellow at the Cohen Center, Eitan Melchior helped me with the research on American Jewish travel to Israel. Eitan was a brilliant scholar and wonderful colleague, whose life was tragically shortened by illness. He is sorely missed.

I am grateful to Jennifer Hammer at NYU Press for championing the book, and to the anonymous reviewers whose suggestions prompted me to rethink and revise parts of the manuscript. The book received indispensable practical support from my home institutions. Brandeis University's Cohen Center supported me during the final several months of full-time writing. The Middlebury College Faculty Professional Development Fund enabled me to make a number of research trips. Students in my Middlebury College course on Diasporas and Homelands introduced me to a wide range of case studies that helped sharpen the book's comparative dimension.

During the latter stages of this project I began working for the Mandel Foundation. My thoughts about Jewish peoplehood and the future of the Israel-diaspora relationship reflect conversations with Mandel colleagues, in particular Jehuda Reinharz, Daniel Pekarsky, and Eli Gottlieb.

I have had seemingly endless conversations with colleagues and friends about the book's core themes. For challenging my thinking—and occasionally agreeing with me—I'd like to thank David and Alisa Dolev, Sharon Cohen Anisfeld and Shimon Anisfeld, Michael and Sara Paasche-Orlow, Jon Levisohn and Emily Beck, Dan Judson and Sandy Falk, Jon Regosin and Randy Berkowitz, Perry Lessing, Robert Schine, David Mittelberg, and Eric Fleisch.

Finally, I would like to thank my wife, Deborah Grant, for her encouragement and support, and my children, Aryeh, Kineret, and Asher, for not teasing me nearly as much as they would have liked about my peculiar preoccupation with American Jews and their attachment to Israel.

have *different* visions for peace in the Middle East, come together united in the support of the state and people of Israel.[1]

The mood in the hall was serious and somber. An Israeli woman studying for the year in Boston as part of a program sponsored by an American Jewish foundation described the challenges she and her family had experienced living in a community in southern Israel within missile range of Gaza. The head of Boston's federation of Jewish communal organizations addressed the assembled crowd by video link from the southern Israeli town of Sderot and described what the Boston Jewish community could do to help.

The hastily assembled crowd, spanning the spectra of age and religious denomination—and including long-time residents as well as new immigrants from Russia and Israel—suggested the ongoing importance of Israel to the Boston Jewish community. The gathering also reflected new currents in American Jews' relationship to Israel. The broad cosponsorship of the event reflected the increased diversity of organizations that mediate the diaspora's connection to the Jewish state. The Israeli speaking from Boston and the Bostonian speaking from southern Israel dramatized the increased circulation of Israelis and American Jews and the role of technology in facilitating more direct contact. Finally, the Rabbi's remarks—highlighting unity on the core issue of "support for the state and people of Israel" but recognizing "diverse political views" and "different visions for peace in the Middle East"—acknowledged the political polarization that in ordinary times preoccupies this community.

In recent years, many journalists and social scientists have described American Jews as "distancing" from Israel. Yet as this book shows, the evidence suggests something perhaps surprisingly closer to the opposite: Across multiple fields, including advocacy, philanthropy, and tourism, American Jews have stepped up their level of engagement with Israel. Attitudinally, they remain as emotionally attached to Israel as they have been at any point during the past quarter century. Nonetheless, the relationship of American Jews to Israel has changed in several important ways. Today, American Jews are more likely to advocate politically on behalf of their own personal views and target their Israel-bound donations to causes they care about personally. They are also more likely to connect to Israel directly, through travel and consumption of Israeli news and entertainment, often through the Internet. With these changes, American Jews are increasingly behaving like other contemporary diaspora communities—they are becoming a *normal* diaspora. As a result, Israel may become more personally meaningful for many American Jews, even as, paradoxically, their capacity to influence American and Israeli policies diminishes as they no longer speak with a unified voice.

* * *

Scholars in the burgeoning academic field of diaspora studies describe the past quarter century as a period of increased diaspora engagement with homeland culture, politics, and society. The digital information revolution, advent of social media, declining cost of international travel, and expansion of multiple citizenship regimes—developments often summarized by the concept of globalization—have made it easier than ever for diasporans to participate in social and political life both "here" and "there" at the same time.[2]

As a result, members of diasporas worldwide remain in regular contact with their friends and relatives abroad, travel frequently between their host and homeland communities, and consume homeland news, sports, and entertainment.[3] In some instances, diaspora communities have united to support newly independent homeland states, to respond to existential threats that affect the homeland, or to support efforts to overthrow oppressive homeland regimes.[4] More commonly, diaspora organizations provide political and philanthropic support for a narrower range of competing homeland projects. South Asian diaspora groups in the United States and the United Kingdom support diverse Hindu, Sikh, and Muslim causes.[5] Mexican, Brazilian, Turkish, and Dominican diaspora groups support rival homeland political parties.[6] Nigerian diaspora groups in the United Kingdom support diverse, often antagonistic, subnational ethnic collectivities.[7]

Throughout the modern period, Jews have in many respects been the prototypical diaspora. Dispersed globally, they maintained connections across diverse centers of diaspora life, with communities in their ancestral homeland, and eventually with the newly established state of Israel.[8] They established hybrid cultures combining their diverse diaspora and religious traditions with the values and customs of their countries of settlement.[9] They also created organizations to promote their own well-being in their countries of settlement, to support the Jewish community of Palestine and eventually the state of Israel, and to assist distressed Jewish communities throughout the world.[10]

During the first four decades of Israel's existence, however, the pattern of American Jewish engagement with the modern state was unusual. In contrast to almost all contemporary diaspora communities, American Jews were not an immigrant diaspora with personal memories of life in Israel. As a result, their knowledge of Israeli culture and society was relatively superficial. No more than one-third ever visited Israel in person, and few had command of the Hebrew language. Rather than draw upon Israeli news sources or firsthand experience, American Jews looked to a leadership cadre of rabbis and organizational functionaries for information about the Jewish state. As a result, American Jews tended to conceive of Israel in highly idealistic terms.

Nonetheless, as the most important center of diaspora life following the destruction of European Jewry, American Jewry played a key role supporting the Zionist enterprise from outside the homeland. American Jews established an unparalleled set of organizations to raise funds and cultivate diplomatic support for the Jewish state. In the philanthropic arena, the United Jewish Appeal coordinated national campaigns that raised billions of dollars to finance immigration, settlement, and economic development. In the diplomatic arena, a small number of elite-dominated organizations, including AIPAC, the Presidents Conference, and the American Jewish Committee, forged consensus around the principle that pro-Israel political advocacy in the United States must support the policies of Israel's elected governments. Although individual Jews might criticize Israel's policy decisions in public, Jewish organizations were effectively discouraged from doing so.

The sociologist Steven M. Cohen and political scientist Charles Liebman described the pattern of American Jewish engagement with Israel during this formative period as the "mobilized model."[11] The model entailed centralized fundraising, consensus-oriented political advocacy, and deference to Israeli political authorities in key areas, including policies on war and peace and how diaspora-supplied funds would be allocated for the purposes of state building. The model rested upon American Jewry's highly idealistic perception of the Jewish state, an orientation that reflected the great cultural, social, and geographic distance that separated American Jewry from Israel.

Over the past quarter century, aspects of the mobilization model have weakened and new forms of engagement, more typical of contemporary diaspora communities, have become increasingly evident. The changes may be characterized in terms of three transformations:

1. *Personalization.* American Jews increasingly relate to Israel personally and experientially rather than through their communal organizations. Today, American Jewish young adults are much more likely than their predecessors to travel to and study and volunteer in Israel—a phenomenon related but not restricted to the popular Birthright Israel program that funds educational tours. At all ages, American Jews are more likely to consume Israeli news and culture (in translation), advocate on behalf of their personal political views, and give to causes of their own choosing.

2. *Organizational diversification.* The organizational vehicles through which American Jews connect to Israel have diversified. The large, umbrella, federated, and representative organizations that long structured the relationship are mostly in a state of decline. They are increasingly replaced by numerous single-purpose organizations now operating in the fields of philanthropy, tourism, and advocacy.

3. *Polarization.* American Jewish advocacy in relation to Israel has become increasingly polarized and contentious. Alongside the centrist advocacy organizations that monopolized the field in the 1970s and 1980s, new groups on the right and left increasingly promote their own partisan political visions and assail one another for threatening Israel's future. Contentious politics have diffused from national advocacy organizations focused on the U.S. government to campus and community organizations where struggles develop over what qualifies as "pro-Israel" and who should be included in the communal tent.

American Jews are thus engaging with Israel more directly, visiting the country, supporting diverse political causes, and targeting their giving. At the same time, the politics of Israel have become more contentious in the American Jewish community, straining community relations. These new forms of engagement are evidence of a gradual paradigm shift. The mobilization model that characterized American Jewish engagement with Israel is in a state of decline. Alongside it, a new "direct engagement" model has emerged, especially among the most active segments of the community. Although American Jewry continues to support comparatively large and influential organizations, American Jewish engagement with Israel increasingly resembles the pattern established by other contemporary diasporas, a pattern characterized by diverse political and philanthropic projects, contentious politics, frequent homeland travel, high levels of consumption of homeland news and entertainment, and realistic rather than idealistic attitudes toward the homeland state and society.

The gradual shift toward direct engagement reflects a variety of political, social, and technological developments. In the 1990s, during implementation of the Oslo Peace Accords, the polarization of the Israeli political establishment and outreach by opposition politicians to their diaspora supporters undermined the American Jewish norm of consensus support for Israel's official positions. In the following decade, the development of the Internet and expansion of educational tourism for young adults provided American Jews with unprecedented access to internal Israeli political debates, often mediated through Israel's partisan news outlets. The overtures by diverse Israeli political actors and the vastly enriched information environment increased the desire of highly engaged American Jews to choose sides in Israel's internal political debates and express their own personal views and values. At the same time, the development of the web and new social media greatly facilitated the launch of new start-up organizations in the fields of advocacy, philanthropy, tourism, and communications.

Changes in how American Jews relate to Israel have been widely observed but generally misunderstood by observers of American Jewish life. As noted, in recent years, scholars, journalists, and organizational leaders have mostly described American Jews as "distancing" from Israel, especially in the younger generation. In this discourse, the concept of distancing has been employed to describe both mounting alienation and diminishing engagement with Israel through political advocacy, philanthropy, and tourism. Those who subscribe to this perspective have attributed the phenomenon to various causes, including intermarriage, the changing historical experience of successive generations, and political alienation.[12]

As this book shows, however, the "discourse on distancing" is rooted in erroneous analysis of the empirical evidence.[13] Writers who allege distancing commonly make two interpretive errors. First, several scholars, observing the weakening of centralized philanthropy and consensus advocacy—practices associated with the mobilization paradigm—deduce diminished American Jewish interest in Israel.[14] However, as we will see, these writers neglect the replacement of these practices by new forms of engagement, for example, partisan advocacy, direct giving, and independently sponsored educational tourism.

Second, many scholars have observed the tendency of emotional attachment to Israel to decline from the oldest to the youngest age cohorts in individual, cross-sectional surveys. These writers have interpreted the pattern as evidence of a steady decline in emotional attachment to Israel across the generations and predicted further decline in the future. For example, in a report on a 2007 national survey, titled *Beyond Distancing: Young Adult American Jews and Their Alienation from Israel*, Steven M. Cohen and the sociologist Ari Y. Kelman wrote, "We are in the midst of a massive shift in attitudes toward Israel, propelled forward by the process of cohort replacement, where the maturing younger cohorts that are the least Israel-engaged are replacing the oldest cohorts that are the most Israel-engaged." They attributed the alleged shift in attitudes to the fading memory of Israel's struggle for existence and rising incidence of intermarriage and predicted a "long-term and ongoing decline in Israel attachment" in the years to come.[15] However, it is important to understand that younger Jews have always been less emotionally attached to Israel than their middle-aged and elderly counterparts, and they have tended to become more emotionally attached as they grow older. In other words, the age-related pattern of attachment to Israel observed in many cross-sectional surveys is not evidence of *decreasing attachment across the generations*; rather, it is evidence of *increasing attachment over the life course*.[16]

Nonetheless the Cohen-Kelman report proved greatly influential. For example, journalism professor Peter Beinart cites the report as the main substantiation for his claim, developed in a *New York Review of Books* article and subsequent book, that young adult Jews have become alienated from Israel.[17] In Beinart's account, however, the alienation of the younger generation is not due primarily to fading memory or intermarriage; rather, it is the result of political disillusionment with the policies of right-wing Israeli governments and their American Jewish apologists. For Beinart, the expansion of West Bank settlements, Israeli foot-dragging in negotiations for a two-state solution, the deterioration of Israeli civil rights and human rights, and—above all else—the failure of American Jewish leaders to vigorously oppose these developments drove American Jewish young adults out of the Zionist camp.[18]

Sparked by these works, a great deal of scholarly and journalistic attention has been paid to the alleged distancing of American Jews from Israel. The journal *Contemporary Jewry* published a special issue on distancing, featuring contributions by nearly two dozen social scientists.[19] A leading Israeli think tank, the Jewish People Policy Institute, assigned a research group to the topic and issued a lengthy report.[20] The American Jewish Committee convened a task force of researchers and practitioners to contemplate the dimensions of the problem and what to do about it. Leading Jewish newspapers and magazines, including *The Forward, Tablet Magazine, Sh'ma,* and *The Jewish Week,* have analyzed the topic; the mainstream press has covered it as well.[21]

Unsurprisingly, the American Jewish connection to Israel has also become a leading concern of Jewish organizations and the Israeli government. Israel's Jewish Agency has reoriented its mission from promoting *aliyah* (immigration) to cultivating diaspora connections to the Jewish state. In 2012, the Israeli Knesset (Parliament) held hearings on how to respond to the distancing of American Jews, and Israel president Shimon Peres convened a conference that addressed the topic. In short, in recent years, the relationship of American Jewry to Israel has become a leading concern of scholars, journalists, and the political and organizational elites of the Jewish world. The dominant theme in this expansive discourse has been that the world's two largest Jewish communities are parting ways. The key challenge has been defined as what to do about it.

In contrast, this book argues that American Jewish engagement with Israel is as strong as ever but developing along new lines that make American Jews more like other contemporary diaspora groups. The book's method is not to present the paradigm shift from mobilization to direct engagement as a neat package without internal strains or contradictions. Instead, I draw upon historical and social scientific evidence (including many studies I conducted with colleagues at Brandeis University's Cohen Center for Modern Jewish Studies) to describe, in as accurate a fashion as I am able, developments in diverse "diaspora-homeland fields."

The notion of *diaspora-homeland fields* borrows a key concept from the sociologist Pierre Bourdieu. As actors in a modern setting, diasporans organize their activities in relation to homelands in distinctive fields, each populated by characteristic organizations, professionals, and practices, and maintained through distinctive funding and training institutions, professional networks, and communications media.[22] This book examines developments in the fields of political advocacy, fundraising, educational tourism, immigration, and communications. Each of these fields is in some sense a world unto itself: it is staffed by its own network of professionals, is responsive to its own achievement criteria, and generates its own internal professional discourse. The diverse fields are linked into a broader network by common sources of funding (e.g., federations and foundations) and as objects of discussion in the nonprofessional Jewish public arena. They are also responsive to the external environment—Jewish and general—and therefore potentially develop along similar trajectories.

The book continues in Chapter 1 with a historical overview of the institutions and practices established by American Jews to support Israel during the two decades before and four decades after the establishment of the state. The aim of this chapter is to describe the rise of the mobilization paradigm as a backdrop against which more recent developments can be measured.

Chapters 2 to 5 then examine trends since the late 1980s in the various diaspora-homeland fields, emphasizing the rise of direct engagement practices. Chapter 2 examines developments in the field of Israel advocacy, tracking in particular the rise of independent political activity on the right and left and describing the fragmented state of the field today. The chapter then explores the diverse arenas in which today's partisan advocacy organizations confront one another while pursuing their political goals, including Congress and the White House, university campuses and community organizations, and the mass media and public opinion.

Chapter 3 describes developments in the field of philanthropy, charting the decline of the federated United Jewish Appeal and the rise of independent fundraising by an ever-expanding number of Israeli and American Jewish nonprofit organizations. The chapter also examines the growing contentiousness regarding what I describe as "political philanthropy"—fundraising for partisan causes of the right and left that increasingly spark controversy in Israel and the United States.

Chapter 4 describes developments in the fields of educational tourism and immigration, examining the privatization of these core Zionist functions through the establishment of new frameworks and the dramatic expansion of the field. The chapter closely examines the main features of Birthright Israel educational tourism, focusing in particular on the ideological messages the program seeks to deliver and the dynamics of *mifgashim* (structured encounters) between American Jewish tourists and their Israeli peers.

Chapter 5 examines developments in the field of mass media and their relation to changing attitudes and feelings. American Jews increasingly consume news of Israel through diverse sources including Israeli media and visits to the country. As a result, they increasingly express a "new realism" that views Israeli society and government policies as imperfect and in need of reform. The chapter describes the views of American Jews on contentious, Israel-related issues, including the conflict with the Palestinians and the issues of religious and minority rights, and examines trends in emotional attachment to Israel.

The book concludes in Chapter 6 by examining how *personalization*, *organizational diversification*, and *polarization* have contributed to the rise of a new direct engagement paradigm. The chapter summarizes the social, technological, and political forces driving the paradigm shift, and explores its implication for the future relationship of American Jews to Israel. As a result of new forms of homeland engagement, American Jews' ties to Israel will likely remain strong even as their political and philanthropic influence, increasingly divided across multiple targets, begins to dissipate. The volume concludes by situating the case of the Jewish diaspora in the broader field of diaspora studies.

Summarizing a book in a very few words is exceedingly difficult. The title *The New American Zionism* has the advantage of focusing readers on new developments in American Jews' relationship to Israel. The title achieves its purpose if readers understand the book's focus to be on changes in the *practical ways* in which American Jews express their attachment to the Jewish state. In the final chapter, I will have a bit to say about Zionist ideology. Analysis of currents in Zionist thought, however, is not a main focus of the book.

Finally, insofar as much of the book explores the changing organizational landscape, the text necessarily mentions dozens of American Jewish organizations. Whenever possible to do so without overburdening the narrative, I provide a few words of explanation about each organization when it is first mentioned. To fill in the gaps, and assist readers who are unfamiliar with the sprawling American Jewish polity, I have also included brief descriptions of the organizations mentioned in the text in the appendix and a list of Hebrew terms in the glossary.

1

Mobilization

Writing in the *Jerusalem Post* in mid-1985, Abba Eban, Israel's former ambassador to the United States, described the reticence of American Jewish leaders to criticize Israeli government policies. "Some Diaspora Jews renounce any analytical role and give blind endorsement to any doctrine or practice that comes out of Israel," Eban observed. "They are thus for everything—and the opposite—according to the rise and fall of the electoral seesaw."[1] The comment aptly captured the posture of American Jewish leaders toward Israel during the two decades that followed the 1967 Six-Day War, a period in which American Jewish organizations achieved a high degree of unity in their advocacy for Israel and did so for the most part by taking their lead from Jerusalem.

But it was not always thus. Prior to the founding of the state of Israel, diverse American Zionist organizations competed politically with their counterparts in Palestine for leadership in the World Zionist Organization, and with non-Zionist and anti-Zionist groups in the United States for the support of rank-and-file American Jews. The formation of a united front of American Jewish organizations to support the Jewish national project began in the 1930s with the United Jewish Appeal, an annual campaign that raised funds for the Jewish settlement in Palestine. After establishment of the state, Israeli officials (including Eban himself) maneuvered to shift responsibility for representing Israel in the U.S. political arena from partisan Zionist organizations to more pliant mainstream American Jewish groups. Together with their American Jewish allies, they established AIPAC to lobby the U.S. Congress and the Presidents Conference to lobby the White House and State Department. The dominance of these organizations played a major role in promoting unconditional support for Israel and deference to the programmatic and policy goals of its government.

The willingness of rank-and-file American Jews to eschew partisan positions regarding Israeli policies reflected their relationship to Israel as well. Few American Jews learned Hebrew, made repeat trips to Israel, or seriously contemplated aliyah. For most, Israel's meaning was less personal and political than symbolic: Israel represented the survival and rebirth of the Jewish people after the Holocaust. For many, it also represented Jewish military valor and a convergence of Jewish and progressive social values. The willingness of American Jews to provide blanket support for Israeli policies reflected their devotion to Israel as a cause, their tendency to idealize the state and its leadership, and their great remove from the political conflicts that, by the mid-1970s, increasingly divided Israelis.

The "mobilization" phase in the relationship of American Jews to Israel reached a high-water mark between the 1967 Six-Day War and the 1987 Palestinian Intifada—the period that is the main focus of this chapter. By the end of the 1980s, Jewish organizations were straining to maintain consensus, and conflicts between American Jewish leaders and Israeli officials were increasingly spilling over into the public arena. The stage was set for the fragmentation that would follow in the decade of the 1990s.

Building Institutions

American Jews were slower than their European and Russian counterparts to embrace Zionism. Focused on achieving full integration within the United States, many feared that declaring support for establishment of a Jewish state would cause their fellow Americans to doubt their loyalty as American citizens.[2] It was only after Louis Brandeis, a lawyer and future Supreme Court justice, crafted a distinctive American version of Zionism that the movement found its footings within the ranks of American Jewry. As the head of the American branch of the World Zionist Organization during World War I, Brandeis recast Zionism as a movement for the rescue and resettlement of persecuted European Jews. The aim of the movement would not be to ingather the entire global Jewish diaspora within a new state, as many European Zionists held, but rather to create a refuge for those who suffered anti-Semitism.[3] American Jews could support the Zionist cause without belying any intention to leave the United States. Moreover, for Brandeis, Zionism was an expression of loyalty to fundamental American values including freedom, democracy, and civil rights. By championing the cause, American Jews could affirm rather than cast into doubt their devotion to the United States.

The leaders of mainstream American Jewish organizations, however, remained unconvinced. In particular, the leadership of the elite and influential American Jewish Committee (AJC) regarded the Zionist project as unworkable and at odds with the need to promote civil rights and equality for Jews in the United States, and relief for European Jewish communities devastated by the war in Europe. At most, they were willing to extend material support to the Jewish community of Palestine, but not to commit political support to the Zionist project to create a fully independent Jewish state.

The United Jewish Appeal

In the 1920s and '30s, Zionist and non-Zionist organizations competed for donations from American Jews for overseas projects. The AJC raised funds primarily for the Joint Distribution Committee (JDC), an agency established during World War I and dedicated primarily to relief and rescue operations in Europe. The Zionist groups—including the Zionist Organization of America (ZOA), Hadassah (a women's group), the Labor Zionists, and the Religious Zionists—raised funds for the United Palestine Appeal (UPA). The UPA in turn supported settlement and development projects in the *Yishuv*—the Jewish community of Palestine.

During the 1930s, at the urging of local federations of Jewish charities, the JDC and the UPA experimented with joint campaigns.[4] The aim was to achieve better overall results than either organization could achieve independently by lowering fundraising costs and reducing duplicative appeals. A formula to divide campaign revenues between the organizations was negotiated in advance, with the JDC as the senior partner. The campaigns were conducted as part of the annual community campaigns of the local federations. The initial results, however, were disappointing, and both organizations resumed independent fundraising.

As the crisis in Europe intensified, the umbrella organization of the local federations again promoted the idea of a joint emergency campaign. The reconstituted United Jewish Appeal (UJA) conducted its first campaign in 1939, for "relief and rehabilitation in overseas lands, the upbuilding and defense of the Jewish homeland in Palestine, and assistance and adjustment for refugees in the United States."[5] The main partners were the JDC and the UPA; a portion of the proceeds was also set aside for refugee resettlement in the United States. The campaign raised $16.25 million, a sum that fell short of the goal but was far greater than the results of previous efforts. The UPA's portion—about one-quarter of the total—was dispersed by the Jewish Agency in Jerusalem, which served as the de facto government of the Jewish community of Palestine.[6]

Reflecting the concern of mainstream American Jewish organizations that fundraising for the UPA not be construed as un-American or evidence of dual loyalty, the campaigns conducted during the war emphasized the UJA's patriotic character. The campaigns featured endorsements by American dignitaries including Eleanor Roosevelt and President Franklin D. Roosevelt. In 1941, President Roosevelt's letter claimed that "the arms of Judea and America are interlocked to bring common victory to the ideals of the ancient prophets which have been enshrined in the American way of life." In 1943, the president wrote that the UJA "sustains the spirit of freedom and democracy."[7]

During the critical period between the end of World War II and the establishment of Israel, the UJA set ever more ambitious campaign goals: $100 million for 1946, $170 million for 1947, $250 million for 1948. To achieve these goals, the UJA, under the leadership of Henry Montor, mobilized thousands of volunteer fundraisers and implemented tactics aimed at eliciting maximum contributions from every potential donor. Major givers were organized into national and local business divisions.[8] Campaign co-captains and lieutenants were assigned to divisions to solicit donors. Private solicitations of major donors were followed by public events that included "card calling"—announcement of each attendee's previous year's pledge amount in the expectation that it should be exceeded in the current campaign. Smaller donors were solicited through door-to-door canvassing. Campaign leaders were sent on missions to visit displaced-persons camps in Europe and the Jewish community in Palestine and to return with firsthand reports. UJA officials, Zionist leaders, and public officials from the Jewish community in Palestine traveled throughout North America speaking at campaign events.

As the attention of American Jews increasingly shifted from Europe to Palestine, the portion of the annual campaign allocated to the UPA increased. Between 1945 and 1948, the UJA raised over $400 million— the equivalent of nearly $4 billion in 2012 dollars—for the development and defense of the Jewish community in Palestine.[9] The funds were used to resettle refugees and transform the Yishuv's paramilitary defense force into a fully equipped army capable of defending the new state against the anticipated Arab onslaught. Had American Jews not committed previously unimaginable sums of money to the cause, it is difficult to believe that the Zionist project in Palestine would have survived.

Zionist Advocacy Organizations

American Zionists also played key political and diplomatic roles in mobilizing support for the Jewish state. By the end of World War II, with the former center of the Zionist movement in Europe shattered, leadership shifted to organizations in Palestine and the United States. The larger American Zionist groups established the Emergency Council, co-chaired by Rabbi Abba Hillel Silver and Rabbi Stephen S. Wise, to coordinate political activities. Membership in American Zionist groups, including Hadassah, the ZOA, and a number of smaller organizations, swelled to over 500,000.[10]

Deeply distressed by the unfolding horror in Europe and their inability to respond in an effective fashion, the American Zionist leaders aligned themselves with the more militant wing of the Zionist movement, demanding open immigration to Palestine and rapid progress toward establishment of an independent Jewish state. With the full scope of the Holocaust increasingly evident, and a half million survivors still languishing in displaced-persons camps, the non-Zionist American groups, including B'nai B'rith (a fraternal association) and the AJC, either embraced the Zionist cause or quietly stepped aside. Only the American Council for Judaism, established in 1942 to express principled opposition to Jewish nationalism, maintained its opposition to Jewish statehood (albeit with a rapidly dwindling membership).[11]

During the run-up to the United Nation's vote to partition Palestine into an Arab and a Jewish state, American Zionist groups intensified their publicity campaigns and lobbying of the Truman administration. On April 29, 1947, American Jews held eighty-eight rallies, with sixty thousand attending the largest gathering in New York City. The Zionist organizations coordinated aggressive publicity campaigns including placement of opinion pieces in major newspapers and distribution of Zionist literature. American Jews sent tens of thousands of letters and telegrams to the White House. Non-Jewish groups organized around the cause as well; three thousand labor unions, church groups, Rotary clubs, and fraternal organizations adopted pro-Zionist resolutions and sent telegrams to Congress.[12] Zionist leaders met with President Truman and other U.S. officials, and with representatives of wavering UN member states. In his memoirs, President Truman wrote that on no other issue was he lobbied so intensely.[13] In the end, American Jewish pressure proved critical in persuading the Truman administration to support partition and to use its influence with other member states to do the same.

Shift to the Mainstream

Following establishment of the state, Israeli prime minister David Ben Gurion engineered a shift of responsibility for fundraising for Israel from Zionist organizations to non-Zionist organizations. The Israeli prime minister believed that since American Zionists did not intend to immigrate to Israel, there was no practical difference between them and the rest of American Jewry. By enlisting mainstream American Jewish organizations, Israel could broaden its base of support in the United States. Ben Gurion also sought to reduce the power of the American Zionist leaders and establish the clear primacy of Israel "as the undisputed source of Zionist decision-making in all major issues affecting political and financial aid."[14] To accomplish the shift, Ben Gurion supported an initiative by UPA director Henry Montor to expand the representation of local charitable federations on the UPA's board of directors. As a result of the reorganization, the ZOA lost its majority voice on the board of the UPA and its effective control over the organization.[15]

In the mid-1950s, a similar shift from Zionist to non-Zionist organizations was accomplished in the diplomatic sphere. In 1943, the ZOA had established a small office in Washington to lobby lawmakers on behalf of the movement. The office was later reconstituted as the lobbying arm of several Zionist organizations and then, in 1954, as the American Zionist Committee for Public Affairs. The first executive director was Isaiah L. Kenen, an American journalist who had been working as press secretary to Abba Eban, then Israel ambassador to the UN and shortly to become ambassador to the United States.[16] The executive committee comprised representatives of Zionist and mainstream organizations, including the AJC and the Anti-Defamation League (an organization established in 1913 to combat bigotry and anti-Semitism). In 1959, to reflect the transition from a Zionist to a more inclusive American Jewish identity, the organization changed its name to the American-Israel Public Affairs Committee (AIPAC). At its inception, although an independent organization, AIPAC was in fact a collaborative project of major American Jewish organizations.

American Jewish leaders also sought to develop a unified voice for communicating with the White House and State Department. According to one account, the idea for the creation of a single mouthpiece for American Jewry came from Henry Byroade, a State Department official who complained that his boss, Secretary of State John Foster Dulles, was confronted by too many disparate organizations purporting to represent American Jewry.[17] According to another version, the initiative came from Israel ambassador Abba Eban, who was repeatedly dismayed to read in American newspapers about the alleged views of the Israeli government—as related to the press by American Jewish leaders.[18] To improve communication and forge consensus positions, Abba

Eban, together with World Zionist Organization president Nahum Goldmann, convened a "Presidents Club" comprising the heads of a number of American Jewish organizations, including both mainstream and Zionist groups. The Presidents Club met periodically after 1955 and, over the next decade, added new organizations (including the three main Jewish religious denominations), hired staff, established formal procedures, and adopted a new name, the Conference of Presidents of Major American Jewish Organizations (hereafter, Presidents Conference).

With responsibility for fundraising and lobbying firmly established in mainstream American Jewish organizations, Zionist organizations (with the exception of Hadassah) lost much of their purpose and began a slow but steady decline. In the future, Israel would be responsible for its own policies and diplomacy, and the American Jewish community, as a whole, would be responsible for raising funds and building political support.

Emergency and Rescue

As the wealthiest Jewish community to emerge from the Second World War, American Jewry assumed the leading role in providing for Jewish needs around the world. During the 1950s and early 1960s, the UJA raised $60 million to $75 million annually for overseas projects, with about two-thirds going to projects in Israel.[19] The UJA campaigns funded housing construction, education, health, and welfare, primarily for Israel's enormous population of refugees from North Africa and the Middle East. Participation in the UJA campaigns expanded, and an annual donation was increasingly viewed as an expectation of all synagogue members.[20]

Between 1963 and 1966, the UJA overhauled its internal organization in order to ensure that contributions it received would continue to be tax deductible for American donors. According to an Internal Revenue Service ruling, American taxpayers could make tax-deductible gifts in support of overseas work if the coordinating body was a nongovernmental organization controlled by American citizens. To conform to these rules, the UJA established the United Israel Appeal (UIA) as a U.S.-based corporation responsible for receiving and distributing funds, and designated the Jewish Agency for Israel (reconstituted as a nongovernmental organization) as the Israel-based subsidiary responsible for project implementation.[21] This basic model for UJA support for Israel has survived more or less intact ever since. The model has also served as a basic template for the myriad "American Friends" organizations established in the ensuing years to support Israeli universities, hospitals, museums, and other institutions.

Six-Day and Yom Kippur Wars

This framework in place, the UJA was ready to respond to the crisis years that shortly followed. Between 1967 and 1973, Israel fought two major wars, and on each occasion American Jews contemplated the destruction of the Jewish state. Barely two decades after the Holocaust, the prospect of Israel's destruction seemed unbearable. As the historian Melvin I. Urofsky put it, "Israel stood, symbolically, as a redemption of the Holocaust; Israel made it possible to endure the memory of Auschwitz. Were Israel to be destroyed, then Hitler would be alive again, the final victory would be his."[22] The wars of 1967 and 1973 afforded American Jewry an opportunity to demonstrate that *this time* they would not remain helpless in the face of Jewish calamity. Animated by the conviction that "Israel must survive"—and that they could make the difference with their donations—they gave as never before. The 1967 emergency drive was launched after the start of the war, and by the time campaign volunteers began streaming into federation headquarters around the country, Israel's victory was already ensured. Nevertheless, the emergency drive collected $173 million, a sum larger than the record-breaking annual campaign that had just been completed a few months earlier.[23]

The sense of crisis was widely shared, as was the presumption that every Jewish person should feel an obligation to give. Both sentiments were evident in the calling script developed for volunteers in one federation campaign, as recorded by historian Marc Lee Raphael. Volunteers in the Columbus, Ohio, campaign were instructed to relate the following to potential donors: "Hello: I'm calling from the UJA headquarters and the following is the latest report we got from Tel Aviv; I want from you $1,000, yes or no, fast, as I have a lot of people to call."[24] Reflecting on the campaign that year, a Jewish leader from Columbus, Ohio, commented, "The UJA did not conduct a campaign, the Jews simply gave and the federation took."[25]

The mood during the 1973 emergency campaign was decidedly more grim, as fundraising proceeded in the context of an uncertain war with a large number of Israeli casualties. During the first twenty-four hours of the war, the UJA and the federations committed to raising $100 million in cash immediately, which they did within one week. The UJA then set the incredible goal of $750 million for 1974, a target that was nearly achieved. The fundraising reached small donors as well as the wealthy. A note written by one Jewish woman along with her check reflected the widespread sense of urgency: "Although I am unemployed and my husband is a grad student, we are sending you about 2/3 of this week's unemployment check because Israel must survive."[26]

The huge sums of money funneled to Israel during the late 1960s and early 1970s reflected not only the emergency campaigns but also a set of decisions by local federations and the UJA regarding allocations. The local federations allocated a large share of the revenues from their regular annual campaigns—often more than 50 percent—to the UJA. In turn, the UJA allocated an increasing share of its revenue to the UIA, which funded the Jewish Agency for Israel, as well as to JDC projects located in Israel.

As the crises of 1967–73 abated, the federations' annual campaigns dipped and then stabilized, and the total sum allocated via the UJA to causes in Israel leveled off at about $300 million annually. In the period that followed, the state of Israel further developed its social welfare capacity, and diaspora funds were increasingly utilized by the Jewish Agency for specialized purposes, including encouraging immigration, resettling refugees, developing Israel's periphery, and providing educational and logistical support to tour groups of diaspora teenagers and young adults.[27]

Resettlement of Soviet Jews

In the 1970s and 1980s, the UJA focused increasing resources on Jews in the Eastern Bloc and Soviet Union. As the gates of the USSR cracked open in the early 1970s, and then again after 1989, American Jews were called upon to fund the exodus of Soviet Jews and their resettlement in Israel and the United States. In the late 1980s, the UJA and the Jewish federations committed to guaranteeing the loans of the Israeli government for financing the immigration of nearly one million Soviet Jews. Jewish organizations quite literally put their property on the line, securing nearly $1 billion in loans against their own buildings and endowment funds.[28]

Making Israel's Case

During the 1950s and 1960s, Israel's closest allies were European countries, especially France and Great Britain, with whom Israel fought the 1956 Suez War. The Jewish state's relationship to the United States was decidedly cooler. The Eisenhower administration placed a priority on developing alliances with Arab states upon whom the United States depended for access to oil. The Kennedy and Johnson administrations adopted a friendlier attitude toward Israel but were preoccupied with the U.S. wars in Southeast Asia. At the conclusion of the 1967 Six-Day War, Israeli leaders expected the United States to insist upon a full Israeli withdrawal from the newly acquired territories, as it had following the 1956 war.[29] Instead, the United States adopted Israel's position— that withdrawal from territories should occur only in the context of a peace deal—and moved decisively to enhance its commitment to the Jewish state.

The context for the warming ties was President Richard Nixon's desire to counter the Soviet Union's influence in the Middle East, in particular with respect to Syria and Egypt. In 1971, following Israel's clandestine military operation to defend Jordan against Syrian and Palestinian threats, the United States boosted Israel's foreign aid package to over $600 million. Following the 1973 war, the United States further increased aid to $2.2 billion annually, a sum many times larger than the annual UJA contribution to Israel. In the words of one observer, "Israel became a virtual U.S. protectorate."[30] The enormous spike in foreign aid was introduced by Secretary of State Henry Kissinger and supported by President Nixon; it was not, notably, an initiative of the still nascent pro-Israel lobby. Maintaining the generous aid package, however, would become a primary focus on the lobby in the years ahead.

In the mid-1970s, national Jewish organizations including AIPAC, the Presidents Conference, and the National Jewish Community Relations Advisory Council (NJCRAC—the advocacy arm of the federations) waged a number of campaigns on Israel's behalf. The pro-Israel groups won legislation to prohibit U.S. businesses from complying with the Arab boycott of Israel.[31] They also persuaded President Gerald Ford to drop his announced "reassessment" of U.S. Middle East policy—the reassessment had tacitly meant to sanction Israel for foot-dragging in negotiations following the 1973 war.[32] The pro-Israel groups were less successful, however, in their attempt to stop the Carter administration's sale of advanced F-15 fighter jets to Saudi Arabia. Finally, throughout the summer 1978 Camp David peace negotiations between Egypt and Israel, the pro-Israel groups kept the pressure on President Carter, supporting Prime Minister Menachem Begin's refusal to recognize the national rights of Palestinians and to negotiate over the future of the West Bank.[33]

Maintaining Unity

In the 1970s, American Jewish organizations twice faced challenges to their united front on Israel. In the first instance, a group comprising mostly young rabbis and graduate students established a dissident Jewish organization named "Breira" or "alternative." Founded with a small budget and staff, Breira aimed to promote dialogue with Palestinian Arabs and mutual recognition of Jewish and Palestinian rights. The group immediately became a lightning rod for intense criticism. The Jewish community's leading figures refused to speak to the group. Some of the campus-based rabbis who joined Breira were threatened with dismissal. "Showing our dirty laundry in public, giving aid and comfort to Israel's enemies, is not allowed in American Jewish life," commented Arthur Samuelson, the editor of Breira's newsletter.[34] The membership peaked at fifteen hundred, and the organization dissolved a few years after its launch.[35]

The crackdown, however, created further discord, and several organizations, including the NJCRAC and the AJC, commissioned internal studies on the limits of legitimate dissent. The AJC's report considered a number of possible justifications for public criticism of Israel by diaspora Jews.[36] The dominant view expressed in the reports, however, was that public dissent suggests disunity and weakness, and must therefore be avoided.[37] Moreover, from a moral standpoint only Israelis have the right to make policy decisions since it is only their lives that are at risk. "These rules were quickly taken up by the Jewish leadership as sacred writ from Jerusalem," commented journalist J. J. Goldberg. "Jews who disagreed found themselves unwelcome in community forums, asked to leave governing boards, shouted down at meetings."[38]

The willingness of American Jewish leaders to adopt Israel's line on policy issues was in sharp contrast to the leading ideological role American Zionists had played prior to the birth of the state. By the 1970s, however, new rules of the game were firmly in place. Israeli policy was to be set in Jerusalem and communicated to the American Jewish leadership through the Presidents Conference and other channels. Less frequently, American Jews could be consulted for their opinions through the same establishment channels. As journalist Edward Tivnan put it, Israel related to the American Jewish community "as a kind of large public-relations agency that would put together pro-Israel demonstrations, prepare releases, or generate telegrams to the U.N., the White House, or congressmen."[39] The arrangement reflected the mood and inclination of American Jewry at the time. As the historian Steven T. Rosenthal explained, the "failure of American Jews to assert themselves in relations with Israel was not an abdication of responsibility, since they had neither the inclination nor the experience to influence Israeli leaders on matters of policy."[40]

When Menachem Begin was elected Israel's prime minister in 1977, unity among the pro-Israel groups was challenged for a second time. Begin was the leader of the right-wing Likud Party, which had led the opposition since the founding of the state. He was known to American Jews as a hard-liner who was unwilling to embrace the "land for peace" formula of previous Israeli governments. President Carter was clearly displeased with the election result, and some in his administration looked to see how the American Jewish leadership, with its impeccable liberal credentials, would respond. The chair of the Presidents Conference, Reform movement head Rabbi Alexander Schindler, immediately flew to Jerusalem to meet with the new prime minister. Upon his return to the United States, Schindler related his favorable impressions to the White House and to the U.S. press. The trip clarified, to any who remained uncertain, that American Jewish leaders would permit no distance between their own positions and those of the Israeli leadership.[41] Later that year, the annual report of the Presidents Conference summarized the basis for Schindler's position: "Dissent ought not and should not be made public because . . . the result is to give aid and comfort to the enemy and to weaken that Jewish unity which is essential for the security of Israel."[42] During the difficult and often stalemated peace talks with Egypt that followed, the American Jewish leadership preserved its unity and expressed consistent support—notwithstanding the private misgivings of some—for Begin's tough negotiating posture.

Throughout this period, dissent was not completely sidelined. The dissidents expressed their views as individuals, however, rather than as representatives of organizations. In 1980, fifty-two prominent American Jews, including three past chairmen of the Presidents Conference, issued a statement in the *New York Times* opposing Israel's policy of settling the territories occupied in the 1967 war. Titled "Our Way Is Not Theirs," the statement charged the Israeli right with chauvinism and distorting Zionism. In response, Presidents Conference chair Harold Squadron expressed the view of the establishment organizations: "I find it most regrettable that American Jewish leaders should engage in this kind of public debate concerning the policies pursued by the government of Israel. Such debate is always unjustified and divisive."[43]

The Rise of AIPAC

In 1981, the Reagan administration proposed to sell to Saudi Arabia an advanced airborne surveillance system, known by the acronym AWACS. The pro-Israel lobby, led by AIPAC, launched a vigorous campaign against the sale, arguing that it would reduce Israel's military edge in the region. The campaign won the support of the House of Representatives, which voted three to one against the sale, but came up short in the Senate. Notwithstanding the campaign's ultimate defeat, the display of Jewish political muscle was noted in the administration and throughout the capital. According to Edward Tivnan, "The result was the end of AIPAC's national obscurity, and the beginning of the revolution in Jewish politics."[44]

Under the leadership of Thomas Dine, who became the organization's executive director during the AWACS struggle, AIPAC developed a membership base of 55,000 grassroots activists who could lobby members of Congress in every congressional district in the country. The organization also expanded its research and publications division and became a major source of information and analysis for members of Congress. Dine understood that lobbying members of Congress in their home districts and controlling the flow of information and ideas were the most effective ways to shape the debate on Israel and Middle East policy.

Dine also stepped up AIPAC's involvement in electoral politics. The organization was not established as a political action committee and therefore could not fund candidates for public office—but AIPAC influenced the decisions of a wide network of pro-Israel donors, including dozens of pro-Israel political action committees. The organization influenced the flow of campaign donations by publishing the views of congressional candidates on issues pertaining to Israel and thereby signaling who were Israel's friends. Then, as now, Jewish donors gave disproportionately to political campaigns, especially to candidates in the Democratic Party, and AIPAC's influence over donations during this period was likely significant.[45]

Throughout the 1980s, AIPAC defeated several presidential initiatives to sell arms to Arab states, in particular Saudi Arabia and Jordan. The organization lobbied for ongoing economic and military aid to Israel (in 1984, Israel's aid package reached $4.5 billion), supported a resolution to move the U.S. embassy from Tel Aviv to Jerusalem, and promoted military and intelligence cooperation between the United States and Israel.[46] It opposed efforts to encourage Israeli negotiations with the Palestine Liberation Organization (PLO), and lobbied successfully for legislation that banned American officials from conducting talks with PLO representatives until certain conditions were met, including PLO recognition of Israel's right to exist.

In the midst of these political campaigns, Dine overhauled AIPAC's structure of governance, transforming the organization "from a small agency, run by the national Jewish organizations as their congressional lobbying arm, into an independent mass membership powerhouse run by its wealthiest donors."[47] He accomplished this by tripling the size of the organization's executive committee and thereby reducing the influence of the original member organizations. With an expanded executive committee, actual power and influence devolved to the "officers' group" composed of a small number of key donors. In the middle of the decade, the NJCRAC curtailed its Israel-related activities and AIPAC became the undisputed flagship of the pro-Israel lobby.

Popular Attitudes

During the decade that followed the 1967 Six-Day War, Israel became an object of great reverence for many American Jews. Political Scientist Daniel Elazar coined the term "Israelolotry" to capture the intensity of pro-Israel feelings, which seemed at times to verge on idolatry.[48] Indeed, because emotional attachment to Israel was so strong, social scientists grappled with how to devise a survey question that could distinguish between various levels of attachment. Thus, in a standard survey question posed toward the end of this period, respondents were asked to agree or disagree with the following statement: "If Israel were destroyed, I would feel as if I had suffered one of the greatest personal tragedies of my life." Notwithstanding the hyperbolic phrasing of the question, large majorities consistently indicated agreement.[49]

Nevertheless, Israel's meaning for American Jews was largely symbolic rather than personal or experiential. For the vast majority, Israel represented the survival and renaissance of the Jewish people after the Holocaust. As well, most regarded Israel as the embodiment of progressive American values. American Jews viewed Israel as a secular democracy that, like the United States, protected minority rights and provided for universal social welfare. They perceived Israelis as scrappy and self-reliant—like Americans—and also, especially after 1967, as exemplary warriors. In a telling if somewhat overdrawn image, Steven T. Rosenthal writes, "It was as if Israel's governmental leaders all combined the revelation of Moses, the wisdom of Solomon, and the moral vision of Isaiah, and were not subject to such human foibles as error, lack of judgment, personal ambition, or momentary political consideration."[50] The broader cultural climate supported these idealistic impressions of the Jewish state, especially after the publication in 1958 of Leon Uris's book *Exodus*. A fictional account of Zionist heroism in the Israeli War of Independence, the book sold four million copies and was made into a popular motion picture. The movie's theme song, which began with the words "This land is mine, God gave this land to me," climbed to the top of the popular music charts.[51]

Construed in an idealistic fashion, support for Israel became a key ingredient in the civil religion of American Jews.[52] Throughout the 1970s and 1980s, the vast majority of American Jews perceived Israel as a just cause. When in 1975 the UN General Assembly adopted a resolution equating Zionism with racism, most American Jews could make sense of the vote only as an expression of resurgent anti-Semitism. Many responded by donning buttons proclaiming "I am a Zionist," and the UJA announced its new campaign slogan, "We Are One!"[53]

Few American Jews, however, had much firsthand contact with Israel or Israelis. Only about one-third had ever visited Israel, and still fewer had visited more than once. (As well, few Israelis traveled in the United States, a fact that further limited contact between the two Jewish communities.) Afternoon Hebrew School was widely understood as a place where Hebrew was not learned—few American Jews ever mastered more than a capacity to read the language phonetically. American Jews acquired news of Israel through the general media or the American Jewish press rather than directly from the Israeli press. Adults learned about Israel from rabbis' sermons. Children learned about Israel in Hebrew School, where the curriculum, as historian Jack Wertheimer notes, "presented an idealized Israel, with little emphasis on teaching about the reality of life in Israel, the religious implications of the establishment of the state, or the value of aliyah."[54]

Marshall Sklare, a leading sociologist of American Jewry, described the dominant orientation of American Jews toward Israel during this period. Returning after the 1967 Six-Day War to a community he had studied in the previous decade, he wrote, "Our respondents were shaken by the threat posed by the Crisis [sic], were unambiguously pro-Israel, were tremendously stirred by the victory. . . . [Yet they] have not shifted in their level of pro-Israel support, and have not evinced any extraordinary eagerness to visit Israel."[55] For the majority, Israel remained largely a symbol and a myth rather than a country that they might soon visit or where they or their children might someday live. "Of all the myths surrounding the Six Day War and its aftermath," wrote J. J. Goldberg, "perhaps the most remarkable is the idea that it transformed the thinking of most American Jews." In reality, only a minority were utterly transformed.[56] The rest continued to relate to Israel in a "wide yet shallow fashion," mostly when visiting Jewish public spaces, such as synagogues and Jewish community centers.[57] Israel moved American Jews deeply, but the Israel to which they responded was an idea, a symbol, and a cause, and not a feature of their everyday lives.

There were exceptions to the dominant pattern. An increasing number of Orthodox Jews traveled to Israel for Jewish holidays, made contributions directly to Orthodox institutions in Israel (alongside or in place of a UJA contribution), and enrolled their children for a year of intensive religious study in an Israeli *yeshiva* (Talmudic academy) during the year before starting college.[58] The youth organizations of the major Jewish denominations sponsored youth travel programs to Israel, and borrowed heavily from Israeli motifs for their summer camps in the United States. The youth travel programs attracted the leadership cadre of Jewish young people: Five to ten thousand high school students participated annually. The typical trips ran for six weeks and included a stay on an Israeli kibbutz (farming collective). The summer camps emphasized the motifs of "pioneering" and kibbutz life, and taught Israeli songs and folk dances. "Housed in a rustic setting and evoking an ambience of communal living where campers might, at any moment, break out in Israeli song and dance, these camps have served as surrogates for an imagined Israel, devoid of warfare, urban blight or poverty."[59] Alongside the youth programs of the Reform, Conservative, and Orthodox movements, there were also trips and summer camps sponsored by the Zionist youth group Young Judea (and its Tel Yehudah summer camp), and by the B'nei Akiva religious Zionist youth movement (and its Moshava summer camp).

Strains and Fractures

The idealization of Israel characteristic of the period following the 1967 Six-Day War was strained in the 1980s by events that challenged existing perceptions. The 1982 Lebanon War and in particular the Sabra and Shatilla massacres of Palestinians by Christian Lebanese fighters operating under Israel's protection shocked many American Jews. The subsequent mass demonstration by 400,000 Israelis demanding a public inquiry indelibly imprinted on the American Jewish consciousness that Israelis were not unified in their own political judgments. Speaking in a private capacity, several prominent American Jews sharply criticized Prime Minister Begin and Defense Minister Ariel Sharon for their failure to prevent the killings, and expressed support for establishing a commission of inquiry.

In the middle of the decade, the conviction of Jonathan Pollard, an American Jewish analyst for the U.S. Navy, for spying for Israel galvanized widespread attention among American Jews. Many expressed amazement over the Israeli leadership's poor judgment and disregard for American Jewish interests.[60] These feelings were compounded a few years later when Prime Minister Yitzhak Shamir announced his intention to adopt a law restricting official recognition of religious conversions to those conducted by Orthodox rabbis. Shamir sought to impose the new restriction in order to attract religious parties to his coalition government. The initiative was interpreted by Reform and Conservative (i.e., non-Orthodox) rabbis in the United States as a direct assault upon their legitimacy as rabbis and on the authenticity of the movements they led. American rabbis blasted the proposal from their pulpits, and Jewish federations in Boston and Atlanta threatened to withhold their UJA contributions. Delegations of American Jewish leaders flew to Israel to lodge complaints.[61]

Israel's response to the first Palestinian Intifada (1987–91) further dismayed many American Jews. Prime Minister Yitzhak Rabin's pledge to subdue protesters with beatings instead of live fire only heighted concern among some American Jews that Israel was losing its moral compass. Rabbi Alexander Schindler described the beatings as "an offense to the Jewish spirit that betrays the Zionist dream" and added, "we plead with you to bring this madness to an end."[62] Albert Vorspan, a prominent lay leader within the Reform movement, published an essay in the *New York Times Magazine* criticizing Israeli actions and the failure of American Jewish organizations to make public their opposition. "We have ceased to be champions of social justice and become cheerleaders for failed Israeli policies," he wrote.[63] Presidents Conference chair Morris Abram warned Rabin that "American Jewish organizations would no longer be able to defend Israel's actions in the territories."[64]

The incidence of public criticism of Israeli policies by prominent individuals was clearly rising. The key organizations in the Jewish world, however, consistently managed to close ranks. During the Lebanon War and the Palestinian Intifada, leaders of major Jewish organizations kept their doubts to themselves and defended Israel in the public arena. Indeed, throughout the 1970s and 1980s, with the exception of short-lived initiatives such as Breira and its successor New Jewish Agenda (founded in 1980), Jewish organizations consistently honored the principle that only the Israeli government should make security decisions, and American Jews should maintain a public face of unity and solidarity.

Conclusion

During the Second World War and the decade that followed, American Jews played a central role in the establishment of the Jewish state. Animated by frustration over their inability to save the Jewish communities of Europe, they mobilized all of their political influence to persuade the Truman administration to support the partition of Palestine and recognize the new state of Israel. The mobilization of American Jewish wealth funded Jewish settlement in Palestine and the creation of a Jewish defense force. Following the creation of the state, American Jewish donations covered the high cost of resettling an enormous refugee population from North Africa and the Middle East.

During the two decades after the 1967 Six-Day War, the fundraising and political influence machinery of American Jewry achieved their full scope. American Jewish organizations mobilized financial and diplomatic support, achieved a united front on most policy issues, and suppressed public dissent. By the late 1980s, however, the signs of fracture were evident. As a result of the Lebanon War, the Pollard spy affair, the conversion debate, and the Palestinian Intifada, the idealization of Israel in the liberal sectors of American Jewish society had diminished. Moreover, as tensions mounted, the willingness of diverse advocacy organizations to subordinate their policy priorities to those of the Israeli government had come under pressure. By the end of the 1980s, the disputes that would soon shatter unity and consensus were well established.

Israel contingent on Israel freezing settlement activity and agreeing to new peace talks. AIPAC, the ZOA, and other leading advocacy organizations either opposed the president or remained silent. Two relatively small Jewish organizations on the left, New Jewish Agenda and Americans for Peace Now (founded 1981), supported Bush's call for a settlement freeze. "I remember trembling as I left the hotel room that morning," recalled the executive director of Americans for Peace Now about the morning he testified on Capitol Hill in support of withholding loan guarantees. "We were doing something that had never been done before. I was scared about what the community would say."[2] In contrast to Breira, which two decades earlier had been drummed out of existence for breaking with the consensus line, in the post–Gulf War context the two peace groups achieved partial acceptance. New Jewish Agenda was invited to make presentations to mainstream groups and Americans for Peace Now was accepted as a member in the Presidents Conference. "Dissent from Israel's policy was becoming accepted, mainstream, and institutionalized," writes Steven T. Rosenthal.[3]

A much more significant break from the united front occurred following the announcement of the Oslo Peace Accords in 1993. The deal struck by the Israeli government of Yitzhak Rabin and the Palestine Liberation Organization called for mutual recognition and phased Israeli withdrawal from the Gaza Strip and West Bank with the aim—not explicit in the agreement—of eventually establishing a Palestinian state alongside Israel. AIPAC and the Presidents Conference were caught off guard by the Israeli about-face on negotiations with the PLO and the possibility of establishment of a Palestinian state. For decades, in accordance with long-standing Israeli policies, the leading advocacy organizations had utterly rejected these notions. After several months of foot-dragging, however, the two groups fell into line with the new Israeli approach, supporting, for example, congressional allocation of funds to the newly established Palestinian Authority.[4]

The announcement of the Oslo Accords precipitated a crisis in the Zionist Organization of America. A shadow of its former self—by the early 1990s there were just a few active chapters and no professional staff—the organization initially signaled its willingness to support Rabin's peace initiative. However, in the election for the ZOA presidency, which coincidentally was scheduled for October 1993, a group of hawkish members organized to support the candidacy of Morton Klein on an anti-Oslo platform. Klein, a mathematician, had been active in a number of Zionist causes but was not at the time a member of the ZOA or employed by any Jewish organization. Following Klein's election, the ZOA came out strongly against the Oslo Accords.[5]

Klein's position was bolstered by Israeli Likud officials who toured the United States in the weeks following the signing of the Oslo Accords. Speaking before Jewish audiences, the new Likud Party leader, Benjamin Netanyahu, declared, "I will lobby in Israel and American Jews will lobby in America. I think that's a good division of labor."[6] Netanyahu was joined by other prominent Likud officials including former minister of defense Ariel Sharon and former prime minister Yitzhak Shamir. Their appeals for action to disrupt the Oslo process were embraced by a coalition of right-wing organizations. The coalition comprised secular advocacy organizations, including the ZOA and Americans for a Safe Israel (founded 1971), and Orthodox religious organizations, including the National Council of Young Israel, the Orthodox Union, and Agudat Yisrael.

Setting their sights on Congress, the groups promoted legislation to make financial assistance to the Palestinian Authority conditional on annual certification of the PA's compliance with the treaty's Declaration of Principles. Prime Minister Rabin, with the support of AIPAC and the Presidents Conference, had lobbied for the American aid, which was to supply one-quarter of a $2 billion fund. The law promoted by the ZOA, adopted the following year as the Specter-Shelby Amendment, ensured that aid to the PA, already unpopular in Congress, would be reconsidered annually. A year later, when the renewal of aid came up for a vote, AIPAC and the Presidents Conference lobbied in favor and the ZOA and the Orthodox Union lobbied against.[7] Speaking at the Council of Jewish Federations annual gathering, Labor Party leader Haim Ramon denounced the aid opponents for "cooperating with the extreme parts of Israel."[8]

The independent lobbying of the right against key elements of the Oslo Accords caused deep dismay in the American Jewish establishment. AIPAC appealed to the Presidents Conference for disciplinary action against the ZOA, claiming that its "amateurish" actions threatened the group's role as the community's official lobby for Israel and "put the entire pro-Israel agenda at risk."[9] ZOA head Morton Klein refused to attend a special meeting called by the Presidents Conference to consider the AIPAC motion, claiming that "in the absence of a consensus in the community, individual groups should be free to pursue their own strategies."[10] The ZOA also rejected new lobbying guidelines that stipulated that positions on Israel-related issues first be cleared with AIPAC. Disturbed by the rapid increase in independent lobbying, Presidents Conference executive director Malcolm Hoenlein worried that lawmakers "may just throw their hands up and say 'forget all of you clowns.'"[11]

In addition to targeting U.S. foreign aid to the Palestinian authority, the right-wing advocacy groups sought to undermine the Oslo Accords by reviving an effort to persuade the U.S. government to move its embassy from Tel Aviv to Jerusalem. The opponents of Oslo knew that both Congress and the Israeli government would find the move difficult to oppose notwithstanding the damage it would cause to ongoing negotiations over the future status of Jerusalem. Nevertheless, the Rabin government made clear its opposition to the measure. In this instance, however, AIPAC joined the right-wing camp, declaring its support for the embassy bill and causing Rabin to lament, "Never have we witnessed an attempt by American Jews to lobby against the policy of a democratically elected Israeli government."[12]

Pendulum Swings

Following the assassination of Prime Minister Rabin in November 1995, the Israeli political pendulum swung right. The new Likud prime minister, Benjamin Netanyahu, announced plans to expand Jewish settlements in the West Bank and Gaza Strip. It was now the turn of the American Jewish left to engage in independent, partisan lobbying. Led by Americans for Peace Now and a new pro-Oslo advocacy group, the Israel Policy Forum (founded 1993), the peace camp persuaded the federations' Washington, D.C., lobby, the National Jewish Community Relations Advisory Council, to adopt a resolution supporting the peace process and urging the Netanyahu government to show "maximum restraint" on Jewish settlements in the West Bank and Gaza Strip. (Netanyahu's drive to expand Jewish settlements in East Jerusalem and the West Bank had previously won the support of the National Council of Young Israel and other Orthodox groups.) Shortly thereafter, one hundred prominent Jews, including leaders of the Reform and Conservative movements, and several past chairmen of the Presidents Conference, took out a *New York Times* advertisement thanking U.S. Secretary of State Madeleine Albright for the leading role of the United States in the peace process. Prior to her Middle East trip, a second letter, signed by a group of forty Jewish leaders, urged Secretary Albright to "press the Likud government for concessions" that would jump-start the stalled peace process.[13]

To keep the Oslo process on track, President Clinton and Secretary Albright urged Netanyahu to agree to Israeli withdrawal from a further 13 percent of the West Bank. Digging in his heels, Netanyahu sought AIPAC and Presidents Conference support for his opposition to the American initiative. AIPAC recruited 81 senators and 150 members of Congress to sign a letter supporting Netanyahu's position, prompting an Israeli Labor Party official to label the organization a "Likud stronghold." In this instance, however, the Presidents Conference refused to toe the Israeli government line. Charging that AIPAC had created an unnecessary sense of crisis, the Presidents Conference opposed the AIPAC letter, issuing instead a call for the Clinton administration to continue its efforts to secure the next phase of the Oslo process. Americans for Peace Now and other left-center Jewish groups signed onto the Presidents Conference call, prompting a *New York Times* headline, "Jewish Groups Go to Washington Squabbling among Themselves."[14]

In spring 1999, in an election focused on getting the Oslo peace negotiations back on track, the Israeli electorate returned the Labor Party, led by Ehud Barak, to power. For American Jews, the political pendulum had swung yet again. Under direct pressure from the new Labor-led government, AIPAC dropped its opposition to the establishment of a Palestinian state. Still, as Palestinian and Israeli leaders convened at Camp David in August 2000 to negotiate a final status agreement, the Jewish press was preoccupied with the question of whether American Jews had been adequately prepared for the compromises Israel now indicated it was willing to make, especially in relation to Jerusalem.

The coalition of right-wing advocacy organizations kicked back into gear. The ZOA published an advertisement signed by thirty prominent

American Jews, including six past chairmen of the Presidents Conference, opposing Prime Minister Barak's Camp David offer of de facto Palestinian sovereignty over the Temple Mount. "Israel Must Not Surrender Judaism's Holiest Site" the advertisement declared. "The Moslems wouldn't dream of giving away part of Mecca or Medina; the Christians wouldn't dream of giving away part of the Vatican. . . . And no Israeli leader has the right to give away the essence of the Jewish people that is embedded in the Temple Mount."[15] By stating that sovereignty over the Temple Mount is an issue for all Jews to decide, the advertisement framed an argument that would be echoed in years to come.

In 2000, the failure of the Camp David Summit and outbreak of the Second Intifada prompted an immediate suspension of partisan lobbying by Israel advocacy organizations. After the lynching of Israeli reservists in Ramallah, American Jews "closed ranks with a fervor that had all but disappeared."[16] During summer 2001 Jewish organizations held solidarity rallies across the United States, including participation of groups spanning the political spectrum from Americans for Peace Now to the Zionist Organization of America. To draw attention to the newly achieved unity against the backdrop of broad disagreement over the peace process, 100,000 American Jews rallied in Washington, D.C., under the slogan "Wherever We Stand, We Stand with Israel."[17]

Gaza Disengagement

In 2003, following two years of intense violence associated with the Second Intifada, Prime Minister Ariel Sharon endorsed the Roadmap for Peace, backed by the United States, Russia, the European Union, and the United Nations, and declared his support for establishment of a Palestinian state in the future. He also announced his plan for unilateral measures by Israel to establish a new international boundary including complete Israeli withdrawal from the Gaza Strip and dismantlement of four settlements in the northern West Bank. The Gaza disengagement would entail dismantling twenty-one settlements and relocating, possibly by force, more than nine thousand Jewish settlers.

Confronted with deep resistance and withering criticism from within Likud, Sharon broke ranks and established a new centrist party, Kadima, to undertake the disengagement. He also looked to American Jewish advocacy organizations for support. As protests in Israel intensified, most of the establishment and center-left American Jewish groups fell into line behind Sharon's plan. In May 2005, the Israel Policy Forum published the roster of pro-disengagement organizations in a full-page advertisement in the *New York Times*, including the American Jewish Committee, the Anti-Defamation League, the Reform and Conservative movements, and the Jewish Council for Public Affairs (formerly, NJCRAC).[18]

AIPAC's support for the Gaza disengagement plan was unequivocal. Journalist Ron Kampeas described how the organization addressed the issue during its 2005 Policy Conference:

> In its opening video montage, AIPAC acknowledged the ambivalence many of its delegates must have felt over the Gaza withdrawal. Wrenching video footage showed settlers weeping as they contemplated leaving their homes. Both sides of the story were thoroughly and fairly presented. But in the end, there was never any doubt about where AIPAC stood. The Israelis appearing in the video, and then live on the AIPAC stage, included a husband and wife who had made up their mind that the possibility of peace was worth the price of leaving Gaza. A mother and daughter who had bitterly resented their evacuation from the Sinai settlement of Yamit in 1982, but who now acknowledged the peace with Egypt that it brought, spoke as well. More stunningly, the video, touting the "reduction in friction" that disengagement would bring, featured footage of Israeli troops lording it over Palestinians at a roadblock. The few seconds of footage were unprecedented from Israel's foremost defender.[19]

AIPAC gave practical support as well. The organization led the effort to secure $2 billion in U.S. aid from Congress for relocation of Israeli military facilities and resettlement of Gaza settlers in the Negev and Galilee.

In contrast, the Presidents Conference was initially unable to reach a consensus position. ZOA leader Morton Klein denounced the plan to "throw Jews out of their home and give a terrorist regime more land."[20] Unable to reach agreement, the Conference issued a tepid statement indicating that a "majority" of its members supported the Gaza withdrawal. The compromise statement prompted ADL leader Abraham

Foxman to remark, "[I]n the 50 years since the Presidents Conference was formed, there had never been a situation in which both the prime minister of Israel and the president of the United States had endorsed an Israeli position and the Presidents' Conference remained mum."[21] A few months later, in August 2005, the Conference finally issued a clear endorsement of the disengagement plan.[22]

Israeli leaders on both sides of the disengagement issue sought to rally their American Jewish supporters. On one occasion, as Prime Minister Sharon addressed fifteen hundred prominent Jews in New York, rightist Knesset member Benny Elon addressed an anti-disengagement rally outside the building. "[Even] if it's kosher, it stinks, and if it's legal, it's illegitimate," Elon told the crowd, referring to the disengagement.[23] Opposition Knesset members Uzi Landau and Natan Sharansky (who quit the government over disengagement) and rightist political activist Moshe Feiglin also traveled to the United States to rally their forces.

Notwithstanding this attention from overseas, the coalition of the right felt abandoned by the mainstream organizations. At a demonstration outside of the UN in August 2005, on the eve of the withdrawal of settlers from Gaza, one protest leader asked, "Where are you, Anti-Defamation League? Where are you, American Jewish Committee? Where is the American Jewish Congress today?"[24]

The main Orthodox congregational association, the Orthodox Union (OU), straddled the fence between the establishment groups, which supported disengagement, and the right-wing groups, which opposed it. "We are trying to serve our constituency, which is divided, in a concrete and constructive way," said Nathan Diament, who directed the OU's Institute for Public Affairs.[25] Although the OU chose against taking a position on the Gaza pullout, it did criticize the Israeli government's treatment of Orthodox Jewish protesters. "We are stunned by reports of security forces singling out persons displaying outward appearances of religious observance for disparate harsh treatment," the OU wrote in a letter to Israeli officials.[26] Dismayed by their organization's failure to take an unequivocal stand against disengagement, OU members subsequently voted to empower their professional leaders to issue statements of criticism concerning Israeli governmental policies.[27] A year later, the OU joined the ZOA and other right-wing groups in lobbying against the division of Jerusalem in any future peace deal.[28]

The bitter divisions over the Gaza disengagement were briefly set aside a year later, during the Second Lebanon War. Israel's rapid response to missile fire and kidnapping of soldiers along the recently evacuated northern border received near-consensus support among Israelis and American Jews, at least at the outset of hostilities. The field of Israel advocacy, however, was about to fracture still further.

J Street

Following the failure of Camp David negotiations and unraveling of the Oslo peace process, leaders in the Israeli and American Jewish peace camps became convinced that greater pressure from the United States was necessary to bring the parties to an agreement. They believed, however, that AIPAC and the rest of the establishment, pro-Israel lobby were effectively preventing the United States from serving as an "honest broker" in the conflict. What was needed, in their view, was a vehicle for demonstrating the broad support of rank-and-file American Jews for a two-state solution and an activist role for the United States in bringing it about. Americans for Peace Now and the Israel Policy Forum had occasionally played this role. In 2002, peace camp activists launched Brit Tzedek V'Shalom as a national grassroots organization to advocate for a two-state solution; by the middle of the decade the organization had dozens of chapters throughout the United States.

From Jeremy Ben-Ami's vantage point in Washington, D.C., however, the peace camp needed a national organization, headquartered in the nation's capital, that could unify the left and challenge AIPAC's standing as the de facto voice of the Jewish community. As a former Clinton administration official with a background in public relations and political consulting, Ben-Ami believed he had the skills and connections to make it happen. With financial support from billionaire investor George Soros and the cooperation of many veteran activists, Ben-Ami established J Street. The organization took its name from the missing street in Washington's alphabetical grid—a gesture signifying the missing voice in the discussion of Israel. It would operate as both professional lobby with a mass base of grassroots supporters (the AIPAC model) and a political action committee that could directly fund candidates for office. During its first year, the organization negotiated a friendly takeover of Brit Tzedek, including its extensive grassroots net-work and rabbinical advisory committee.

J Street's early successes galvanizing the left and attracting fund-ing, support, and attention can be attributed not only to the skills of its founders but also to the immediate political context. J Street's launch coincided with the presidential campaign of Barack Obama. As a can-didate, Obama emphasized his intention to restore the Israeli-Palestin-ian peace process to the center of the U.S. foreign policy agenda. His subsequent election with the support of the vast majority of American Jews signaled an opening for the peace camp. Furthermore, the elec-tion during the same year of a right-wing Israeli government made plausible J Street's claim that establishment Jewish organizations that defended Israeli policies were out of step with mainstream Jewish opin-ion. To make the point, the new organization commissioned a national survey revealing broad support among American Jews for a two-state solution and a majority in favor of the United States "pressuring" both the Israelis and the Palestinians to come to an agreement. Poll results in hand, Ben-Ami explained J Street's strategy. The organization would "act as the president's blocking back" in Congress, neutralizing pressure from AIPAC and others to automatically embrace Israeli government positions.[29]

Nonetheless, J Street assiduously described itself as "pro-Israel." By this the organization meant not only that it supported Israel's right to exist but also that a two-state solution was in Israel's best interests. Later, when J Street began branching out to address a broader range of Israeli political and social issues, including civil rights, Ben-Ami distinguished between knee-jerk advocacy in support of all policies favored by the Israeli government and advocacy that supports Israel as conceived in its Declaration of Independence. To be pro-Israel, J Street eventually argued, is to champion policies that secure Israel's future as a Jewish and democratic state. In interviews, Ben-Ami also vigorously defended the right of American Jews to lobby the U.S. government to promote a two-state solution:

> The view that Jewish Americans don't have a right to express views on Israel because they live here is a fallacy. It's a fallacy because, first of all, we're Americans and as Americans we have every right to express

ourselves on foreign policy as it relates to Israel. And as Jewish Americans we happen to care a little bit more deeply about Israel. . . . But I also think that the state of Israel is the state of the Jewish people. They talk about it that way, whether you live there or not. The government officials there will say "we are a state that does represent you." I do believe, as a Jew who lives here, whose life and experience is impacted by Israel—by the way Israel is perceived and the way that Israel acts—both as an American and as a Jew that we do have a right to express our opinions and talk about these issues.[30]

The organization has grown steadily since its founding, increasing attendance at annual conventions, establishing chapters on campuses in Jewish communities across the country, and raising millions for congressional candidates. The group's "rabbinical cabinet" includes nearly seven hundred rabbis and cantors. The organization's annual gatherings draw delegations of Knesset members from center-left opposition parties. The group has also received support from prominent Israeli literary and cultural figures including the writers Amos Oz and A. B. Yehoshua. In short, J Street quickly established itself in many quarters as the loyal opposition—an accomplishment without precedent on the Jewish left.

Nonetheless, the group's self-designation as "pro-Israel" has been vigorously challenged. Writing in the *Jerusalem Post*, columnist Isi Leibler described J Street as the "enemy within" and likened the group's leadership to medieval apostate Jews "who fabricated blood libels" resulting in massacres.[31] Israel's U.S. ambassador Michael Oren repeatedly declined requests to speak at the group's annual gatherings. Heads of several establishment groups refused to appear on the same podium with Ben-Ami.

During hearings held in the Israeli Knesset to examine J Street's pro-Israel bona fides, Ben-Ami argued that the organization contributes to Israel's cause by engaging young people who would otherwise be entirely alienated from Israel and Judaism. He further argued that the organization sets a clear boundary between the pro-Israel left (i.e., J Street), which supports Israel's right to exist and opposes international efforts to pressure Israel through Boycott, Divestment and Sanctions (BDS) and the non-Zionist left, which promotes BDS and rejects or takes no stance on Israel's right to exist.

The latter stance is exemplified by the organization Jewish Voice for Peace (JVP, founded 1996), which also gained ground during the early years of the Obama presidency. JVP expresses the views of Jews who are already part of the broader American left, especially on college campuses and as part of the Occupy Wall Street movement. In contrast to J Street, JVP refuses to declare its support for a particular version of Israeli-Palestinian peace, leaving the door open to a one-state "democratic" solution to the conflict. The organization also supports boycotts of products produced in West Bank settlements and cooperates with organizations that call for a more comprehensive BDS strategy.

Contentious Advocacy

The new organizations of the Jewish left have been joined in recent years by a raft of single-purpose Israel advocacy groups on the right and in the center.[32] On the right, these groups include the neoconservative Emergency Committee for Israel (founded 2010), which was created expressly to counter J Street. (The group's founder, political commentator William Kristol, ironically describes it as "the pro-Israel wing of the pro-Israel community.") The new groups also include the David Project (founded 2002), created to combat anti-Israel bias on university campuses, and Stand With Us (founded 2001), created to encourage grassroots responses to anti-Israel activities. Closer to the center, the new groups include the Israel Project (founded 2002), a well-funded organization that promotes favorable news coverage of Israel. Table 2.1 provides an overview of the contemporary field of Israel advocacy, highlighting the salient political divisions.[33]

In terms of revenue (Figure 2.1) and grassroots participation (Figure 2.2), the organizations of the center tower over the rest of the field. AIPAC's operating budget increased annually from $14.5 million in 2000 to $67 million in 2010. The organization boasts more than 100,000 paying members and an endowment of more than $140 million. Participation in AIPAC annual policy conferences has increased year after year, reaching 14,000 in 2012. The other major organizations of the center grew more moderately during the 2000s but continue to dwarf their more partisan rivals. For example, the American Jewish Committee,

Table 2.1. The Field of Israel Advocacy

Left	Center	Right
Americans for Peace Now	American Israel Public Affairs Committee	Americans for a Safe Israel
Ameinu	American Jewish Committee	Committee for Accuracy in Middle East Reporting
Israel Policy Forum	Anti-Defamation League	David Project
J Street	Conference of Presidents	Emergency Committee for Israel
Partners for Progressive Israel	Israel Project	Jewish Institute for National Security Affairs
Jewish Voice for Peace[a]	Jewish Council for Public Affairs	Stand With Us
		Zionist Organization of America

a. Jewish Voice for Peace does not define itself as "pro-Israel."

with a mandate that includes but is not limited to pro-Israel advocacy, has 175,000 paying members, a staff of 250, and an annual budget of about $40 million.

Several organizations of the right and left grew significantly during the decade of the 2000s, but the partisan organizations still command far fewer resources. On the right, Stand With Us grew to a staff of fifty and budget of $7 million. The David Project grew to a staff of twenty-five and budget of $4 million. The ZOA held steady with a professional staff of about fifty and $4 million in revenue. On the left, J Street similarly grew to a staff of fifty and total budget (including its educational and political divisions) of about $7 million. Americans for Peace Now and Ameinu (formerly the Labor Zionist Alliance) held steady, each with about six staff and a few million dollars in revenue.

Today, Israel advocacy organizations clash with one another over various issues in diverse arenas. In the following sections, we consider three arenas of conflict: Congress and the White House, campus and community organizations, and the media and public opinion. In relation to each arena, we examine the core issues in contention and the overall balance of power.

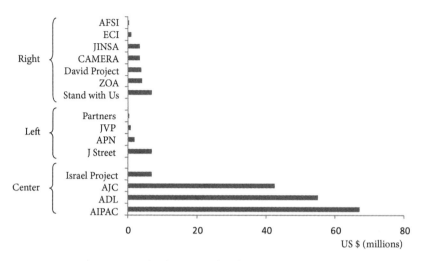

Figure 2.1. Revenue of Select Israel Advocacy Organizations, 2010
Source: U.S. Internal Revenue Service documents, except for J Street and ZOA. J Street estimate combines the group's political and educational activities, as described in the group's annual report. ZOA estimate is from an interview with the group's president, Morton Klein.

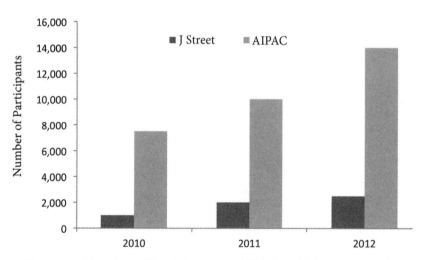

Figure 2.2. Number of Participants in AIPAC and J Street Annual Conferences

Congress and the White House

As a consequence of the institutionalization of organizations engaged in independent, partisan advocacy on the right and left, Israel advocacy organizations routinely clash with one another as they seek to mobilize supporters and influence Congress and the White House. In recent years, the most conspicuous struggles have been waged over three major issues: the Gaza War, West Bank settlements, and Iran.

The Gaza War, initiated by Israel in December 2008 in response to years of rocket fire on southern Israeli towns and villages, sparked diametrically opposing responses by the leading advocacy organizations. At the very start of the conflict, J Street issued a press release declaring "real friends of Israel recognize that . . . only diplomacy and negotiations can end rockets and terror." The statement called for "strong diplomatic intervention" by the United States and other parties to negotiate an immediate ceasefire. From the opposite end of the political spectrum, the ZOA encouraged Israel to "defeat Hamas" and permanently reoccupy borderline areas of Gaza—war aims that exceeded Israel's stated objectives in the conflict.[34] Of the three groups, only AIPAC expressed unconditional support for Israel's conduct and war aims. On Capitol Hill, more than one hundred members of Congress signed a policy letter issued by AIPAC; just seven expressed support for J Street's call for an immediate ceasefire.[35]

The major organizations have also clashed over the direction of U.S. policy on West Bank settlements. In 2009, in an effort to restart negotiations between Israel and the Palestinian Authority, President Obama called on Israel to freeze new construction in East Jerusalem and the West Bank. Some centrist organizations, including the Anti-Defamation League, joined right-wing groups in opposing the president's demand. The ADL published an advertisement with the headline "Mr. President, the problem isn't settlements, it's Arab rejection." J Street immediately issued a letter in response to the ADL advertisement, declaring that "peace isn't advanced by pointing fingers at either side." J Street, the Reform rabbinical association (representing two thousand rabbis), and a number of other left-leaning groups declared support for a settlement freeze.[36]

The conflict over the direction of U.S. policy on settlements came to the fore again in 2011 over a United Nations Security Council resolution condemning Israel for expansion of West Bank settlements. AIPAC and groups to its right lobbied the Obama administration to veto the resolution—as the United States has done in response to most previous UN resolutions condemning Israel. J Street, however, came out against the veto: "We cannot support a U.S. veto of a resolution that closely tracks long-standing American policy and that appropriately condemns Israeli settlement policy." For many establishment and right-wing figures, J Street's stance, which effectively enabled if not endorsed UN condemnation of Israel, confirmed the organization's status as outside the Jewish mainstream.

Finally, the national advocacy organizations have also clashed over the United States' Iran policy. The organizations on the right, including the ZOA and the Emergency Committee, have pressed relentlessly for a military response to Iran's nuclear program, including support either for U.S. military action or for an Israeli strike. AIPAC has not yet gone that far. In 2010, the organization collected signatures from three-quarters of the U.S. Congress (363 members of the House and 76 members of the Senate) calling for "crippling sanctions against Iran."[37] Two years later, speakers at the group's 2012 policy conference urged President Obama to delineate the "red lines" that would trigger a U.S. military response. This was too much for J Street, which responded with a video featuring American and Israeli military experts expressing doubt about the efficacy of a military strike. Interviewed in the *New York Times*, J Street director Jeremy Ben-Ami called for diplomacy and sanctions but drew the line at military action. "We're trying to calm down the drumbeat of war," said Ben-Ami.[38] After the conference, Dylan Williams, head of government affairs for J Street, commented on the dynamic between the pro-Israel organizations: "A lot of people talk about the 'Israel lobby' as if it's a monolithic thing," he said. "It's a myth. There is a deep division between those who support military action at this point and those who support diplomacy."[39]

In relation to Congress and the White House, the balance of power clearly tips toward the center. This is evident in the dominance of AIPAC in securing congressional signatures on its policy letters, as we have seen. For AIPAC and J Street, "inside the Beltway" influence can also be measured in terms of the number of public officials attending annual meetings and campaign donations.[40] President Obama and the four leading Republican presidential candidates addressed the 2012 AIPAC meeting; for the president, this was the fifth time that he addressed the gathering. More than half the members of the U.S. Congress also attended at least part of the three-day event. In contrast, the administration sent Anthony J. Blinken, national security advisor to Vice President Biden, to address the J Street conference; and only a handful of members of Congress visited the J Street event.

Campaign donations are a more problematic index of influence. J Street claims to be the largest pro-Israel political action committee (PAC), but this is true only in a limited sense: AIPAC is not a PAC and does not directly fund candidates. However, AIPAC's activists and board members are influential among the leaders of approximately two dozen pro-Israel PACs, and the organization is often credited with shaping their decisions about which candidates to endorse and which to support with campaign contributions.[41] In 2010, J Street contributed $1.5 million to congressional races; the other pro-Israel PACs contributed a total of $3.5 million.

Campus and Community Organizations

Outside of Washington, D.C., on college campuses and among community organizations, the proliferation of new organizations spanning the political spectrum has sparked an intense debate over what counts as "pro-Israel" and where the boundaries of legitimate dissent should be drawn. Should Hillel, the umbrella Jewish organization on college campuses, accept for membership Jewish groups that disavow the label "Zionist" and support boycotts of West Bank products? Should Jewish community institutions, such as synagogues and Jewish community centers, host events that criticize Israel's record on human rights and religious freedom? How large a tent should the Jewish community pitch? Where exactly should the tent stakes be nailed down and who should decide?

Consider the following anecdotes, drawn from press accounts of struggles on college campuses:

- The decision by the University of Pennsylvania Hillel to allow the school's J Street group to rent space for a lecture by Jeremy Ben-Ami sparked a wave of protest. Hillel board members and community activists demanded that Hillel rescind the rental agreement. "To me, it gave a hekscher [a kosher seal] that J Street is a mainstream Jewish organization, which I don't believe it is," explained Lori Lowenthal Marcus, a member of Philadelphia Hillel's executive committee. Rabbi Howard Albert, the campus Hillel director, countered that "these students deserve our trust." The lecture went ahead as planned and critics held a parallel event—a lecture by a former AIPAC staff member. In response to the incident, the University of Pennsylvania Hillel promulgated new rules for rental of its building to Jewish groups: To be eligible to rent the space, groups must support Israel's right to exists as a Jewish state, not advocate for boycotts or sanctions against Israel, and present viewpoints with civility.[42]

- The J Street group at the University of California, Berkeley is a member in good standing of the campus Hillel organization. In a highly contentious vote, however, the University's Jewish Student Union elected to keep J Street out. A student-run organization, the Jewish Student Union is governed by representatives of the university's Jewish organizations. Jacob Lewis, co-president of the student Israel advocacy group Tikvah, explained his decision to vote "no" on J Street's request for membership: "J Street is not pro-Israel but an anti-Israel organization that, as part of the mainstream Jewish community, I could not support." Members of the spurned J Street chapter responded in an op-ed in *The Forward* newspaper: "We often ask ourselves, 'Why are we fighting to be part of a community that doesn't want us?' Some have stopped asking the question and have simply walked away. We refuse. We demand a place in this community. We are still here."[43]

- At Brandeis University, where the J Street chapter is fully integrated into the larger bodies of Jewish campus life, contentiousness has focused on a group to its left, the Jewish Voice for Peace. Citing guidelines issued by the international Hillel organization that discourage affiliation with groups that support "boycotts of, divestment from or sanctions against the State of Israel," the Brandeis Hillel board voted not to admit the local JVP chapter. "We are a pro-Israel organization," said student Hillel president Andrea Wexler, "and while that can mean different things to different people, our definitions differed too much." Student members of the JVP chapter objected, explaining that their support for boycotts includes only products produced in the West Bank. "We were rejected on the grounds that boycotting settlement goods is the same thing as boycotting Israel," said Morgan Conley, a member of the

Brandeis JVP chapter. "The reality, however, is that the settlements are not in Israel—they are in the occupied Palestinian territories."[44]

Beyond the campuses, Jewish communal organizations also grapple with the question of which groups can legitimately be included in the "pro-Israel" community and should receive community funding. The struggle has been waged within and between federations, Jewish community centers, Jewish film festivals, synagogues, and communal umbrella organizations (e.g., Jewish community relations councils). Consider the following anecdotes culled, as above, from the Jewish press:

- In Washington, D.C., a group calling itself Committee Opposed to Propaganda Masquerading as Art campaigned to ban Jewish federation funding of a Jewish theatrical group, Theatre J, for staging plays deemed too critical of Israel. The group was especially incensed by Theatre J's decision to stage Caryl Churchill's Seven Jewish Children, a play described by its critics as "virulently anti-Semitic." Theater J artistic director Ari Roth responded that it "is not the prerogative of the donor" to intervene in artistic content. A member of the local Jewish community relations council responded in The Forward, "There are things a Jewish community shouldn't be doing, like serving a bacon cheeseburger on Yom Kippur. Putting on an anti-Semitic play is one of these things."[45]
- In New York, a group calling itself JCC Watch similarly urged the New York Federation to suspend support for the Manhattan Jewish Community Center. The Manhattan JCC's offense was to host events sponsored by organizations that the activists viewed as anti-Israel, including B'Tselem, an Israeli human rights organization, and Breaking the Silence, a group of Israeli army veterans opposed to the occupation. Citing its commitment to supporting diverse Jewish viewpoints, the Federation refused to cave in to the pressure.[46]
- In Newton, Massachusetts, a Reform synagogue cancelled at the last minute a lecture by J Street's Jeremy Ben-Ami. The synagogue's rabbi explained that intense pressure by a few prominent members of the congregation made holding the event impossible. Ben-Ami lectured down the street, at a neighborhood elementary school, to a standing-room-only crowd. (Although banned from the Reform synagogue, Boston's J Street chapter

was subsequently inducted into the Boston Jewish Community Relations Council.)

The intense contentiousness over who should be inside the communal tent may create a distorted impression of organizational influence at the local level. On the whole, the large advocacy organizations of the political center maintain much stronger footholds in communities and on campuses than the partisan groups to the right and left. The ADL, AJC, and AIPAC, for example, maintain chapters and regional offices throughout North America, employing hundreds of professionals and engaging the support of thousands of grassroots activists. In contrast, J Street inherited Brit Tzedek's grassroots network and built it up to forty-four volunteer-led local chapters; the ZOA reports twenty-six volunteer-led local chapters. I attended a meeting of the Boston J Street chapter in spring 2012 that drew several hundred participants, including much of the community's mainstream leadership. The show of support for the dissident organization was impressive but does not yet put it in league with its better-established and more centrist counterparts.

The situation is much the same on the college campuses. On the left, J Street has chapters on forty campuses and drew 650 college activists to its 2012 national conference.[47] On the right, the ZOA has twenty-four campus chapters and reports increased participation in its training workshops and Israel trip. The right-leaning organizations Stand With Us, the David Project, and Hasbara Fellowships have all beefed up their campus outreach and organizing. AIPAC, however, continues to tower over the rest, drawing 1,600 college students from fifty states to its 2012 policy conference (with 600 more on a waiting list). The organization drew an additional 9,000 students to its advocacy training seminars, including the Saban Leadership Conference and a dozen similar events. College campuses have become much more contentious sites for debates among student activists representing an expanding spectrum of opinion; however, on college campuses, as in Washington, D.C., AIPAC still dominates.

Mass Media and Public Opinion

Contestation among Israel advocacy organizations extends to the fundamental question, "Who speaks for the Jews?" Since the authority to represent the views of the community is largely a matter of perception, competition among the groups extends into the domains of media coverage and public opinion.

To assess media coverage, we conducted a modest content analysis of news outlets that roughly represent the general U.S. media, the Israeli media, and the American Jewish media. To represent the general U.S. media, we included the *New York Times* and the *Wall Street Journal*. To represent the Israeli news media, we included the *Jerusalem Post* and the English-language version of *Haaretz*. To represent the American Jewish press, we included the weekly newspapers *The Jewish Week* and *The Forward*. Our focus was on coverage of three organizations— AIPAC, the ZOA, and J Street—that roughly represent the spectrum of Israel advocacy. We included all news stories and opinion pieces published during the period 2009–11.

Figure 2.3 shows coverage in the sample of news stories. In general, coverage in the Israeli newspapers was the most extensive, followed by the American Jewish papers (notwithstanding the fact that they are weeklies rather than dailies) and the U.S. general press. In terms of the distribution of coverage, AIPAC was mentioned in the largest number of columns but J Street also received substantial attention (generally two-thirds as much as AIPAC). Most AIPAC stories reported news from the group's annual policy conference, including quotations from speeches and policy statements. In contrast, most stories about J Street reported on the organization itself, including stories about its policy positions, organizational growth, and future prospects. The ZOA was much less visible in this sample of news stories. In my view, the gap between AIPAC and J Street is rather small in light of the latter's newcomer status.

As shown in Figure 2.4, the pattern of coverage in opinion pieces and editorials is similar, with AIPAC receiving the most attention, followed by J Street. The ZOA again appears as a distant third. In addition to the numerical tally, we coded the opinion pieces and editorials for their editorial content in relation to the advocacy organizations. The direction of editorial opinion generally reflected the news outlets' political orientations, in particular with respect to the Israeli news outlets. As shown in Figure 2.5, in the right-leaning *Jerusalem Post*, most editorial mentions of AIPAC were neutral or positive, whereas most mentions

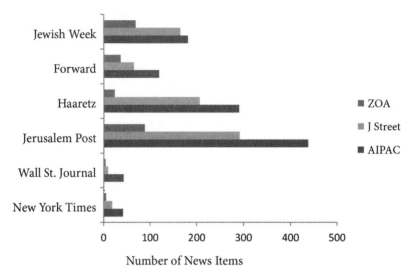

Figure 2.3. Mentions of Leading Advocacy Organizations in News
Stories, 2009–2011

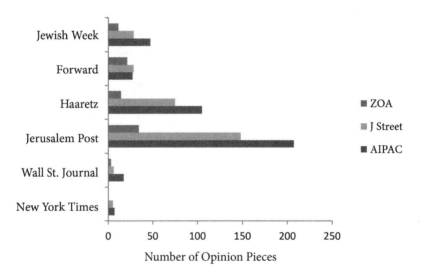

Figure 2.4. Mentions of Leading Advocacy Organizations in
Opinion Pieces, 2009–2011

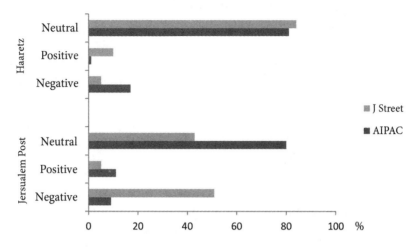

Figure 2.5. Direction of Editorial Opinion in Israeli English-Language News Outlets

of J Street were neutral or negative. Much of the negative commentary on J Street came from a few regular columnists who describe the organization as "anti-Israel." In contrast, in the left-leaning *Haaretz*, most mentions of J Street were neutral or positive, whereas most mentions of AIPAC were neutral or negative. In *Haaretz*, the negative depictions of AIPAC were by a variety of columnists who described the organization's political activities as harmful to Israel's interests.

To what extent does this pattern of media coverage influence the consciousness of American Jews about the rival Israel advocacy organizations? Later, I devote a chapter to the political opinions of American Jews on Israel-related issues. Here I want to report the limited information we have on the attitudes of American Jews about AIPAC and J Street. There are just two studies that examined Jewish attitudes regarding these organizations. The first is a survey conducted by Brandeis University's Cohen Center of a sample of American Jewish young adults who applied to the Birthright Israel program between the years 2001 and 2006. The respondents to the survey—about two-thirds of whom actually went on a Birthright trip—were between the ages of twenty-three and thirty-six at the time we administered the survey. We asked, in reference to AIPAC and J Street, whether respondents had heard of each organization and whether they supported its mission. Overall, 58 percent of respondents had heard of AIPAC, compared to 29 percent who had heard of J Street. Among the minority of respondents who had heard of both organizations and had opinions regarding their missions, 36 percent "very much" supported AIPAC, compared to 26 percent who "very much" supported J Street.[48]

In the leadership cadre of the American Jewish community, however, the situation is more complex. In a 2011 survey of ordained rabbis and current rabbinical students of the Conservative movement's Jewish Theological Seminary, Steven M. Cohen reported sharp generational differences in attitudes toward AIPAC and J Street. In the following summary of findings, Cohen contrasts the responses of older rabbis (ordained 1980–94), younger rabbis (1995–2011), and current rabbinical students:

> In moving from older rabbis to the students, we see marked shifts in their attitudes toward . . . AIPAC and J Street. . . . The levels of support (the percent somewhat or very favorable) for AIPAC drop from 80 percent among the older rabbis, to 64 percent among younger rabbis, to 42 percent among the students. In contrast, the comparable support levels for J Street mount from 32 percent to 54 percent to 58 percent, respectively. In other words, among older rabbis, AIPAC strongly out-polls J Street (80 percent to 32 percent). Among younger rabbis, the gap narrows with AIPAC still leading (64 percent to 54 percent). But among the students, AIPAC falls behind J Street in favorability ratings (42 percent to 58 percent).[49]

Notably, the survey found no significant differences among the older rabbis, younger rabbis, and rabbinical students in their level of emotional connection to Israel. The generational differences in attitudes toward AIPAC and J Street express political differences and not declining emotional attachment to the Jewish state.

To summarize, in two of the three major arenas of competition, the centrist advocacy groups, led by AIPAC, clearly retain the upper hand. In fact, AIPAC has been increasing its organizational power in recent years. However, the advocacy organizations of the left and right have

achieved firm footholds in Washington, D.C., on campuses and in Jewish communities across the country, and in the mass media. Most pro-
vocatively, a key segment of the leadership cadre of the Jewish community—Conservative rabbis and rabbinical students—is evenly divided
in its sympathies for AIPAC and J Street, with the next generation of
rabbis expressing more favorable attitudes toward the dovish advocacy
group. In short, the balance of power still tilts toward the center, but the
united front characteristic of the pre-Oslo years has been shattered.

Advocacy in Israel

Alongside the rising tide of partisan advocacy aimed at influencing
the policies of the U.S. government, American Jewish organizations
have increasingly sought to directly influence the policies of the Israeli
government. Direct lobbying of the Israeli government began with
struggles over conversion. In the late 1980s—and then again in the late
1990s—Israeli religious parties introduced legislation in the Knesset to
grant legal authority over conversion to the Orthodox rabbinate. The
religious parties were motivated, in part, by a desire to prevent large-
scale conversion of Russian immigrants via non-Orthodox procedures. The Reform and Conservative movements, joined by the leading establishment organizations (e.g., the AJC, the ADL, and AIPAC),
mobilized intense political opposition to the proposed conversion laws.
Delegations of diaspora leaders trekked to Israel to lobby Israeli officials; rabbis delivered sermons warning of an irreversible break in the
diaspora's relationship to the Jewish state; the New Israel Fund called
for donations to be diverted from the Jewish Agency to its fund in support of religious pluralism. Reform movement leader Rabbi Eric Yoffie
explained the intensity of opposition to the proposed conversion laws:
"If Reform rabbis in Israel are not rabbis and their conversions are not
conversions that means our Judaism is not Judaism and that we are
second class Jews." It mattered little that authority over conversions in
Israel was, de facto, already in the hands of Orthodox authorities.[50]

The drama over conversion unfolded for a third time at the end of the
2000s as a broad alliance of American Jewish groups, including the leading rabbinical, advocacy, and philanthropic arms of American Jewry,
lobbied against Knesset legislation that promised to ease conversion

standards inside of Israel for hundreds of thousands of Russian Jews. Sponsored by the Russian-led Yisrael Beiteinu Party, the so-called Rotem Bill proposed to empower municipal rabbis, some of whom opposed the restrictive approach of the state's official rabbinical courts, to conduct conversions. The Chief Rabbinate expressed willingness to embrace the plan but on the condition that, for the first time, ultimate legal authority for approval of conversions conducted inside the state of Israel be placed in its hands. Although the legislation would not have altered the status of conversions conducted by non-Orthodox rabbis outside of Israel, which are recognized by the state of Israel, the symbolic degradation of their movements inside the state was unacceptable. As in the past, the broad and intense opposition of mainstream American Jewish groups killed the effort to alter the status quo on conversion.[51]

In the 2000s, mainstream groups began adopting partisan positions on additional aspects of Israeli society and the conflict with Palestinians. For example, a broad coalition of organizations from the political center, including the large federations and most of the mainstream advocacy organizations, created the Inter-Agency Task Force on Israeli Arab Issues. The aim of the group, which has a small professional staff, is to advocate for civic equality in Israel and promote education about Arab-Israeli civil rights issues in the North American Jewish community. The centrist, mainstream groups that support the coalition embrace the view that American Jews have a special contribution to make to Israel concerning the issue of minority rights: "American Jews can play a key role in encouraging greater engagement by Israel's leaders and the Israeli public on this crucial challenge. American Jews are able to draw upon a wealth of practical experience informed by their long struggle as a minority fighting discrimination and working to optimize opportunities for all Americans."[52]

American Jewish organizations also directly lobby the Israeli government concerning the future of Jerusalem. Left-leaning advocacy organizations, including J Street, Ameinu, and Americans for Peace Now, consistently support the principle that Jerusalem will serve as the capital of two states. They were joined in the late 2000s by the Reform movement. The Orthodox Union, the ADL, and a raft of other center and right-wing organizations have either opposed territorial division of Jerusalem or argued that because of Jerusalem's religious significance, diaspora Jews must be consulted about its future. "Since Jerusalem belongs to all the Jewish people," said ADL head Abraham Foxman, "decisions about its future are not just an Israeli decision."[53] (Political scientist Ofira Seliktar describes this position as the "doctrine of limited sovereignty."[54])

More recently, a number of mainstream organizations, including ADL, AJC, and the Reform movement, have taken stands against proposed Knesset laws that would restrict civil liberties or limit funding to Israeli human rights NGOs. On the day after a preliminary Knesset vote on legislation calling for investigation of the funding sources of NGOs that criticize the Israeli army, AJC president David Harris declared, "The Knesset's action today contravenes the democratic principles that are Israel's greatest strength. Israel's vibrant democracy not only can survive criticism, it also thrives and is improved by it." The Reform movement and the ADL issued complementary statements. Explaining the trend toward outspoken critique of some of Israel's policies by mainstream organizations, William Daroff, director of the Washington Office of the Jewish Federations of North America, commented, "Diaspora Jewry has an obligation to stand up. People should not be *hasbara* (propaganda) agents."[55]

Today, American Jewish groups seem to weigh in on almost every domestic Israeli issue. The ADL's Abraham Foxman traveled to a Tel Aviv school to announce his opposition to the planned deportation of 400 children of foreign workers. "Everything about the values of Israel and the Jewish people screams to us: Do not send these children away! The biblical injunction to treat the stranger in your midst as you treat your own rings loud and clear." He then explained his rationale for taking a stand on the treatment of foreign workers in Israel: "On an issue like this, where the well-being of 400 children is at state, it is important for American Jews and American Jewish leaders to weigh in. And so I am here with you today in solidarity, not against the government of Israel but in standing up for what is best in the Jewish people, what is best in Jewish values, what is best in the Jewish and democratic State of Israel." In the same vein, the ADL and AJC issued statements blasting some ultra-Orthodox rabbis for instructing Jews not to rent apartments to African migrants.[56] Following rioting against African migrants in spring 2012, J Street, the ADL, and numerous other left and mainstream groups issued statements condemning the violence.[57]

Conclusion

After the announcement of the Oslo Accords, the consensus model for Israel advocacy previously embraced by American Jewish organizations fractured. In the mid-1990s, the American Jewish right, led by the ZOA, lobbied the U.S. Congress for policies that subverted the priorities of the center-left Israeli government. It did so in part at the urging of Israeli Likud Party officials, then in the opposition. For its role in breaking the consensus, the right earned the opprobrium of the Jewish establishment, including harsh criticism in the Jewish press and efforts to sanction its leadership in the Presidents Conference. A decade later, the American Jewish left, led by the newly established J Street, followed much the same script, criticizing the policies of Israel's center-right government. As in the earlier period, the dissident groups were supported by Israeli opposition party officials and were subjected to reproach in the press and by the leadership of establishment organizations.

Notwithstanding the addition of many new advocacy organizations representing positions across the political spectrum, the centrist advocacy organizations, led by AIPAC, continue to dominate the field of Israel advocacy. They raise more money, employ larger professional staffs, and have more paying members than their rivals on the right and left. They also wield greater influence in Washington, D.C., on college campuses, and in Jewish communal organizations. The two documented exceptions to this pattern of dominance concern media coverage and the political sympathies of Conservative rabbis and rabbinical students. The latter finding—that Conservative rabbis and rabbinical students are divided in their sympathies for J Street and AIPAC—is especially significant. Perhaps more than any other single factor, the broad support of younger rabbis and rabbinical students for J Street indicates that polarization is more than surface deep.

Alongside increased partisan lobbying of the U.S. government, the past two decades have witnessed a rise in direct lobbying by U.S. Jewish organizations of the Israeli government and intervention in Israeli political debates. This kind of direct engagement began with the Reform movement's opposition to Israeli policies on marriage and conversion but has since spread to a wide range of Jewish organizations engaged in advocacy concerning an ever-expanding range of issues. Increasingly,

American Jews, including representatives of the establishment, stake out clear positions on issues that were once commonly viewed as the purview of Israeli citizens alone. They declare their views not as American citizens seeking to influence the U.S. government but as Jews seeking to influence the Israeli government. More broadly, they seek to shape Israel's future after their own particular (and often conflicting) visions of the ideal Jewish state.

3

Fundraising and Philanthropy

During the run-up to the establishment of Israel, and then during the first four decades of the state's existence, American Jews provided vital financial assistance. Called upon by their local federations and the United Jewish Appeal to support Israel, American Jews donated generously and without strings attached. Over the past quarter century, the federations' annual campaigns have stagnated, the donor pool has shrunk, and the portion allocated to Israel has reached a historic nadir. The overall amount of money American Jews give to causes in Israel, however, has actually *increased*. It has done so as American Jews have elected to give directly to an ever-expanding number of Israeli nonprofit organizations that appeal for their support. In the emerging system of direct giving, moreover, a significant portion of philanthropic money flows to causes associated with the political right or left rather than to support Israel—the state and its citizens—more generally. The new partisan fundraising, in turn, has produced considerable legal and political controversy, in both Israel and the United States.

Federations and United Jewish Appeal

Throughout the 1990s and 2000s, the collective fundraising of the North American Jewish federations for local and overseas Jewish needs hovered just shy of $1 billion annually. At this level, the federations joined the largest charitable organizations in the United States, and their annual campaigns, although not increasing year by year, nevertheless reflected a significant fundraising achievement.[1]

The stable level of year-by-year fundraising, however, masks a sharp decline in the overall number of donors to the federation campaigns. Over the past two decades, the number of donors to federation campaigns has decreased from nearly 900,000 to fewer than 500,000.[2] During these years, the larger contributions from donors who remained loyal to the federation system offset the decline in absolute number of donors. In part, the shrinking number of donors is a consequence of federation strategy that has focused on maximizing the gifts of large donors who are much less costly to court.[3] The shrinking donor pool, however, is also a reflection of broader dynamics, including the rapid development of information technologies associated with the Internet. Among smaller donors, an increased awareness of the work of diverse charitable organizations reduced the perceived need for the federations' key function—to identify worthy causes and package and deliver donations.[4] Donors increasingly perceived the federations as "overhead" that reduced the effectiveness of their gifts. Similar dynamics have reduced the number of individual donors to United Way campaigns (which were originally modeled on the federation system).[5]

Individual federations (there are 157 of them) make their own determinations about the portion of their annual campaigns they will allocate to "overseas needs," which in the early 1990s still meant the United Jewish Appeal (UJA).[6] The UJA in turn divided the pooled overseas contributions between the United Israel Appeal (UIA), which received 75 percent, and the American Jewish Joint Distribution Committee (JDC), which received 25 percent. According to U.S. law, tax-deductible donations cannot be made directly to an overseas organization but must be channeled through a U.S.-based nonprofit organization that retains control over allocations overseas. The UIA is the U.S.-based affiliate of the Jewish Agency for Israel (JAFI) and serves the dual function of channeling tax-deductible contributions to JAFI and appointing one-third of its directors. The JDC, in contrast, is an American organization and therefore able to receive UJA funds directly. Although it was once the senior partner in the UJA, the JDC's share decreased following the founding of the state of Israel, and the 75–25 percent split between JAFI and the JDC continued throughout the 1990s and 2000s.

As discussed in Chapter 1, donations to JAFI via the UIA have historically supported new immigration, community development, social welfare, and Zionist education. A large quasi-public agency with hundreds of staff and an annual budget of more than $500 million, JAFI has been the preeminent vehicle for diaspora Jewish contributions to the state of Israel. Donations to the JDC, in contrast, have supported the organization's work in destitute Jewish communities throughout the world. Although the JDC mostly focused on providing relief to Jewish communities in the former Communist Bloc countries, the organization has also sponsored projects in Israel. As a result, in a typical year well over 80 percent of the total UJA-federation system's allocation for "overseas needs" in fact makes its way to the Jewish state.

As federations' annual campaigns leveled off, their perceptions of proper balance between local and overseas needs shifted rather dramatically. The 1990 National Jewish Population Study, which reported an intermarriage rate of 52 percent (subsequently adjusted downward a bit), galvanized concern over assimilation and "continuity." The Oslo Accords and Israel's economic growth provided additional impetus for an inward turn by the federations. Peace with the Palestinians seemed close at hand, and Israelis seemed increasingly capable of caring for their own social welfare needs. Confirming the impression, Deputy Foreign Minister Yossi Beilin urged American Jewish audiences to divert their donations from Israeli causes to Jewish education in the diaspora, including trips for diaspora young adults to Israel to strengthen Jewish identity and ties to the Jewish state.[7]

During the early 1990s the federations continued to fund overseas needs at a high level largely in support of the immigration of the Jews of the former Soviet Union to Israel. (Between 1990 and 1995, federations raised nearly $1 billion for resettlement of Soviet Jews.[8]) By the middle of the decade, however, the federations were shifting their resources to local needs including Jewish education.[9] The proportion of the federations' annual campaigns donated to the UIA steadily decreased from 47 percent in 1990 to 38 percent in 1997 and to 23 percent in 2004.[10] This downward slide reflected the cumulative decision making of dozens of individual federations throughout the United States and Canada regarding priorities and allocations.

By the end of the 1990s, supporters of the federations' overseas role were ready to try a new approach. In 1999, the Council of Jewish Federations (CJF), the UJA, and the UIA merged to form a new organization, the United Jewish Communities (UJC). (A decade later, the UJC changed its name to Jewish Federations of North America.) One goal of the merger was to increase federation support for overseas allocations to JAFI and the JDC by giving the federations more direct ownership of those organizations. The notion was that the federations would view JAFI and the JDC as equivalent to their local agencies and therefore remain committed to allocating for their needs.[11] From a practical standpoint, the change meant that the federations would have a direct role in the governance of JAFI by gaining the right to appoint the UIA's portion of its directors (the rest are appointed by Keren Hayesod—the equivalent of the federation movement in Europe and Latin America—and by the World Zionist Organization).

At the time of the merger, the federations also created the Overseas Needs Assessment and Distribution (ONAD) committee to systematically review the overseas activities. The aim was to address federation concerns that JAFI and the JDC were engaged in duplicative activities and that JAFI's operations were politicized by the Israeli government and overly bureaucratic. The ONAD process was intended to professionalize decision making regarding the federations' overseas activities—to assess needs and improve oversight. It also introduced a degree of flexibility, permitting, for the first time, the federations to earmark a small portion of their overseas donations to particular projects. In practice, ONAD did little to change the cultures and operating styles of the federations' overseas partners. Nor did the new system motivate federations to devote larger shares of their budgets to overseas needs.[12]

Throughout the 2000s, combined federation donations to overseas causes (i.e., to JAFI and the JDC) averaged about one-quarter of the federation annual campaigns, which translated to about $200 million annually to the JAFI and $65 million to the JDC. Donations spiked higher during years that included "emergency campaigns," for example, during the Second Intifada (2001–3) and during the Second Lebanon War (2006), but then returned to previous levels. With the pressure of settling immigrants from the former Soviet Union who arrived in the previous decade greatly diminished, JAFI was able to live within its budgetary constraints. The JDC, however, was not. With its mission of providing assistance to Israel's poor still urgent—and already chafing at the lopsided split of federation-raised funds—the JDC chose to step up its own independent fundraising and expand its activities in Israel. We will discuss its work below, in the context of the huge expansion of direct fundraising and targeted giving that developed in recent decades. Later, we will return to the centralized, federation-JAFI system and consider its future.

The Rise of Direct Giving

A handful of Israeli organizations, including a number of Israel's leading universities and hospitals, had long operated outside of the federation-UJA framework, appealing directly to American Jews for support. The UJA sought to limit the number of such competing fundraising efforts through its Committee for the Control and Authorization of Campaigns.[13] By alternatively threatening and cajoling, the committee was able to limit the number of organizations engaged in independent fundraising. In 1985, the committee published a list of "classically approved charities" that were permitted to continue direct solicitation of American Jewish donors alongside the federation campaigns. The list included organizations such as Hadassah, American Friends of the Hebrew University, and the Jewish National Fund.

By the 1980s, however, the UJA's capacity to limit independent fundraising was already unraveling. In 1980, the New Israel Fund (NIF), created to support progressive causes in Israel including civil rights, women's rights, and Arab-Jewish coexistence, was established with $80,000 from eighty donors. Like the federations, the NIF accepted gifts in every permutation from unrestricted donations to bequests, trusts, and designated giving. By 1995 the fund had allocated $106 million.[14] Israeli social welfare, educational, cultural, and religious organizations followed suit, hiring fundraisers and establishing American Friends fundraising affiliates in the United States. By the end of the 1980s the number of American Friends organizations increased to 265, by 2000 it reached 436, and by 2010 it was 667.[15]

The huge increase in the number of Israeli organizations fundraising among American Jews through U.S.-based affiliate organizations must be understood in relation to the growth of the Israeli nonprofit sector as a whole. Following its 1977 victory, Israel's right-wing Likud government began dismantling the Israeli welfare state, preferring to contract services privately rather than operate through quasi–state agencies with strong political ties to the Labor Party. As Israel's nonprofit sector expanded in the 1980s and 1990s, it looked increasingly to American Jewry for support.[16] U.S. Internal Revenue Service regulations that treat donations to foreign charities as tax deductible so long as they flow through American nonprofit organizations provided the regulatory framework for this practice.[17]

The surge in direct fundraising by Israeli nonprofit organizations also reflected an increased desire on the part of donors to target their contributions. Donors were increasingly dissatisfied with giving through the umbrella UJA and instead wanted to "see and feel their money at work."[18] They increasingly wanted to choose the specific causes they supported within Israel: a program for at-risk teenagers; a soup kitchen; a dance company; a secular Jewish learning center; and so forth. The increase in the number and diversity of Israeli organizations fundraising in the United States made such broad choice possible for the first time. It also made donations targeted at Israeli charities and nonprofit organizations as easy as a donation to the UJA.

Trends in Total Giving

The diversification of fundraising means that a full account of American Jewish donations to causes in Israel must include not only the UJA but other fundraising vehicles as well. A reasonably complete list must include the following:

- American Friends organizations. These are American nonprofit organizations established to support one specific charitable or nonprofit organization abroad.
- Ideological umbrella funds. These are organizations that fundraise to serve a particular ideological or political purpose in Israel, for example, to support West Bank settlers or to promote democracy and human rights.

Table 3.1. Donations to Israeli Organizations by Year

Year	Jewish Agency (UJA)	Direct donations to Israeli NGOs	Total (current dollars)	Total (2010 dollars)
1975	223 M	*60 M*	*283 M*	*1.147 B*
1985	261 M	*200 M*	*461 M*	*934 M*
1994	224 M	*550 M*	*774 M*	*1.139 B*
2007	330 M	1.729 B	2.059 B	2.165 B
2010	169 M	1.281 B	1.450 B	1.450 B

Note: Values in italics are estimates. All values are in U.S. dollars.

- Pass-through funds. These funds function as vehicles for donations to Israeli charities or nonprofit organizations that, by and large, do not have their own American Friends groups.
- Foundation and federation projects in Israel. In some instances, foundations and federations operate their own projects in Israel or make contributions directly to Israeli organizations rather than through their American Friends affiliates.[19]

Researchers have tried to estimate total giving, including both UJA giving and giving that goes through these additional fundraising/fund-allocating vehicles. Table 3.1 shows contemporaneous estimates for select years and the equivalent sums in 2010 dollars. Goldberg reported that in 1975 American Jews donated $223 million to the UJA to support the JAFI; in that same year, he estimated that American Jews donated an additional $60 million to other Israeli organizations.[20] Kosmin reported that in 1985 American Jews donated $261 million to the UJA-JAFI; in that same year, he estimated that American Jews donated an additional $200 million to other Israeli organizations. Wertheimer reported that in 1994 American Jews donated $224 million to the UJA-JAFI. In that same year, Wertheimer estimated that, *worldwide,* Jews donated an additional $690 million to other Israeli organizations; for our own purposes, we estimate the American share at 80 percent, or $550 million.[21]

For 2007 and 2010, Table 3.1 reports the findings of research I conducted with Eric Fleisch examining the tax filings of organizations that raise money for causes in Israel. We chose 2007, the year before the beginning of the severe recession, in order to include a peak year for American Jewish donations, and 2010, which was the most recent year for which complete data were available. Through a combination of keyword searches of Internal Revenue Service databases such as Guidestar, searches of the web, and key-informant interviews, we identified 774 American Jewish organizations that transfer funds to Israel. This figure includes the 667 American Friends groups mentioned above plus dozens of umbrella funds, pass-through funds, and direct-donating foundations and federations.[22] We then examined IRS tax filings (990 forms), noting the dollar amount donated to these organizations for select years.[23] According to this research, in 2007 American Jews donated more than $2 billion to causes in Israel. In 2010, following a postrecession dip, the figure was $1.45 billion.[24]

As Table 3.1 shows, the overall trend, in inflation-adjusted dollars, is toward increased giving: a doubling between 1994 and 2007 and then a falling partway back during the recession years that followed.[25] By 2007, direct giving by American Jews to Israeli causes was more than five times greater than giving through annual campaigns of the federations. The gains in direct giving have more than offset declines in donations through the federations, and overall giving to Israel-based causes was greater in 2010 than in the 1990s, notwithstanding the postrecession slump.[26]

Do increasing donations mean that the proportion of American Jews giving to causes in Israel is, contrary to the prevailing view, actually increasing? One survey administered on behalf of J Street reports that 32 percent of respondents gave to a cause in Israel.[27] Unfortunately, surveys of American Jews only rarely ask specifically about such donations. It is therefore impossible to double-check the figure from the J Street survey or determine whether it indicates a change from the past. However, findings from a pair of surveys of the New York Jewish population conducted in 2002 and 2011 identify a relevant trend. According to these surveys, the number of households donating to any Jewish cause held steady while the number donating to the UJA-federation declined.[28] This finding lends plausibility to the hypothesis that during the same period, the pool of donors for causes in Israel either held steady or increased even as the donor base to the federation campaigns contracted.

Giving by Category

What causes do American Jews support with their targeted donations? To find out, we categorized donations reported in the IRS 990
forms. Figure 3.1 shows total donations to Israeli organizations for
2010, by category.[29] In the sections that follow, we unpack the categories and describe the largest fundraising organizations. The dollar sums
reported in parentheses reflect funds raised in 2010 and shown in Figure 3.1. The substantial group of uncategorized donations deserves
mention up front. This category mostly comprises donations to the PEF
Israel Endowment, an organization established in 1923 by Justice Louis
Brandeis. In recent decades, the fund has channeled donations to hundreds of Israeli nonprofit organizations that do not have their own U.S.
affiliates. The PEF beneficiaries run the gamut of charitable organizations and are active in most of the fields described below. In 2010, the
PEF transferred about $45 million in earmarked donations to Israeli
nonprofit organizations.[30]

Zionist Organizations

The leading category of donations, with more than $300 million raised,
is composed of historic Zionist organizations plus a few recent additions that share the same purposes. These are charities created for the
purpose of building the Jewish state through land acquisition, immigration, resettlement, economic development, and Zionist education.
The group is dominated by the UIA, which received $169 million from
the federations in 2010. Notwithstanding its steady decline over the past
two decades, the UIA remains the single largest organizational vehicle
for American Jewish donations to causes in Israel. As in the past, the
funds raised by the UIA are transferred to the JAFI.

The category includes the Jewish National Fund ($37 million), an
organization established in 1901 to purchase land in Palestine for Jewish settlement and which today raises funds primarily for forestation,
water, land management, and community development projects. Long
a consensus charity identified by its iconic blue boxes and campaigns to
plant trees in Israel, the JNF in recent years has been challenged for its

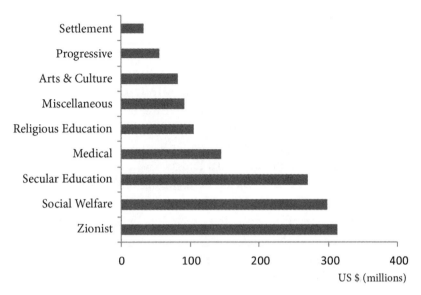

Figure 3.1. Federated and Direct Giving, by Category, 2010

policy against selling land to non-Jews and for displacing Bedouin in the Negev.[31] Nevertheless, the organization reports enormous growth. During the 2000s, the donor base increased from fewer than 100,000 to more than a half million, and revenue from fundraising increased from the $15 to $20 million range in the late 1990s, to the $40 million range for most of the 2000s, reaching $65 million for 2011. Director Russell Robinson attributes the JNF's fundraising success to improved outreach by the group's sixty-five-person fundraising staff, innovative use of the Internet and direct mail, and the organization's commitment to cultivating small donors and younger donors. (Indeed, as the group's donor base expanded in the 2000s, the average donor age dropped from seventy-four to fifty-nine.[32])

The category also includes two much newer organizations whose work we examine in Chapter 4: Birthright Israel ($52 million), which raises funds to support educational tours of Israel for diaspora young adults, and Nefesh B'Nefesh ($14.3 million), which promotes and facilitates aliyah from North America.

Welfare and Development

The American Jewish Joint Distribution Committee ($57 million) is the leading private philanthropic actor in the Israeli social welfare field. Although one of the founders of the UJA (see Chapter 1), the JDC embarked in the late 1990s on independent fundraising, courting especially a relatively small number of very wealthy Jewish donors. Most of its annual budget is now raised directly rather than through the centralized federation system.[33] With an annual budget for its Israel-based projects of more than $125 million (including contributions by the Israeli government and other partners), the JDC operates a far-flung network of programs for vulnerable populations, including immigrants, the elderly, at-risk children, the disabled, and the unemployed. The organization approaches its service work in a strategic fashion, seeking partners and striving over time to persuade municipal and national governments to assume greater responsibility.[34] The JDC's programs for at-risk children and Ethiopian immigrants have also attracted federation partners—but as direct donors rather than through the centralized federation system (more on this below). The JDC's systematic approach to Israel's social welfare needs is reflected in its support for two of Israel's leading social research institutes, the Taub Center and the Brookdale Institute.

The social services category also includes American Friends of the Israel Defense Forces ($57 million), an organization that funds academic scholarships, social services, and recreational facilities for soldiers and veterans. With fourteen regional offices and chapters spread across the United States, the AFIDF is among the largest fundraising operations for an Israeli cause. More than 25,000 donors contributed to the organization in 2010—a nearly fourfold increase in fundraising from a decade ago. The 2010 gala dinner at the Waldorf Astoria Hotel in New York attracted 1,500 donors and raised nearly $23.5 million. Minister of Defense Ehud Barak delivered the keynote address. Six former chiefs of staff of the Israeli armed forces were in attendance, and Prime Minister Benjamin Netanyahu addressed the gathering by video link.

Each of Israel's largest cities hosts a foundation that supports local educational, recreational, and medical institutions, as well as community development in its many diverse forms. The largest of these, the Jerusalem Foundation ($10 million), raises funds for a variety of projects. As a philanthropic organization serving a mixed city, the Jerusalem Foundation stresses its work in both Jewish and Arab parts of Israel's capital, although the allocation of grants reflects the concerns of its mostly Jewish donors more than the composition of the city.

Finally, alongside these relatively large organizations, American Jews give to dozens of funds and organizations, many under religious auspices, to address the needs of Israel's poor and vulnerable populations. Some such organizations, including Meir Panim ($3 million), which runs food and social service programs for poor families, and Yad Sarah ($2 million), which provides free medical equipment for home use, have U.S. affiliate offices in New York but operate with minimal professional staff. Others have no official presence in the United States and instead collect earmarked donations through a pass-through fund such as the PEF Israel Endowment.[35]

Secular Education

Among Israel's major universities, two scientific research centers lead the field in fundraising among American Jews. The Weizmann Institute of Science ($37 million) and Technion-Israel Institute of Technology ($60 million) each raised $35 to $75 million annually in the United States during most of the 2000s. Technion reports having raised $1 billion for its Shaping Israel's Future campaign (1996–2010), and the Weizmann Institute reports donations of over $100 million for 2007. To raise these remarkable sums, the U.S.-based affiliates employ dozens of professional fundraisers in regional offices throughout North America (the Technion Society has one hundred fundraisers in eighteen regional offices). The organizations engage in what one senior fundraiser described as a "good news" campaign. Building on Israel's reputation as a "start-up nation," the professional fundraisers invite donors to "participate in Israel's remarkable scientific achievements."[36] The two organizations also emphasize their institutions' contributions to universal well-being in the areas of medicine and the environment.

Israel's five other major universities—Hebrew University of Jerusalem ($35 million), Bar Ilan University ($24 million), Haifa University ($4 million), Ben Gurion University of the Negev ($20 million), and Tel Aviv University ($8 million)—take a similar approach, albeit on a smaller scale. Each of these universities has an American Friends affili-ate in the United States employing a staff of professional fundraisers (generally ten to twenty each), working out of a national office in New York and several regional offices. In 2011, Hebrew University announced a $22 million gift by the Cleveland-based Mandel Foundation to estab-lish a new school for the humanities and Bar Ilan University launched a capital campaign in the United States to build a new medical school in the northern town of Tsfat.

The Secular Education category also includes organizations that sup-port independent primary and secondary schools in Israel, including Amit Women, which operates a network of ninety-eight schools ($7.2 million), and Boys Town, which operates a boarding school in Jerusa-lem ($3.5 million).

Medical Institutions

Fundraising for medical institutions is dominated by two large organi-zations, Hadassah Medical Relief Association ($65 million) and Magen David Adom ($23 million). The success of these organizations reflects their deep histories as independent fundraisers as well as their particu-lar contributions to Israeli society.

Established by Baltimore, Maryland, native Henrietta Szold in 1912, the Hadassah Women's Zionist Organization has been a major force in the development of the Israeli health care system. The organiza-tion built, owns, and supports two large medical centers in Jerusalem (one at Mount Scopus and one in Ein Kerem) as well as a number of smaller institutions, including a vocational college and, until recently, the Young Judaea youth organization.

A grassroots organization with about 300,000 members, Hadassah is organized into dozens of chapters throughout the United States. In recent years, the organization has struggled with a graying membership (several chapters are organized in nursing homes) and financial turmoil resulting from its investments with the convicted swindler Bernard Madoff. In 2011, Hadassah agreed to a "clawback" payment of $45 mil-lion to a fund for Madoff's victims—a sum representing about half of the organization's unwitting profits from the notorious Ponzi scheme. In anticipation of this debt, the loss of $90 million in paper profits, and the 2008 recession, Hadassah fired its chief executive and one-quarter of its staff of more than three hundred people.[37] The organization also closed a number of regional offices, sold Jerusalem properties, and spun off the Young Judaea youth organization. Still, these troubles notwithstanding, Hadassah boasted annual fundraising receipts of $75 to $100 million throughout the 2000s and successful completion of its $300 million capital campaign to build a major addition to its Ein Kerem hospital. As the organization prepared to celebrate its centennial it reported registering 28,000 new members.[38]

Alongside Hadassah, during the 2000s American Jews donated $20 to $30 million annually to the American Friends of Magen David Adom (AFMDA). Established in 1940 to support Israel's version of the Red Cross (the Red Star of David), the AFMDA built and pays the operating expenses for Israel's national blood bank. The organization also supplies and maintains a fleet of 800 ambulances, many emblazoned with the names of American Jewish donors, and other emergency medical equipment. In Israel, the AFMDA provides tourists with an opportunity to donate a pint of blood, and more than 2,000 did so in 2009.[39] The organization's donor base has roughly doubled to more than 60,000 per year since the late 1980s, a trend the director, Arnold Gerson, attributes to Israel's highly visible national emergencies and increased fundraising activity through the Internet.[40] The donor base reflects the mainstream of American Jewry—most donors are affiliated with the Conservative or Reform movements—and although most are older than sixty-five the trend is toward younger donors. In 2011, the AFMDA announced a capital campaign to build a new $50 to $70 million National Blood Services Center to replace an aging facility. Other medical institutions that raised significant support among American Jews in 2010 include Shaarei Tzedek Hospital ($17.6 million), the Souarsky Medical Center ($12 million), and the Rambam Medical Center ($3.3 million).[41]

Religious Education

The American affiliates of Israel's religious educational institutions tend to be run by volunteers and raise far smaller sums of money than their secular university counterparts. Our search for American Friends organizations identified 236 affiliates of Israeli *yeshivot* and *midrashot* (academies for religious learning for male and female students, respectively). Leading this group are large Jerusalem institutions that attract many American students, including Mir Yeshiva ($11 million), Hebron Yeshiva Jerusalem ($3.1 million), Shalom Hartman Institute ($4 million), and Pardes Institute ($3 million). The full spectrum extends from the institutions supported by the Ger Hassidic sect ($10 million) to dozens of small Torah academies with fundraising revenues of less than $100,000 each.

In many instances, these organizations have post–high school ("gap year") programs for American students and are represented in the United States by parents of program alumni and rabbis of the communities that send students. A number of yeshivot and midrashot are located in the West Bank, and donations to support their programs are counted below, in the section on "partisan giving," although support for settlement may or may not be a factor in the motivations of their American supporters.

Arts and Culture

Many of Israel's cultural institutions raise money among American Jews, but only a handful do so on a large scale. The U.S. affiliate of the Israel Museum ($33 million) is by far the largest of these entities. With a professional staff in New York and Los Angeles, the group has raised between $20 and $35 million annually since 2005. In 2010, 550 donors attended the museum's signature fundraising event, a gala dinner in New York City. In that same year, the museum completed a $100 million capital campaign for a major renovation of its Jerusalem campus, the largest such campaign ever for an Israeli cultural institution. The project doubled the museum's gallery space and created a new visitor's center. The list of major donors includes the names of many of the best-known American Jewish philanthropic families, including the Bronfmans, Steinhardts, Wexners, Mandels, and Schustermans.[42]

American Jews have also been strong supporters of Yad Vashem, Israel's national Holocaust museum and memorial ($10 million). Over the years, the American Society for Yad Vashem, with more than 150,000 paying members, has raised funds in support of dozens of projects in the museum complex, including the Monument to Jewish

Fighters (1983), the Children's Memorial (1987), and the Institute for Holocaust Research (1993). Other Israeli arts and culture institutions engaged in significant fundraising among American Jews include the Tel Aviv Museum of Art ($2.7 million) and the Israel Philharmonic Orchestra ($3.4 million).

Partisan Giving

During the 1990s and 2000s, as American Jewish advocacy organizations became increasing polarized over negotiations with the Palestinians, the Second Lebanon and Gaza Wars, civil rights, and religious pluralism, direct giving began taking on more partisan forms. On the right, giving to settler organizations and institutions located in the settlements increased, and donors were recruited to acquire properties for Jews in Arab sections of East Jerusalem. On the left, giving to organizations that advocate for human rights in the Occupied Territories, civil rights for Israel's minority Arab population, and other progressive causes similarly increased. These forms of partisan giving, which we might term "political philanthropy," have generated controversies in both the United States and Israel.

West Bank Settlements and East Jerusalem Enclaves

The centralized federation system does not make contributions to Jewish settlements beyond the 1967 "Green Line," but a number of other American organizations have sought to fill the gap. In recent years, fundraising for Jewish settlement has focused especially on East Jerusalem and the Old City, as international pressure mounts for a two-state solution with Arab-majority East Jerusalem as the capital of Palestine. In general the organizations that raise money for settlements beyond Israel's 1967 borders are volunteer-run or employ a small number of professional staff. We focus on the larger ones.

Daniel Luria, the director of Ateret Cohanim (Crown of the Priests; $1 million), an organization that promotes Jewish settlement in East Jerusalem, describes his work as "holy real estate."[43] The group's Jerusalem Reclamation Project does not purchase real estate directly but instead encourages Jewish investors to purchase buildings and Jewish families to settle in them as tenants. Most of the group's efforts have focused on former Jewish properties in the Muslim Quarter of the Old City and surrounding Arab neighborhoods, including apartments, synagogues, and yeshivot that were in Jewish hands prior to the 1948 War of Independence. After matching donors to properties, the organization provides services to Jewish families that settle in the newly established enclaves, including rooftop playgrounds for children, nurseries, security services, and yeshivot.

Luria, who immigrated to Israel from the United Kingdom in the 1990s, views Ateret Cohanim's work in terms of an epic struggle over the future character of the capital city—a "battle over every centimeter of Jerusalem." The only way to ensure that Jerusalem will remain united under Jewish sovereignty, Luria insists, is to settle Jews in Arab neighborhoods in the Old City and East Jerusalem. The surrounding Arab states grasp the nature of the struggle, he explains, and provide ample funding to Muslim associations seeking to acquire East Jerusalem properties. In recent years, as competition for properties has increased and international pressure to divide the city has intensified, the "urgency of the moment" has prompted Ateret Cohanim to raise its public profile. Still, the transfer of properties from Arab to Jewish hands is controversial in Israel and illegal in the Palestinian Authority. Ateret Cohanim's Jerusalem office has a clandestine feel to it—the organization's name does not appear on the outside of the building, and the interior office door still bears the nameplate of the former tenant.

Ateret Cohanim raises $1 to $2 million annually in the United States—more than half of its operating budget. Funds are primarily raised through parlor meetings in the New York area and tours of Ateret-supported projects in Jerusalem. Most donors to the organization are Orthodox Jews, the segment of the American Jewish population most supportive of the Israeli settler movement. Luria explains that his supporters include many former UJA and JNF donors who are no longer willing to pay the costs associated with big charities. "The days of giving to the big *kupah* (fund) are over!" Luria declares, "Donors will give to a soup kitchen or for *geulat yerushalayim* (redemption of Jerusalem) but they won't pay for overhead!"

The Ir David Foundation ($5.5 million) similarly promotes Jewish settlement in East Jerusalem, focusing especially in the Arab neighborhood of Silwan, site of the ancient City of David. The organization sponsors archeological digs, educational programs, and tours alongside its work to establish a Jewish residential enclave. Like Ateret, Ir David seeks to deepen Jewish claims to East Jerusalem by emphasizing both historic ties and contemporary settlement. The group has long enjoyed the support of Dr. Irving Moskowitz, a Florida hospital developer who has invested millions of dollars acquiring East Jerusalem buildings in support of the organization's settlement projects. Overall, since 2005, American Jewish supporters have donated $3 to $6 million annually to the Ir David Foundation.

Beyond East Jerusalem, American Jewish donors also give to projects in West Bank settlements. As in the case of Ateret Cohanim, American donors to West Bank settlements are mostly Orthodox Jews. Donations go through a number of umbrella funds. The Central Fund for Israel ($12 million) functions much like the PEF—donors specify the organizations they wish to support—but with a substantial portion of funds flowing to Jewish settlements in the West Bank.[44] In contrast, the One Israel Fund ($2.3 million) gathers donations for its own West Bank projects including building recreation, education, and community centers and supplying medical, firefighting, and security equipment. The fund has raised more than $20 million since its inception. Finally, the Hebron Fund ($1 million) raises contributions in support of the Jewish enclave in the West Bank city of Hebron, one of the major flash points of the Palestinian-Israeli conflict.

Among the largest of the West Bank recipients of American Jewish support are a number of yeshivot. In some instances the West Bank location is incidental to donor support. For example, the Har Etzion Yeshiva ($2 million), located in a settlement close to Jerusalem that is expected to remain part of Israel in any future peace deal, is widely regarded as one of Israel's top religious seminaries. The same can be said for the Ohr Torah Stone ($4.8 million) network of seminaries and religious-educational institutions that includes sites in both Jerusalem and the West Bank. Donations to such institutions do not necessarily reflect a desire to support the settler movement. By contrast, donations to the Beth El Yeshiva Center ($2 million), located in a much more controversial settlement near Ramallah, are properly viewed as an expression of support for the settler movement.

American Jewish financial support for Jewish settlements in East Jerusalem and the West Bank is a common topic of articles and exposés in the Israeli and the American press. An article on the front page of the *New York Times* in 2010 for example, called into question the legality of tax-exempt donations beyond the Green Line that contravene U.S. policy objectives.[45] The U.S. government views Jewish settlement in the West Bank as an obstacle to a peace deal. Nevertheless, under the prevailing interpretation of U.S. tax law, such contributions remain tax deductible. Jewish critics, such as Peter Beinart, and left-leaning advocacy organizations, including Americans for Peace Now, have urged that the tax exemption for such donations be cancelled.[46]

The controversy over tax policy aside, as best we can ascertain, the amount given by American Jews to the settlement enterprise is relatively small compared to the amount invested by the Israeli government (about $17 billion overall) and compared to donations by American Jews to more mainstream causes in Israel.[47] But in the estimation of former U.S. ambassador to Israel Daniel C. Kurtzer, "a couple of hundred million dollars makes a huge difference" and "creates a new reality on the ground."[48] As of this writing, notwithstanding demands for change, there is no evidence that U.S. public officials are reviewing the legality of these donations.

Civil Rights, Human Rights, and Coexistence

Like their counterparts on the right, liberal American Jews increasingly spend their philanthropic dollars in ways calculated to mold Israel according to their own particular vision. In practice, this has meant supporting organizations that promote a cluster of progressive causes including civil and human rights, religious pluralism, democracy, Arab-Jewish coexistence, and social equality.

Since its establishment in 1980 as an alternative to the UJA (see above), the NIF ($38 million) has been the largest philanthropic vehicle for progressive causes in Israel. The NIF is an American charitable organization that raises about 95 percent of its annual budget in the United States. The CEO of the organization is an American, and a network of professional fundraisers work out of regional offices in each of the major centers of Jewish life in the United States. Donors include both individuals and Jewish foundations (e.g., Nathan Cummings Foundation). These legal and financial realities aside, the organization represents itself as a full partnership between American Jews and Israelis. The board of directors is divided evenly between the two groups, and the professional staff is mostly Israeli.

The NIF provides direct support to more than one hundred Israeli nonprofit organizations and operates Shatil (Seedling), a capacity-building organization that provides consulting services to more than one thousand more. Through these activities, the NIF has had an enormous influence over the development of the Israeli nonprofit field as a whole. Over the years, NIF professionals have introduced—often in Hebrew tinged with an American accent—concepts and methods derived from the American nonprofit arena. To the extent that Americans and Israelis speak a shared language regarding the role of nonprofit organizations—including concepts like "grassroots action," "social change," "community development," and "accountability"—it is largely due to the influence of the NIF.[49]

Itzik Shanan, a veteran member of the Israeli staff, describes the organization's accomplishments in Israel along a continuum. The pluralism and coexistence initiatives have met with the least success. The non-Orthodox Israeli Reform and *Masorati* (Conservative) movements have grown at a lackadaisical pace. Coexistence initiatives fell apart during the Second Intifada, and many leaders in the field have since soured on the value of person-to-person dialogue in the context of intense and ongoing national conflict. Today, NIF professionals view coexistence activities—what Shanan describes as "Jews and Arabs eating humus together"—as less valuable than advocating for the civil rights of Israel's Arab minority. In contrast, according to Shanan, the organization boasts very strong accomplishments in the areas of women's rights and gay and lesbian rights. Harassment of women is taken more seriously in Israel today than in the past, and gays and lesbians are much less stigmatized, according to Shanan.[50]

The NIF is a major sponsor of Israel's leading human rights and civil rights organizations, including the Association for Civil Rights in Israel (ACRI) and B'Tselem (In God's Image—a reference to Genesis 1:27). These organizations, which receive additional support from European states and private foundations, monitor and issue reports on

Israel's compliance with international human rights norms. In addition, ACRI monitors compliance with international law on the protection of civilians in armed conflict and litigates in defense of civil rights and the rights of women, gays and lesbians, migrant workers, and Palestinian citizens of the state. The NIF also supports a number of additional civil rights and human rights organizations, including Adalah, an organization that advocates that Israel should be a neutral democratic state ("a state of all its citizens").[51]

In recent years, the NIF's support for Israel's human rights and civil rights advocacy groups has made the fund a target of right-wing activists and officials. Critics include the American-born political science professor Gerald Steinberg and the Israeli organization he established, NGO Monitor. Steinberg charges that NIF and its beneficiary organizations behave as agents of foreign governments and engage in political activism under the guise of impartial human rights advocacy.[52] In 2010, Steinberg's critique was picked up by Im Tirtzu, an Israeli right-wing advocacy organization.[53] The activists of Im Tirtzu were particularly incensed that NIF-funded human rights groups had supplied information critical of Israel to the United Nation's Goldstone investigation of the Gaza War. Israel had refused to cooperate with the UN investigation, calling the tribunal biased, and in the absence of official Israeli participation, the information provided by the human rights groups proved especially important in the final report. The Im Tirtzu campaign against the NIF, which received extensive press coverage in Israel and the United States, featured a cartoon image of NIF President Naomi Chazan with a rhinoceros horn extending from her forehead—an image the NIF described as anti-Semitic. (Im Tirtzu viewed the matter differently; the group pointed out that the Hebrew word *keren* means both "fund" and "horn.")

More recently, Israeli lawmakers from the Yisrael Beiteinu Party initiated legislation to establish a parliamentary inquiry into foreign government support for Israeli human rights organizations. The aim was to publicly investigate the funding of organizations that supplied information to the Goldstone commission. The Israeli human rights organizations and their supporters in Israel and the United States cried foul, charging the Israeli right with a "witch-hunt" and "McCarthyism" that threatened Israeli democracy. The NIF rallied several thousand of its

American Jewish supporters to contact fence-sitting Israeli lawmakers. The legislation ultimately failed to garner sufficient support, as Prime Minister Netanyahu and several other Likud Knesset members refused to endorse an inquiry targeted exclusively at left-wing organizations. Notably, the failed legislation focused only on donations by foreign governments. A broader mandate to investigate *all foreign funding* of Israeli nonprofits was not discussed, perhaps because such an inquiry would have included American Jewish support for West Bank and East Jerusalem settlements.[54]

Beyond the NIF, American Jews give directly to a number of progressive organizations in Israel. These include the Israel Democracy Institute ($9 million), which promotes democratic values and the development of a constitution (Israel does not have one), and the Abraham Fund ($4 million), which sponsors initiatives to promote Arab-Jewish coexistence and equal rights for Israel's Palestinian minority.

New Directions for Federations and JAFI

As the Israeli nonprofit sector expanded and stepped up outreach to American Jews, the federations and the Jewish Agency struggled to remain relevant. The federation system remains the largest fundraising operation in the Jewish world and the biggest single donor to causes in Israel. Major staff reductions and budget cuts aside, the Jewish Agency likewise remains the largest independent organization in the Jewish world and an important bridge between diaspora Jewry and Israel. Although Jewish philanthropic activity in Israel has become more fragmented and polarized, these core institutions continue to play a prominent role. In the sections that follow, we examine how the federations and JAFI have adapted to the changing field of diaspora philanthropy.

Federation Direct Engagement

In the early 1990s, in response to donor demand for greater control over overseas contributions, the larger federations began locating permanent staff in Israel and directly funding their own projects. The New York, Los Angeles, and Chicago federations were the first, followed shortly by Boston. By the mid-2000s, thirty federations had professional staff permanently stationed in Israel, the larger ones in their own offices and the smaller ones in a shared office of the Jewish Federations of North America (JFNA). The federation-sponsored projects run the gamut of social service and educational initiatives. Cleveland founded and funds a significant women's health initiative. New York created and supports a network of Jewish renewal congregations and learning centers for secular Jews. Chicago supports a campaign against domestic violence. Atlanta funds social services for Ethiopian immigrants. Several federation-supported projects provide services to Arab Israelis as well as Jews, including the JFNA's fund for Jewish-Arab Equality and Shared Society, which distributed several million dollars during its first three years.

In some instances the targeted giving of individual federations flows directly to Israeli organizations; more frequently it is channeled through the UIA and JAFI and therefore credited to the centralized philanthropic system. In either case, however, the donations are viewed by the federations as their own special projects rather than as projects of the ubiquitous Jewish Agency. As JFNA director of Israel programs Rebecca Caspi explained to me, the aim is to show donors that "this is ours" and cultivate a personal connection between the donors and the work of their particular federation. "The federations once depended on JAFI and JDC to identify and address Jewish needs—this was a compact," Caspi explained. "Today, the world has flattened and information spreads more easily . . . and people want direct connection and control."[55]

In addition to increased direct engagement in Israel, the JFNA is rethinking its exclusive commitment to its partnership with JAFI and the JDC. The federations recently established a "global planning table" to identify and prioritize the challenges facing the Jewish world, evaluate the basic model for overseas giving, and consider directing funds to additional Israeli nonprofit organizations.[56] "What worked magnificently in 1975 may not work so well in 2010, not to mention 2025," wrote the federation movement's chief executive in a letter to the Jewish Agency. "The Jewish world here and in Israel, is substantially different today than it was decades ago. By itself, the sheer growth of wealth and civil society in Israel—developments we can take great pride in—challenges the way we do business and also creates new opportunities for us."[57]

JAFI Reengineered

Just as the federations have begun reassessing their exclusive commitment to their "historic partners," the Jewish Agency has embarked upon a fundamental overhaul of its mission and strategy. The new strategic plan, drafted in 2010, describes the Agency's central mission in the coming years as promoting Jewish identity in both Israel and diaspora. The revised strategy reflects the priorities of Natan Sharansky, the former Soviet political prisoner and one-time Israeli cabinet minister who was nominated by Prime Minister Netanyahu to head the Agency, and his deputy, Alan Hoffman, who for many years directed the Agency's division for Jewish Zionist education. According to the new plan, although JAFI will continue to support new immigrants in a limited fashion, the organization's main focus will be on supporting a full complement of educational programs geared to diaspora and Israeli youth and young adults.[58]

From a practical standpoint, this vision will entail deepening the Jewish Agency's involvement in Israel experience programming for diaspora high school students, college students, and young adults. As Hoffman, now the Agency's director general, explained, "The goal is an ever-increasing number of young people coming to Israel in a spiral from teen-age to post college years."[59] The Jewish Agency has long played a key role in organizing Israel experience programs for diaspora students and young adults. The new strategic plan elevates these functions to the organization's top priority. Programs for Israeli young adults will emphasize social action, including national service in Israel and opportunities for service in Jewish communities abroad. Most new programs will include diaspora and Israeli participants in cooperative frameworks, for example, a new "Global Tikkun Olam" initiative—a kind of Jewish Peace Corps to serve distressed Jewish and non-Jewish communities in poor countries—will be staffed in equal measure by Israeli and diaspora young adults.

Hoffman described the Jewish Agency's shifting focus as a natural reaction to changes in the Jewish world. The Russian migration was likely the last major wave of immigration by a distressed Jewish community to Israel. The role of Israel as the site for the ingathering of the Jewish diaspora has been largely achieved, and although individual Jews from rich democratic countries may choose to move to Israel, the age of large-scale Jewish rescue has drawn to a close. At the same time, according to Hoffman, the Jewish identities of non-Orthodox diaspora Jews and their connection to Israel are weakening. In Hoffman's metaphor, the diaspora "roots" that for generations nourished the Israeli "tree" are withering. Israelis, who long picked the fruits of the tree, must now do their share to tend to the roots. Moreover, the Jewish identities of secular Israelis, who tend to see themselves as Israelis rather than Jews and feel little natural solidarity with Jews outside of Israel, must be nurtured as well. In this changing context, building up the Jewish state, which has always been JAFI's overarching mission, requires a shift in focus from aliyah to strengthening Jewish identity.

However elegant, Hoffman's explanation for the Jewish Agency's shifting focus does not quite fit the time line. The last major aliyah of Russian Jews peaked in the early 1990s, just as the continuity agenda was coming to the fore in the diaspora. The Jewish Agency did not propose a shift in focus to cultivating diaspora Jewish identity until 2010. The decisive factors were more likely the success of Birthright Israel, which developed outside of the JAFI framework (see Chapter 4), and the 2008 recession, which prompted sharp budget cuts. In this context, a reorientation that emphasizes educational tourism and mifgashim (encounters) between Israeli and diaspora young adults makes good sense. Educational tourism is a well-funded enterprise that has broad support in the federations and the Israeli government. The new focus may enable the Jewish Agency to protect its core funding streams while still pursuing aspects of its historic mission.

Beyond Diaspora Donations

The focus in this chapter has been on trends in Jewish giving to Israel. We digress here to examine several related phenomena. Christian Zionist contributions to Israel are increasingly significant. Christians United for Israel, led by Pastor John Hagee, reportedly donates to West Bank settlements as well as Im Tirtzu, the organization that led the attack against the NIF.[60] However, the larger share of Christian support for Israel is channeled to more mainstream causes. The International Fellowship of Christians and Jews, headed by Rabbi Yechiel Eckstein, raised nearly $96 million in 2010—although after fundraising expenses just a little over half that sum made its way to Israel.[61] Notably, the International Fellowship gives the lion's share of its contributions to the federations' partner organizations, the Jewish Agency and the JDC.

We have also neglected Israel Bonds. Israel Bonds are issued by the Ministry of Finance to support capital projects in Israel, including the national water carrier, airports, and power plants. Strictly speaking, the purchase of Israel Bonds is a financial investment rather than a donation. However, for many American Jews, the purchase and gift of an Israel Bond—for example, on the occasion of a bar or bat mitzvah—is viewed more as an expression of Jewish identity and solidarity with Israel than as a sound financial investment. During the 1967 Six-Day War, Israel sold $250 million in bonds; during the 1973 Yom Kippur War it sold double that amount. By 1991, the year of the Gulf War, the sale of Israel Bonds had increased to over $1 billion. Since then, Israel has consistently sold over $1 billion in bonds annually, creeping up to $1.2 billion in 2010. However, increasingly purchasers of bonds include not only Jews but also diverse organizations and funds including American labor unions and state and municipal governments (the latter purchased $143 million in 2010).

Finally, Israel is a major recipient of foreign direct investment. The high-tech sector benefits from huge infusions of capital by technology companies such as Google, Intel, and Microsoft and by venture capital funds such as Warren Buffett's Berkshire Hathaway.[62] However, at the margins, there is much "diaspora direct investment," a category that includes investments made by diaspora Jews with the intention (at least in part) of benefiting the homeland.[63] For example, Morton Mandel, an American Jewish philanthropist, contributes tens of millions of dollars annually to Israeli institutions of higher education and the arts, as well as to a network of Mandel Foundation–operated leadership institutes. He has also invested in an Israeli bottling plant and a network of private medical clinics.[64] No one knows how much investment of this sort occurs, but anecdotal evidence suggests that it must be a significant amount.

Conclusion

Under the mobilization paradigm, American Jews were often cast by Israelis into the role of a rich but distant uncle. Their job was to write checks and not ask too many questions—knowing that the money was "going to Israel" was enough. This is less often the case today. Transnational alliances and collaborative efforts between Israelis and American Jews are increasingly the rule. The federations are funding and supervising their own projects in Israel. The NIF touts its mixed board of directors, comprising in equal number Israelis and American Jews. The JDC, although an American organization, has both Israelis and Americans on its staff. Many Israeli nonprofit organizations that raise funds in the United States are staffed in Israel by American Jewish immigrants.

The trend is clearly toward more targeted giving and hands-on American Jewish involvement. Even federation gifts are now given with the understanding that the federations' overseas partners will need to justify the expenditure of every shekel, and that diaspora concerns will need to be considered. The federations are also directly involved with their own projects, enabling American Jews to see their philanthropic dollars at work, and to feel direct ownership. For better or worse, American Jews are on the ground in Israel, running projects for the JDC, collaborating with Israeli partners in shaping priorities for the NIF, purchasing buildings in Jerusalem's Arab neighborhoods, and helping to establish the new Magen David Adom blood center. As the local experts, Israelis still take the lead in most endeavors, but American Jews are no longer the passive donors of UJA lore.

Taken as a whole, the complex field of philanthropy reflects the broad range of trends shaping the relationship between American Jews and Israel. The field has decentralized with the core institutions weakening and myriad Israeli nonprofit organizations jostling alongside the Jewish Agency to raise funds among American Jews. Although most giving continues to support mainstream and noncontroversial institutions (the universities and hospitals still dominate the field), political philanthropy aimed at shaping Israel according to particular ideological visions is increasing. Finally, American Jews are more personally involved in Israel-oriented philanthropy, choosing among causes to support, directing federation donations, and forming transnational alliances with Israeli counterparts. The master trend in philanthropy, as in the field of advocacy, is from mobilization to direct engagement.

4

Tourism and Immigration

During the period extending from the early 1950s until the late 1990s, the Jewish Agency for Israel (JAFI) served as the central address for both educational tourism and aliyah (Jewish immigration, literally "ascent"). As such, it was the linchpin organization responsible for bringing young people to Israel and for recruiting new immigrants. Today, the Jewish Agency remains active in these endeavors, and has launched a new entity, Masa, which coordinates and subsidizes long-term study, volunteer, and internship programs for Jewish young adults. In recent years, however, the fields of educational tourism and immigration have grown and diversified to include new, privately funded organizations such as Taglit-Birthright Israel, which brings Jewish young adults on free ten-day educational tours, and Nefesh B'Nefesh, which promotes aliyah and provides support to new immigrants. The new organizations have designed attractive, consumer-oriented programs and devised new schemes to fund and market them. As a result of these innovations, the number of North American participants in educational tourism in Israel has jumped more than fourfold, and the number of new immigrants has doubled. More American Jews from a wider range of backgrounds are spending time in Israel than ever before, and a small but growing number are choosing to live there.

The Jewish Agency System

Until recently, the system for educational tourism was relatively compact and centralized. A handful of American Jewish youth organizations, including the denominationally based organizations of the
Reform (National Federation of Temple Youth), Conservative (United
Synagogue Youth), and Orthodox (National Council of Synagogue
Youth) movements, together with Hadassah's Young Judea, sponsored
most educational tourism programs. These organizations mounted their
trips in conjunction with the Jewish Agency and its parent body, the
World Zionist Organization.[1] Most participants registered for the programs sponsored by the organizations to which they already belonged
and were only dimly aware of the role played by the Israel-based, quasi-
public JAFI-WZO in providing infrastructure and delivering much of
the educational program. Programs were geared to the leadership cad-
res of the youth movements. Participation varied between 5,000 and
9,000 during the period 1970–85 and between 6,000 and 10,000 during
the period 1986–2000.[2]

The most common type of program throughout this period was the
four- to eight-week summer tour for high school students.[3] The trips
typically consisted of several weeks of volunteer work on a kibbutz combined with several weeks touring the country by bus. Travel logistics
and the educational program were mostly organized in Israel by JAFI-
WZO. Direct costs for the trip were borne by parents of participants,
often with the assistance of scholarships from federations, synagogues,
and other U.S.-based Jewish organizations. The indirect costs for overhead, including marketing, tourist infrastructure, and educational program, were covered by the JAFI-WZO with funds raised through the
community campaigns of the United Jewish Appeal (UJA).

The JAFI-WZO provided these services through a number of separate entities, each geared to a specific age category and program type.
The Youth and Pioneer division was responsible for high school programs. Other divisions were responsible for programs for college and
older students and for educational initiatives in religious and secular
settings. Each organization had its own office in Jerusalem and emissaries in the United States. In addition, JAFI-WZO had an overseas

affiliate in the United States that was responsible for marketing trips, the American Zionist Youth Federation (AZYF).[4]

By the early 1990s, the system came under intense criticism from U.S.-based philanthropists and federations for redundancy, bureaucracy, and waste. An initial reform resulted in a Joint Authority for Jewish Zionist Education. Subsequently, in 1998, the separate divisions of the JAFI-WZO responsible for educational programming were consolidated into a new Department of Jewish Zionist Education. Alan Hoffman, a South African–born Jewish educator who had once directed the Young Judea Year Course (see below), was appointed as its director. (Hoffman went on to become the director general of JAFI, as discussed in Chapter 3.) The purpose of the new department was to serve as a policy and planning mechanism for Israel experience programming. As part of the same reform, the AZYF was closed and all logistical functions (e.g., scheduling flights, hotels, buses, and tour guides) previously performed by the JAFI-WZO were outsourced to a newly established entity, Israel Experience, Inc. The latter would operate as a private, for-profit subsidiary of the Jewish Agency.[5]

In contrast to educational tourism, the Jewish Agency managed aliyah on its own. There were nearly three hundred JAFI emissaries working in North America in the mid-1980s. The emissaries were often political appointees, and turnover was rapid. According to critics, emissaries did not typically develop adequate knowledge of the American Jewish community until their term of service was set to expire. Reflecting classic Zionist ideology, many were described as having disdain for American Jewish life. The annual number of new immigrants to Israel from North America hovered between two and three thousand.[6]

Responding to complaints from diaspora funders and UJA executives about the aliyah system's tremendous expense, a commission of inquiry was established in the mid-1980s. Headed by former Israeli chief justice Moshe Landau, the commission reported that the number of emissaries was excessive in relation to the number of people they served, that emissaries had little aptitude for their work and lacked familiarity with the American Jewish scene, and that many tasks could be accomplished by local personnel at lower cost. The report called for sweeping changes in the aliyah system in North America.[7]

By the mid-1990s, pressure was building for a fundamental overhaul in the Jewish Agency–dominated fields of educational tourism and aliyah. In both arenas, diaspora frustration was mounting and new frameworks for bringing diaspora Jews to Israel were sought. The fundamental break with the past occurred, however, only after the establishment, outside of the JAFI system, of Taglit-Birthright Israel.

Birthright Israel

In 1993, during the same year he was deeply involved in behind-the-scenes negotiations with the Palestine Liberation Organization that would shortly produce the Oslo Accords, Deputy Foreign Minister Yossi Beilin launched a critique of the UJA (see Chapter 3). Appearing before diaspora Jewish audiences, Beilin blasted the UJA campaigns for characterizing Israel as an impoverished state in desperate need of diaspora charity. The imagery associated with such appeals created the erroneous impression that Israel was incapable of addressing its own needs, Beilin claimed. It also perpetuated a distorted relationship in which Israel was the perennial supplicant of its rich "American uncle." Beilin argued that funds raised for Israel in the diaspora could be more wisely used to enable every Jewish teenager to visit the Jewish state. Such an initiative would strengthen the Jewish identities of diaspora visitors and help counter assimilation, an issue that had recently come to the fore with the publication of a national study that reported the intermarriage rate to be over 50 percent.[8] To implement his vision of trips to Israel as a universal rite of passage, Beilin proposed replacing the UJA and Jewish Agency with a new, democratically elected body of world Jewry whose primary purpose would be mounting educational trips to Israel for diaspora Jewish teenagers.[9]

Beilin's proposal to replace the UJA and JAFI never gained traction. However, the initiative to dramatically increase participation in educational trips to Israel was taken up within a few years by Jewish philanthropists Charles Bronfman and Michael Steinhardt. Bronfman, scion of the Seagram liquor fortune, had been active in the field of Israel experience programs for many years, most recently as founder of the Mifgashim Center (which promoted encounters between Israeli and diaspora youth) and as a supporter of Israel Experience, Inc. Bronfman believed strongly in the identity-forging impact of Israel experience tourism and was committed to making it more widely available. Although initially skeptical about Beilin's proposal to make trips to Israel absolutely free to diaspora Jewish young adults, he warmed to the idea when approached by Michael Steinhardt, a Wall Street hedge fund manager who had recently closed his firm to devote his energy and fortune to initiatives to strengthen Jewish identity.

In 1998, Steinhardt and Bronfman persuaded the Israeli government and Jewish federations to join them in funding the initial years of Birthright Israel. The founders' goal was to employ Israel experience tourism as a tactic for combating assimilation. Their belief that educational tourism in Israel could strengthen the Jewish identities of young adults was rooted in their experience with existing programs and a fairly large body of evaluation research.[10] In their view, the trips could provide a "last chance" for young adults who were already on their way out of the fold. The focus would therefore be on older participants, eighteen to twenty-six years of age, who had never before participated in an educational program in Israel. The definition of "Jewish" would include anyone with one Jewish parent, mother or father. The aim would be to make an experience in Israel a normative part of the lives of Jewish young adults. The first trips were announced in 1999, and the first flights landed in Israel in January 2000.

Shimshon Shoshani, a former director general of Israel's Ministry of Education, was recruited as Birthright's chief executive officer. Shoshani established the organization's basic structure and operating procedures: Birthright would not run its own trips but instead operate as a funding and regulatory agency that contracted with private tour providers. The latter would qualify to participate in the program by designing trips that met Birthright's basic requirements, including the quality of travel amenities as well as the organization's educational program. By outsourcing the trips, Birthright could avoid becoming a massive JAFI-like bureaucracy and at the same time ensure that a wide variety of tours could be offered to meet diverse interests and needs.[11]

Barry Chazan, a professor of education who had written on the impact of Israel experience programs, was recruited to design Birthright's educational guidelines.[12] The initial guidelines specified that every bus group—comprising about forty diaspora Jewish visitors,

often from a single university or city—be accompanied by a certi-
fied Israeli tour guide. Tours would vary in terms of thematic focus
and religious orientation, but all would include certain core features,
including a visit to a Holocaust memorial site (e.g., Yad Vashem), a
Jewish historical site (e.g., the City of David), and a site related to
Zionist history (e.g., Independence Hall, where David Ben Gurion
declared Israeli statehood in 1948). All trips would also visit the Western Wall, Masada, and a site related to the modern state of Israel,
such as the Knesset or the Supreme Court. In addition, all trips would
include some kind of Shabbat observance, an encounter with Israeli
peers, and opportunities for group reflection on the meaning of the
trip experience.[13]

During Birthright's first decade, the number of participating tour
organizations increased and diversified. Hillel, the leading organization
of Jewish university students, became a key organizer of the first Birthright tours and continued as one of the largest U.S.-based trip sponsors.
The organization recruited participants and contracted logistical services from Israeli tour companies. Other U.S.-based organizations also
mounted trips, including Kesher (the Reform movement) and Mayanot
(the Chabad-Hassidic movement). Israeli educational and tour companies soon entered the Birthright market offering their own trips without the mediation of U.S. organizations.

By the mid-2000s, the single largest of the two dozen trip providers was Oranim, a private for-profit Israeli tour company. Oranim trips
developed a reputation for visits to beaches, pubs, and the resort city of
Eilat. The organization also became famous for its charismatic director, Shlomo "Momo" Lifshitz, who lectured personally to every visiting
Oranim tour group. Momo's message to the young adult diaspora visitors was that they must stand up to anti-Semites, defend Israel against
its detractors, and raise Jewish children. "Today, there are not enough
leaders that say to you that you must raise your children Jewish, keep
our faith alive!"[14] (Oranim was the trip provider most responsible for
Birthright earning the moniker "birthrate"; the organization no longer
participates in the Birthright program.)

Tour providers emphasized disparate themes. Israel Experts
mounted trips that emphasized seminar-like learning about Israeli

history and archeology. Shorashim led trips that included groups of Israeli young adults for the full duration of the tour. AIPAC organized trips that focused on public affairs. Other tour providers arranged trips for special constituencies, including gays and lesbians, young professionals, and the developmentally disabled. The right-wing Zionist Organization of America and the left-wing Union of Progressive Zionists each offered trips until Birthright banned programs with overt political content.[15]

Banning overtly political trips did not, however, result in tours devoid of political content. Rather, the trips' political messages were delivered more subtly as part of the tourist experience, through the tour guides' narratives at tourist sites but also through the structure of the tour itself. As the largest educational tourism program bringing North American young adults to Israel, Birthright's curriculum—what it teaches about Israel, including but not limited to its political messages—is of particular significance. In the sections that follow, we examine the tour guides' narratives and then return to the question of Birthright's political significance.

Master Narratives

The trips' core themes and narratives are the work of independent tour guides and not scripted by the program. However, as I learned from a large ethnographic study I conducted with colleagues in the mid-2000s, most guides develop three master narratives over the course of the Birthright tour. The master narratives are developed throughout the tours, but each is most closely associated with a small number of tour sites. In some cases, the master narratives overlap and meld into a single story line. They are "meta-narratives" in the sense that they link together and provide coherence to the more detailed historical explanations associated with particular sites. The following are thumbnail sketches of the master narratives culled from field notes of participant observers of a sample of twenty-two Birthright trips.[16]

1. *Land of Israel* is the narrative for Jewish archeological sites including, for example, the Western Wall and the City of David.

LAND OF ISRAEL

The roots of the Jewish people are in the Land of Israel. It is here that the Jewish people first established a national home. David established his kingdom here and united the twelve tribes of Israel into a single nation. It is here that Solomon built the First Temple. Our holiest sites can be found here, including the Temple Mount—the rock upon which God tested the faith of Abraham, and the Western Wall—the remains of the Second Temple. Jews were twice driven from the land, following the destruction of the First and Second Temples, and twice returned. Jews have lived in the Land of Israel continuously; following the destruction of Jerusalem they created Yavneh and communities in the Galilee. They returned to Jerusalem in small numbers in the Middle Ages. During the years of exile, Jews longed to return to the Land of Israel and restore Jewish sovereignty. The Land of Israel is the birthright of every Jew. "Under us we found 2,700-year-old roots," explained one guide. "Above us, Jews are living today and once again there is Jewish life in the Old City."

2. *Ashes to Redemption* is the narrative for Zionist historical and Holocaust memorial sites including Yad Vashem, the Mount Herzl national military cemetery, and Independence Hall.

ASHES TO REDEMPTION

An assimilated Jewish journalist, Theodor Herzl, was the founding visionary and organizer of the modern Zionist movement. In 1894, while covering the anti-Semitic show-trial of the French Jewish Captain Alfred Dreyfus, Herzl came to the realization that the only way to eliminate anti-Semitism was for the Jews to create a state of their own. Herzl declared, "If you will it, it is no mere legend," and that, "in Basel [Switzerland, the site of the first Zionist conference] I have founded the Jewish state." The Nazi Holocaust culminated centuries of persecution of the Jews of Europe. European Jewry was totally devastated. Indeed, Herzl's own children perished in the Holocaust. But from the ashes of destruction his vision was fulfilled. The modern state of Israel was established following World War II as a refuge for hundreds of thousands of

survivors of the Holocaust. It was built by idealistic young pio-
neers and achieved its independence through the self-sacrifice "on
a silver platter" of thousands of Jewish soldiers. Today, the state
of Israel remains a refuge for persecuted Jews the world over. One
participant summed up this narrative during a group discussion:
"The thing that is most amazing is that they are trying to kill us
all the time and do not succeed. They tried to kill us in the Holo-
caust, they tried in Masada and still the Jewish people continue
and survive and we even have a state."

3. *Besieged Israel* is the core narrative for war memorials and battle sites
such as Latrun (the site of a battle to lift the siege of Jewish Jerusalem
in 1948) and the Golan Heights (the site of key battles in 1967 and
1973).

BESIEGED ISRAEL

Even before the declaration of statehood, the surrounding Arab
world rejected the presence of Jews in Palestine. Following the
UN vote to create Jewish and Arab states, the Arabs declared,
"What is written in ink shall be erased in blood." Six Arab armies
attacked the Yishuv. Since the War of Independence, Israel has
fought many additional wars, including in 1967, 1973, 1982, and
the recent Lebanon and Gaza Wars. In fact, Israel has more or
less fought a continuous war for its existence against the sur-
rounding Arab countries, all of which have vowed time and again
to drive the Jews into the sea. The latest wars, which followed Isra-
el's withdrawals from Lebanon and Gaza, are but the most recent
installments in this long saga.

At their core, the Birthright master narratives emphasize the roots and
continuous presence of the Jews in the Land of Israel, the triumphant
rise of modern Israel from the ashes of the Holocaust, and the struggle of Israel against its hostile neighbors. Birthright guides strike other
themes as well, including describing Israel as a "refuge for persecuted
Jews," a "multicultural society," and a "high-tech powerhouse." During
the period of our field research, however, these alternative themes typically received less emphasis.[17]

Masada Narratives

Beyond the master narratives, the educational content and political tenor of individual trips depends in large measure on the decisions of individual tour guides. This was dramatized during our field research by the guides' diverse presentations on the summit of Masada.

All Birthright trips visit the desert fortress, with most ascending before dawn to witness the sunrise. Long associated with the Besieged Israel narrative, Masada was the site of the Jews' last stand following Rome's conquest of Jerusalem in 70 CE. According to the conventional account, after a long and heroic struggle, the Masada defenders chose to take their own lives and those of their family members rather than submit to the imperial power of Rome. In Israeli political culture, Masada's central message has been that Jewish sovereignty, regained with the establishment of Israel, must be protected at all costs. In a phrase, "Masada must not fall again."[18]

Field observers in our 2005 ethnographic study recorded several instances of this conventional account. As one guide explained to his group (here paraphrased from the observer's field notes),

> In Israeli society they say that there will not be a second Masada, there will not be a situation where someone will surround us for three years [and] that in the end we'll have to commit suicide. . . . As soldiers, we are faithful to the warriors of Masada . . . this is what Israel is all about. In our culture, we use the lessons of Masada from the past to protect us and teach us about the future.[19]

To our surprise, however, as often as not the guides we observed delivered an alternative, dissident account of Masada's significance—one fine-tuned to the political debate then raging in Israel over the evacuation of Jewish settlements from the Gaza Strip. According to the alternative, counternarrative, the defenders of Masada were Jewish political extremists who assassinated a number of their more moderate Jewish compatriots and triggered an unnecessary and hopeless confrontation with Rome. The significance of Masada, according to this account, is as a warning against the dangers of Jewish political extremism. Consider the fascinating narrative told by a tour guide named Eran, a doctoral student in Bible, who began lecturing on the theme of Masada during his group's visit to the late prime minister Yitzhak Rabin's grave at the Mount Herzl national cemetery. The following rather lengthy account is from an observer's field notes:

> We went first to the graves of Israel's leaders and their spouses, walking among the graves while Eran explained who could be and was buried there. At Rabin's grave Eran's tone changed. Whereas before he provided occasional conversational explanations of the cemetery, here he stopped and adopted a more serious, grave tone. He told us that Rabin was "murdered by a religious zealot," and that "that was the greatest shock, I think, to our society." At Masada, he told us, we would talk about "what happens when someone takes religion and becomes a zealot."

A few days later, at Masada, Eran picked up the theme of the dangers of zealotry. "In a way," he told the group, "I was building the tour up to this moment." He then continued, arguing that Zionists, who embraced Masada as a symbol during their struggle for statehood, ignored the Zealots' messianic religious convictions and the disastrous choices that they produced. Today, however, religious extremists once again threaten fellow Jews:

> Two thousand years later, the Jews . . . looked for a symbol and they found Masada, a place surrounded by enemies where the people put religion before everything else. However . . . there was one thing [the Zionists] left out: that these people [Masada's defenders] believed that God would save them and were therefore willing to do irrational things. Eran told us that this fact is important because there are zealots around today. They are the people who believe that "if you return land God has given you, you are sacrilegious traitors." He said "the modern day zealots I know better than the old time zealots, their devotion should not confuse anybody, they are terrorists . . . and eventually (if they continue to push) just like we lost the first and second Temples, we will lose Israel." Eran talked about "the day Rabin was murdered," how he was murdered by a zealot, how this was a failure of democracy, and how even though the signs were there that something like this might happen, nobody really heeded them. He told us then, "It's the mission of my life to warn the world from zealots; they are willing to take everything to the edge and then march forward."[20]

What then is the meaning of Masada on a Birthright Israel trip? For some groups, the lesson of Masada is that Jews throughout the world must stand united to defend Israel against its enemies. For others, it is that Jewish political and religious fanaticism must be opposed lest it lead to Israel's self-destruction. In the tours included in our study sample, about half heard the conventional narrative and half heard the counternarrative or the counternarrative in combination with the conventional narrative. Taken together, these alternatives define a fairly broad spectrum of political discourse.

Birthright's Politics

Birthright's official policy is that guides should avoid politically one-sided presentations and aim for balance. In practice, some trips lean to the right or left, depending on the trip sponsor or the tour guide. Overall, though, the norm is to offer a variety of viewpoints on the political issues that divide Jews, drawing a line at the basic issue of the Israel's legitimacy. The Jewish people are depicted as a nation with a right to a homeland, and the Zionist movement is depicted as the national movement of the Jewish people. Whether the homeland ought to include the Occupied Territories and where the boundary should be drawn between religion and state are typically treated as open questions about which reasonable people disagree.

In *Tours That Bind*, the sociologist Shaul Kelner argues that although Birthright tour guides express diverse views that run the gamut of Israeli Jewish opinion, the ideological action in the program is not in the guides' formal narratives. In practice, participants are often inattentive to the guides' lessons but derive a crucial political message from the program nevertheless. The ideological work is accomplished by the bodily experience of being a Jewish tourist on an Israeli tour. Even when guides present the "Palestinian view," they locate it unselfconsciously and matter-of-factly as the view of the "other." The emplacement of tourists on the Jewish-Israeli side, literally as well as figuratively, is more important than the guide's specific ideological pronouncements.[21]

Kelner's analysis unravels an interesting paradox. According to evaluation studies, Birthright's effect on participants' emotional attachment to Israel is much stronger and more consistent than its impact on

their views on contentious issues related to the Israeli-Palestinian conflict. For example, in a posttrip survey, participants were roughly three
times more likely to feel "very much" connected to Israel than a control
group of applicants to the program who did not go on to participate. In
contrast, participants were equally likely to oppose dismantling West
Bank settlements for the sake of peace and just 13 percent more likely to
oppose dividing Jerusalem.[22] Birthright's main effect is thus to heighten
emotional attachment to Israel and not to convey a particular political
outlook with respect to more narrowly drawn political issues.

Nonetheless, critics on the left charge that Birthright soft-pedals
Israel's occupation of the West Bank and offers scant attention to the
Palestinian experience. On tour to promote his book *The Crisis of Zionism,* journalism professor Peter Beinart criticized the program as "intellectually insulting and dishonest" for not introducing participants to
the Palestinian point of view. "Ethically, how do we explain the fact that
we send all of these kids to Israel and pretend as if essentially Palestinians don't exist?"[23] Writing in *The Economist,* David Landau, the former
editor-in-chief of the Israeli newspaper *Haaretz,* expresses the concern
that Birthright's efforts to strengthen Jewish identity may be "coloured
by [Israel's] rightist religious *Zeitgeist.*" If so, he fears that the program
"will shore up an aggressive pro-Israel loyalism that denies the only fea-
sible future for a Jewish, democratic Israel: sharing the land with a Palestinian state."[24] A few organizations, including the group Encounter,
seek to redress the perceived imbalance by bringing American Jews to
the West Bank to hear the Palestinian viewpoint. A small number of
Birthright participants join such trips after their ten-day tour of Israel.

The Mifgash

Birthright's impact on participants' feelings about Israel is shaped not
only by the experience of visiting sites and hearing the guides' explanations. It is also shaped by the *mifgash* (pl. *mifgashim*), or encounter
with Israeli peers. Initially, mifgashim were a relatively minor part of
the Birthright program. During the program's early years, tour groups
typically met with groups of Israeli counterparts for a formal discussion
over lunch and perhaps a single related activity. Over time, however,
largely as a result of experimentation that highlighted its impact, the

mifgash has become a central component of the Birthright program. In recent years, all groups have included a delegation of five to eight Israelis for at least half of the duration of the tour. The Israelis are typically soldiers who, because of Israel's universal conscription, are the age-group peers of the diaspora visitors. As soldiers on active duty, they are easily recruited for participation in the trips, minimizing the logistical challenge of incorporating Israelis on the tours. Moreover, as soldiers, they also enjoy a great deal of instant cachet with many diaspora Jewish visitors.

Although mifgashim entail some formal programming, the essence of the encounter is informal interaction, especially conversation. On the bus, while walking to and from tour sites, over meals, and in hotel lobbies, Israeli and North American participants discuss their lives, exploring their similarities and differences. The diaspora visitors look to their Israeli counterparts as key informants about Israeli society. One Israeli participant recorded some of the typical exchanges in a diary she kept as part of a research project.[25]

> The [North Americans] used the bus rides for quick naps along with questions such as, "How was it in the Army? How was it in the recent Lebanon War?" . . . I was also asked if all the bananas are green or just not ripe yet, and [they were] impressed by the cultivation of black sun-flower seeds in Israel. We ended the day at the hotel bar. It was nice to talk over a glass of beer and to get to know them better.

The exchanges often include discussion of contentious political issues, and the encounters provide diaspora visitors with an opportunity to hear a range of Israeli opinions. As the diarist quoted above also recorded in her notebook,

> There was a discussion on whether Jerusalem should be the capital of Israel or [whether it should be] Tel Aviv. . . . I expressed my opinion (opposition) and said that we need to leave the past behind us, there is an Israeli identity which should be the primary identity in Israel, and that after all Israel is very diverse. . . . Many people approached me afterwards and told me that they weren't aware of the diversity of opinions on this matter in Israel and bombarded me with questions.

Although the impact on Israelis was not an original goal of the program, Israeli participants in the encounters often report having been deeply moved by the experience. In a posttrip survey, soldiers who had participated in the program indicated that the experience made them feel "proud to be Israeli" and "proud to serve in the Israel Defense Forces."[26] Such feelings are undoubtedly a response, at least in part, to tour guides' narratives that feature Israeli soldiers as heroic defenders of the Jewish state and Jewish people. They also stem from the experience of seeing their country from the vantage point of visiting tourists. Here is how one Israeli participant described the experience in a focus group interview:

> I've already been to all of the places we visited . . . and still, I was amazed by how moved I was each time at every place. Being at the Kotel [Western Wall] . . . it becomes ordinary, [but] suddenly I was really moved. Or at Yad Vashem [Holocaust memorial], I was really moved. . . . Even at the Dead Sea. I was suddenly excited that you can float! I just saw it through their eyes. And something that really moved me was that on the bus, on our way back, I asked someone how would you describe [the trip] in one word, and he said that the thing that had the greatest impact on him was actually to see *us* in all these places, like the opposite from me. For me, the thing that had the most impact was seeing them!

Surveys of North American participants similarly underscore the central importance of the encounter with Israeli peers. In response to questionnaires administered at the conclusion of the winter 2012 trips, North American participants indicated that the participation of Israeli peers "contributed to the trip's success" and "taught me about my Jewish identity."[27] In follow-up surveys administered up to 18 months after the trips, nearly three-quarters indicated that they had been in touch with Israeli participants since the trip; 43 percent indicated that they had been in touch on three or more occasions.[28]

Birthright participants from abroad are exposed not only to Israelis but also to other visiting diaspora groups. Such encounters happen routinely at tourist sites that often host several groups at once. More dramatically, several times a season Birthright holds a "Mega Event" of performances and speeches for all Birthright groups in the country on a given date. At the Mega Event, American visitors encounter delegations from throughout the Jewish world. As part of the evening's routine format, the names of countries represented by Birthright groups are announced and one at a time the delegations rise to their feet. Argentina is cheered, followed by Brazil, and then Chile, all the way through to the United States. In this fashion, Birthright participants from throughout the world encounter one another in person, transforming "world Jewry" from an abstract concept into a concrete reality.

A Normative Jewish Experience

At Birthright's inception, Steinhardt and Bronfman envisioned a program that, much like a bar mitzvah ceremony, would become a rite of passage. They set a goal of eventually sending half of all diaspora Jewish young adults on an Israel tour. Reinforced by evaluation studies showing strong program impact, the founders expanded the circle of large donors.[29] Lynn Schusterman, founder, together with her husband Charles, of an Oklahoma-based oil and gas business, and Sheldon Adelson, a Las Vegas developer, joined the group of leading donors. Adelson gave $100 million to the program in the mid-2000s. The state of Israel increased its contribution and, in 2010, announced its intention to fund one-third of the program for a five-year period. The American Jewish federations continued to give, albeit at a level below what the founders had initially hoped.

At the end of the Birthright's first decade, the founders' vision appears to be within reach. More than 340,000 diaspora Jewish young adults—two thirds from the United States—have participated in the ten-day trips. About 60,000 Israeli young adults have joined the trips as participants in mifgashim. During the seven-day registration period for summer 2012 trips, more than 45,000 American Jewish young adults completed online applications.[30] Overall, in 2012 Birthright brought more than 31,000 North American visitors, a figure that likely exceeds the target necessary to ensure that half of all American Jewish young adults will eventually participate in an educational program in Israel.[31]

As a result of Birthright's unprecedented scale, a wider range of Jewish young adults have traveled to Israel than ever before. Rather than representing the leadership cadre of diaspora youth (as in the days before Birthright), today's visitors reflect the full spectrum of diaspora Jewry. Among participants in the summer 2011 trips, 23 percent had no formal Jewish education while growing up, 70 percent attended a supplementary religious school or Hebrew School, and 15 percent attended a full-time Jewish day school.[32] A 2010 national survey of American Jews demonstrates the program's impact on the age cohort as a whole: 40 percent of those ages eighteen to twenty-nine reported having been to Israel, a proportion higher than any other age group except the oldest, and half of those eighteen to twenty-nine who had been to Israel had gone on a Birthright trip.[33]

Masa: Israel Journey

One concern expressed about Birthright was that the program would claim market share from other Israel programs, effectively substituting a ten-day experience for the more substantial four- to eight-week programs geared toward high school students and the academic year programs for college students. Who would be willing to pay for an Israel trip if they could join one for free? For several years during the mid-2000s, participation in many kinds of Israel programs did indeed decline. It was unclear, however, whether the cause was Birthright or the violence associated with the Second Intifada. By the end of the decade, however, participation in a range of long-term programs began increasing. Together with the diminished violence, two new factors were responsible for increased participation in long-term programs: Birthright, which motivated many young adults to seek ways to return to Israel for a longer experience, and the inauguration of a new Jewish Agency program, Masa: Israel Journey.

Masa was created by the Jewish Agency in 2003 as a nonprofit subsidiary to promote participation in long-term (four months or longer) study and internship experiences in Israel. Established a few years after Birthright, Masa reflects JAFI's desire to remain an active force in the field of educational tourism. The initiative was funded by the government of Israel to settle a legal dispute over the state's acquisition of lands that had been improved by JAFI (with UJA funds). The settlement entailed the Israeli government's commitment to fund an educational program for diaspora Jews—viewed as part of JAFI's and the UJA's mission—in perpetuity.

As Masa developed in the mid-2000s, the organization sought to promote diaspora participation in long-term programs by providing partial subsidies directly to participants, funding the development of new programs, and marketing long-term programs through its website and targeted advertising. Through these practices, Masa helped spur growth in the field of long-term programs, including "gap year" programs for students between high school and college; study abroad programs for university students during the junior year; and internship, volunteer, and career development programs for recent college graduates.

Gap year programs in Israel had long included yeshiva study for Orthodox students, and Masa provided subsidies for participants in such programs. Masa also supported programs that serve a non-Orthodox population, such as Young Judea's Year Course. Established in 1956, Year Course mixes academic classes in Hebrew and Jewish studies with travel and community service. During the 2000s, participation in the program—previously limited to the elite of the Young Judea youth movement—increased from 150 to more than 500 annually.[34] The program diversified its offerings, narrowly targeting disparate interest groups with special tracks in visual, culinary, and performing arts, athletics, business, and medicine. In addition to Young Judea, Masa supported the establishment of new gap year programs including several that are based in Israel but offer travel to Jewish communities throughout Europe and beyond (e.g., the program Kivunim, or "Directions").

Alongside support for gap year programs, Masa provided funding and scholarships for study abroad programs that attract diaspora Jewish students to Israel's universities, and career development and social justice programs for recent college graduates. The latter include programs such as Career Israel, which places North American Jewish graduates in internships in Israeli companies, government agencies, and nonprofit organizations. Other programs emphasize organic farming, peace and social justice, Jewish studies, and Hebrew and Arabic studies. Participants in college and postcollege programs are much more diverse, in terms of Jewish background, than gap year program participants, who remain disproportionately Orthodox. Half of all participants in the postcollege programs are alumni of Birthright Israel.[35]

Since its inception, Masa has spurred growth in the field of long-term programs and increased the participation of North American young adults from four thousand to six thousand annually, with growth in particular in the non-Orthodox segment of the population.[36] Following a decision in 2012 to cancel OTZMA, a federation-sponsored program established in the mid-1980s that no longer competed effectively in the increasingly crowded field, JFNA CEO Jerry Silverman wrote, "Today, there are more than 200 Israel programs for young Jewish adults, built upon OTZMA's shoulders, and many offer similarly extraordinary experiences."[37]

Recent research on alumni of long-term programs finds that most are highly engaged in the Jewish community both before and after their Israel experiences. Indeed, research on young adults who hold leadership positions in the Jewish community finds that more than half (56 percent) are alumni of long-term Israel programs. In contrast, just 30 percent of older Jewish leaders queried in the same study had spent the equivalent of four months or longer in Israel.[38] Similarly, the proportion of younger leaders who described their facility with Hebrew as "excellent" or "good" was more than twice as large (48 versus 21 percent) as that among older leaders.[39]

Building on the notion that repeated experiences in Israel deepen commitment to Jewish identity and the Jewish state, new emphasis has recently been placed on long-neglected high school programs. A new initiative to organize high school programs into an independent framework (like Birthright and Masa) is now under way under the name Lapid (Torch). Programs for ninth and tenth grade students from North American Jewish day schools have become increasingly common.[40] Like Birthright, high school programs increasingly include a mifgash with Israeli peers.[41] In 2011, eleven thousand North American high school students participated in educational tourism programs in Israel, surpassing the pre-Birthright level and contradicting the expectation that Birthright would eliminate the market for such programs.[42]

Birthright, Masa, and Israel Tourism

Overall, taking into account Birthright, Masa, and programs for high school students, the field of educational tourism in Israel has expanded dramatically during the past decade. From a peak of about ten thousand North American participants before the turn of the twenty-first century, the number of participants in such programs increased to an estimated fifty thousand in 2008 (Figure 4.1). Spending time in Israel is increasingly a normative part of growing up Jewish in North America.

Moreover, program evaluation studies that compare Birthright participants to control groups of applicants who did not go on to participate report significant impact: up to ten years after the trip, Birthright participants are more likely than comparable nonparticipants to feel connected to Israel, to participate in Jewish communal life, and to marry a person who is Jewish or converts to Judaism.[43] Although the full impact of scaled-up Israel travel on the future relationship of American Jewry to Israel cannot yet be determined with certainty, the early evidence suggests that it will be considerable.

The increase in young adult educational tourism occurred in the context of a more general increase in American Jewish tourism in Israel; indeed, it was a partial driver of it. As shown in Figure 4.2, American Jewish travel to Israel averaged between 150,000 and 200,000 during the 1990s. Following a dip between 1998 and 2003 (partially due to the Second Intifada), American Jewish tourism increased to an average of about 250,000 annually in the latter half of the 2000s.[44] The overall increase for the period as a whole is almost 50 percent, about a quarter or third of which is due to the surge in youth tourism that is the subject of this chapter.

Nefesh B'Nefesh

During the 2000s, as the field of Israel experience programs expanded and diversified, comparable developments were under way in the field of aliyah. Immigration from North America to Israel had long lagged behind the rest of the diaspora, with an average of just two to three thousand new immigrants annually during the 1990s.[45] The retention rate for this small immigrant population had also been notoriously low, with an estimated half of all immigrants eventually returning to North America, often because they could not find adequate employment. The Jewish Agency's work in the field of North American aliyah was ripe for takeover like a struggling company.

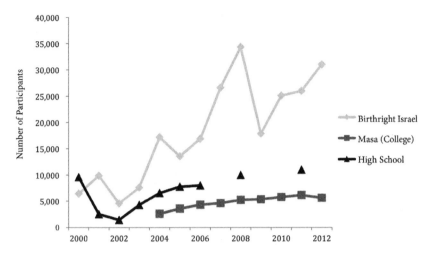

Figure 4.1. North American Participation in Israel Experience Programs, by Type

Sources: High school: For North American participation, 2000–2006, see Cohen, *Youth Tourism in Israel* (North American participation is here estimated as 70 percent of worldwide participation). For North America participation in 2011, see Arian, *Mapping the Field of Israel Travel*. For North American participation, 2008, see Kopelowitz, Wolf, and Markowitz, *High School Israel Experience Programs*. Masa: North American participation is based on data supplied by Masa; for 2004–6, North American participation is estimated as 65 percent of worldwide participation. Birthright Israel: North American participation is based on data supplied by Taglit.

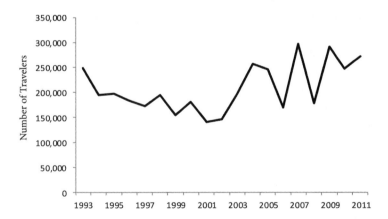

Figure 4.2. Number of American Jewish Travelers to Israel by Year

Source: Data supplied by the Israel Ministry of Tourism and published in the ministry's annual publication *Tayarut Le Yisrael*. The estimate Jewish travelers is derived from an annual survey conducted at border crossings.

The initiative to take a fresh approach came from two Florida residents, Yehoshua Fass, the rabbi of a Boca Raton synagogue, and Tony Gelbart, an investment fund manager. The impetus for Rabbi Fass was the death of his cousin, Naftali, in a suicide bombing. "Naftali's death made me want to stand in his stead in Israel," explained Fass, who determined to move to Israel and establish an organization to promote aliyah.[46] Fass and Gelbart commissioned research on the obstacles to aliyah among young families from the United States, Canada, and the United Kingdom. The research identified a number of barriers including employment, government bureaucracy, cost and, social integration. Fass and Gelbart established Nefesh B'Nefesh—"Soul to Soul"—with the aim of systematically lowering the barriers to aliyah for Jews from English-speaking countries.

In its first year, 2002, the new organization chartered an El Al 747 jet to bring 510 new immigrants, Rabbi Fass and his family among them. The organization enlisted the support of key figures across the Israeli political spectrum, including then prime minister Ariel Sharon and Jewish Agency chairman Sallai Meridor. The vision was to create a "business-like" organization that would deliver aliyah services efficiently and in a consumer-friendly fashion, with the goal of increasing immigration from English-speaking countries and improving retention of new immigrants.

For the next four years, the new organization alternately competed and collaborated with the Jewish Agency. In 2006, at the behest of the Israeli government, the two entities reached an agreement: Nefesh B'Nefesh would become responsible for promoting aliyah in the United States, Canada, and the United Kingdom and supporting new immigrants. The Jewish Agency, in turn, would retain responsibility for determining the eligibility of prospective immigrants under the Law of Return, and for processing their immigration paperwork. The Nefesh B'Nefesh budget would be supplied jointly by private donors, mostly from the United States, and the Israeli government.

In the ensuing years, Nefesh B'Nefesh developed programs and strategies to promote aliyah in its target countries. Today, the organization publishes extensive information about aliyah on its website. Nefesh staff (there are ninety in the Israel office) travel continuously throughout North America hosting information sessions and meeting potential *olim* (immigrants, literally, ascenders). Once olim have begun the immigration process, members of the Nefesh staff remain in regular contact, providing advice on handling all aspects of the immigration experience. Nefesh operates an employment bank linking immigrants and employers and also provides job and career counseling, advice on communities and schools, and information about immigrant benefits made available by the Israeli government.

In addition to providing practical assistance, members of the Nefesh professional staff seek to reinforce the pro-aliyah motivations of new immigrants. In contrast to most other immigrant groups, olim from English-speaking countries come to Israel for religious and ideological reasons rather than fleeing persecution or poor economic circumstances. As olim by choice, they are vulnerable to second thoughts and the temptation to return to their diaspora homes. Understanding this dynamic, Nefesh provides ongoing ideological and emotional encouragement in a way that the more bureaucratic Jewish Agency could not. It arranges for olim to arrive on chartered flights with other immigrants and for dignitaries to greet their arrival in a celebratory manner. It hires as staff other English-speaking immigrants who feel positively about their own choices and communicate their enthusiasm to potential and actual new immigrants. It also encourages olim to remain in touch with one another and Nefesh staff in the years following their immigration and, in some instances, to establish communities of like-minded olim.

Nefesh settles immigrants throughout Israel and in the West Bank.[47] The organization also has programs that encourage olim to relocate to areas identified by the Israeli government as high priority for Jewish settlement, including the Galilee. The "Go North" (Galilee) initiative provides special benefits to immigrants from English-speaking countries and supports a small number of mostly Anglo settlements. Finally, Nefesh engages in advocacy to simplify the aliyah process, reduce the necessary paperwork, and shorten bureaucratic processes. In many instances, Nefesh olim can finish their immigration paperwork during their flight to Israel and receive Israeli ID cards within thirty-six hours of arrival.

During its first decade, Nefesh brought roughly 33,000 new immigrants from English-speaking countries, an estimated 90 percent of whom have remained in the country. In 2010, the organization brought

3,980 new immigrants from North America, a larger number than arrived in any single year since 1973, and more than double the number that arrived in 2001, the year before the organization was established.[48] The largest category of olim consisted of families with young children, most of whom were Orthodox. The overrepresentation of young Orthodox families among new immigrants predates Nefesh and reflects their greater level of religious and ideological motivation; it also reflects the high cost of Orthodox living—especially the cost of private day school tuition—in the United States. The next largest category consisted of more than 1,000 unmarried young adults. According to Nefesh, the latter group was mostly secular and comprised individuals who came to Israel for the first time on a Birthright tour.[49]

Conclusion

The developments in educational tourism and aliyah described in this chapter have a number of common features. The central role of the Jewish Agency, funded by the annual campaigns of Jewish federations and philanthropies worldwide, is in relative decline. Alongside the Jewish Agency, new private and semiprivate initiatives of philanthropists and organizational entrepreneurs have emerged and play an increasingly influential role. The new organizations, including the dozens of tour companies that offer programs through Birthright and Masa, as well as Nefesh B'Nefesh, are consumer-friendly, market-savvy, and oriented to niche markets.

Privatization, entrepreneurship, and the infusion of new philanthropic funds have contributed to a modest increase in the annual number of new immigrants from North America, especially among Orthodox families and young adults. These processes, however, have had their greatest impact in the field of educational tourism. More American Jewish young adults from a wider variety of backgrounds are traveling, studying, and volunteering in Israel than at any previous time since the founding of the state. Increasingly, a trip to Israel in the context of an organized, educational program is a normal part of growing up Jewish in North America.

Like their predecessors, the new educational tourism programs stress core Zionist themes, especially the Ashes to Redemption narrative that describes the state of Israel as a culmination of diaspora Jewish history. The scant attention to Palestinian perspectives has prompted some to criticize Birthright's educational program as one-sided. The leading role of professional tour guides, however, has meant that core Zionist themes tend to be inflected in ways that reflect, minimally, the spectrum of Israeli-Jewish political opinion. As a result, although Birthright trips foster emotional attachment to Israel, they do not have a strong influence on participants' political views on contentious issues. Instead, the programs tend to reinforce the diversity of American Jewish viewpoints, a topic we explore in Chapter 5.

Finally, in contrast to the previous generation of Israel experience programs, the new initiatives (including both Birthright and Masa) place greater emphasis on mifgashim—direct encounters—between diaspora visitors and their Israeli counterparts. The increasing number of diaspora visitors to Israel and their encounters with Israeli counterparts are core dimensions of the new direct engagement paradigm, a theme to be explored further in Chapter 6.

5

Attitudes and Attachment

During the 1970s and 1980s, social scientists stressed the symbolic significance of Israel for American Jews. According to these accounts, Israel
represented the revival of the Jewish people following the Holocaust and
Israel's existence meant that Jews would never again find themselves
defenseless and bereft of a sanctuary from anti-Semitism. As a young
democracy with a strong welfare state, Israel represented the Jewish commitment to social justice and progressive values. As a regional military
power, evidenced most dramatically in the 1967 Six-Day War, Israel represented the emergence of a new kind of Jew, tough and resourceful—the
antithesis of diaspora bookishness. American Jews viewed Israelis as
"young, tough, hardworking, idealistic pioneers, struggling in the midst of
a backward and hostile world, balancing a reverence for Jewish tradition
with a socially progressive commitment to build a modern, democratic
society and make the desert bloom."[1] In this context, Israel became a source
of personal pride for millions of Jews the world over.

According to some observers, many of the features that contributed to Israel's symbolic significance have long since faded or dissi-
pated. The Holocaust and founding of the state have receded into history, and American Jews have achieved ever higher levels of security
and integration within American society. Israel's image as a progressive,

democratic country has been challenged by news of corruption, mounting social inequality, and discrimination against the Arab minority and non-Orthodox Jews. Israel's vulnerability to terror and, in recent years, bombardment from Lebanon and Gaza—not to mention the menace of a potentially nuclear-armed Iran—increasingly cast doubt on its capacity to serve as a refuge. Finally, Israel's moral standing in the world has been eroded by allegations that its forces committed war crimes during the 2008 Gaza War and, more generally, by the claim that its ongoing occupation of the West Bank will transform it into an apartheid state. What, in this changing context, does Israel mean for contemporary American Jews? What are their views regarding Israel's contemporary policy dilemmas? How close do American Jews feel toward Israel, and what do current trends tell us about the future?

What Israel Means

Asked about Israel's personal meaning, many American Jews respond by striking classical Zionist themes about anti-Semitism and Israel's role as a refuge for persecuted Jews. These themes were prevalent, for example, in focus group discussions I moderated among diverse sets of Jews in the Boston area.[2] In particular, the *Israel as refuge* theme was expressed by discussion participants who had little firsthand experience with Israel, including those who had never visited the country and those who did not closely follow news about Israel in their everyday lives. As an example of this discourse, consider the following comments from the focus group discussions. The first is by Jonathan, a physician in his mid-fifties:

> I am the child of a Holocaust survivor, so Israel has been, you know, important, an emotional sanctuary for me, growing up. . . . A watershed moment for everybody is when you have children, and though we haven't yet made it to Israel, I'd like our children to think of Israel as a home for them also. And that makes . . . me feel more motivated to visit there . . . to help them feel as though that's a place they belong.

The second comment, striking the same theme, comes from Michael, a lawyer in his late thirties:

Did you ever see how they kill baby seals in Scandinavia with the sticks? This is how they killed Jewish children in the Holocaust. And I have two little boys, and I can imagine. . . . I consider myself a liberal person, however, sometimes you lose your liberalism when your back is against the wall and you're under threat. People think the Holocaust is a long time ago, and the problem of anti-Semitism has faded away, but they really haven't.

In the above comments, both speakers invoked the Holocaust and described Israel as a potentially important refuge for their children. In the next comment, Steve—a mental health counselor in his early fifties—also describes Israel's importance in reference to the history of anti-Semitism. Notably, Steve describes his commitment to Israel's survival as totally independent of his feelings about contemporary Israeli society:

I've been to Israel once and I didn't particularly enjoy the experience. I found the Israelis to be obnoxious and generally rude and in your face. . . . Israel has become much more important to me as a consequence of studying Jewish history and that will remain so regardless of my personal level of comfort in visiting Israel, being there or having a direct connection with the actual place. And it is because, as I say, of this certainty that we should never again have to live at someone else's pleasure. And I feel I've made just a commitment for myself to do what I can from this end to make sure that it remains the case.

Similarly building on classical Zionist themes, some discussion participants described Israel as a source of self-assurance and pride for contemporary Jews. In the following comment, Ralph, a law professor in his early fifties, evokes the 1967 Six-Day War as a pivotal event that led to Jewish self-assertiveness in the United States.

My bar mitzvah year was 1967. You know, there's always sort of this history of hiding underneath the bed, and if you don't rock the boat, you won't get into trouble, which at least in '67, as far as I was concerned was a dead issue. That all of a sudden, you don't have to hide underneath the bed, and yes, you can rock the boat. And there's something extraordinarily valuable as a people in doing that.

Such conventional rationales for support of the Jewish state might seem anachronistic to observers who doubt Israel's role as a safe haven and moral exemplar but not to many of the participants in the discussion groups. Indeed, their support for conventional Zionist positions explains, in large measure, why they seek to reconcile their sometimes critical orientations toward policies of the Israeli government with their ongoing feelings of attachment to and support of the Jewish state— themes to which we will return below.

Focus group participants who have had more intensive experiences with Israel often touched on additional themes, including Israel's significance as a state with a Jewish majority and Hebrew culture and its accomplishments as a democracy, welfare state, and innovative society. The following comment illustrates this discourse, emphasizing Israel's significance as a Jewish-majority state. The speaker is Martha, a graduate student in her late twenties.

> It's like Disney World! [laughter]. I love being there . . . because, you know, when you grow up with no Jews, to think that there is a country that celebrates Purim is like a dream! And it definitely has gotten more significant to me as I've gotten older and traveled there and learned more about it. . . . It's definitely a love relationship, it's very serious [laughter].

New Realism

In addition to the above comments, however, the discourse on Israel's significance among those who know the country well and follow its affairs closely was often tinged with ambivalence. In these accounts, Israel is a country that boasts remarkable accomplishments as well as serious flaws and social problems. Many on the political right perceive Israelis to be drifting away from Jewish and Zionist commitments in favor of the comfortable lifestyles of the West. In contrast, many liberals perceive Israel to be losing its democratic character due to the occupation of Palestinian lands and undemocratic practices regarding minorities and the role of religion in the state. Across the spectrum, there is recognition of yawning social gaps and worsening environmental problems. The following comment illustrates this perspective, albeit with an emphasis on the positive. The speaker is Robert, an investment manager in his early fifties:

I've probably been back [to Israel] eight or ten times since [my first visit]. I certainly know the country much better today than I did then, pluses and minuses. But, I'll tell you, as aware as I am of Israel's flaws, I still feel like I'm coming home every time I go. And I think I have at least an average to above-average sense of the flaws and challenges, as well as the other side of the coin. But it's a very special place to me and I think [that] held up against any reasonable lens, that modern Israel exists is just an unbelievable miracle.

Focus group participants who discussed Israel's shortcomings often did so as part of a coming-of-age narrative—a tale of moving beyond youthful idealism to embrace realism about the Jewish state. Consider the following examples of this *idealism to realism* theme. The first speaker is Jean, a forty-year-old pediatrician.

Well, I think when you're very young . . . you see things in very simplistic terms. I think when I was young, there was this land flowing with milk and honey to protect everyone from further Holocausts, and there was dancing and singing and the planting of trees. . . . I mean to a certain extent some of those are still engraved in your psyche. But as you get older of course, you come to understand history a bit better. . . . And you have a more balanced view of the world, and you know other people suffered because of these glorious victories, and that there were these really messy political and geographical developments. Not that I don't still have very strong, very positive feelings towards Israel but they're somewhat down by the current political situation. I definitely do not agree [that] everything Israel does makes sense. I guess one of the big things that changed is there is "Israel the image" and "Israel the reality." [I] still consider myself possibly a strong supporter of Israel the entity. I have to say that I do not always agree politically with what is going on but I could say the same thing about . . . America.

Jean describes embracing a "balanced" view of Israel as she matured, one that entails criticism of Israeli policies (which do not all make sense to her) alongside ongoing support for Israel's existence. Notably, she compares her feelings for Israel to her attachment to the United States; in both cases, she feels loyalty to a country whose government pursues policies she does not always support.

Marci, a software engineer in her mid-forties, similarly describes her ongoing attachment to Israel notwithstanding her increasingly critical perspective:

> I think Israel's as important to me now as I've grown up. But, I have a very different perspective. As a child, you know, it was played up as a homeland and a beautiful place, and ours, and now I see it through less rose-colored glasses—but as equally important—the importance of it existing hasn't diminished. But I see the struggles a little more clearly, and it's not just this fantasy land, it's not Disney Land that you know [is] always going to be there, like I think I thought when I was little.

Notably, evidence from surveys underscores a major theme in the new realism discourse, namely, the relative autonomy of feelings of attachment from political judgments about specific policies. For example, for the period 1986 to 2010, the annual surveys of the American Jewish Committee show remarkable stability in the overall level of attachment to Israel. Throughout this period, the proportion of American Jews who reported feeling "close to Israel" fluctuated up and down within a relatively narrow band (between three-fifths and three-quarters) and there was no consistent relationship between political ideology (when measured on the liberal-to-conservative continuum or in terms of political party affiliation) and emotional attachment to Israel.[3] In short, the claims of many focus group participants that their attitudes on policy issues have little bearing on their feelings of connection to the Jewish state are borne out by the survey research evidence.[4]

Information Environment

The new realism about Israel derives, at least in part, from a much enhanced information environment. This includes increased exposure to Israel through travel, as described in Chapter 4. It also includes increased access to Israeli newspapers, newscasts, films, and music, which are all much more readily available and widely distributed today than in the past.

The increasing availability of news directly from Israel—especially via online newspapers—is especially noteworthy. Since the late 1990s, Israeli newspapers *Haaretz* and the *Jerusalem Post* have published online

English editions. *Yedioth Ahronot*, until recently Israel's largest circulation daily paper, added a web-based English version of its newspaper in 2005. In 2009, the *Jerusalem Post* began publishing a weekly U.S. edition, distributed in select New York metropolitan neighborhoods together with the *New York Post*. These news outlets provide American Jews a "warts and all" view of the Jewish state. They also tend to express strong editorial positions, with the *Jerusalem Post*, for example, tending toward the political right and *Haaretz* tending toward the political left.

Two new additions to the burgeoning ranks of Israel's English-language news outlets are funded by American Jewish philanthropists with ties to the political right. *Israel Hayom*, a free Hebrew-language newspaper launched in 2007 and now Israel's largest circulation daily, recently added an online English-language edition. The paper is owned by Sheldon Adelson, a prominent supporter of the Zionist Organization of America and a major donor to Republican politicians (as well as Taglit-Birthright Israel). The *Times of Israel*, launched by a former *Jerusalem Post* editor in 2012, publishes online, in an English-only format. The new venture is funded by Seth Klarman, a prominent hedge fund executive who served as chairman for the right-leaning advocacy group The David Project and has supported a number of prosettler charities (as well as mainstream Jewish causes). Both publications describe their editorial stances as independent and neutral, but critics charge, in particular in reference to Israel Hayom, a pro-Likud bias.[5]

Israeli English-language newspapers have become the news outlets of choice for highly engaged diaspora Jews both for news of Israel as well as for news of diaspora Jewish communities. Steven M. Cohen's survey of Conservative rabbis (see Chapter 2) reported that during the previous month 58 percent frequently or sometimes read *Haaretz*, 46 percent the *Jerusalem Post*, and 29 percent *Yedioth Ahronot*.[6] Indeed, a study of Jewish websites reports that the *Jerusalem Post* and *Haaretz* were hubs in American Jewish cyberspace and the most visited sites.[7] Research on Birthright Israel participants also finds fairly widespread use of Israeli English-language websites. In surveys conducted five to eight years after the ten-day trips, 40 percent of respondents reported having checked Israeli websites for news of Israel.[8]

The richer information environment is a major factor in the diffusion of more nuanced views of Israel among the more engaged segment of the American Jewish community. It is also a factor in the increasing polarization of American Jewry with respect to Israel-related policy issues. Indeed, American Jewry increasingly reflects the divisions in Israeli society over policy issues. In the sections that follow, we examine American Jews' views regarding three sets of policy issues: the Israeli-Palestinian conflict, the relationship between religion and state, and the issue of minority civil rights.

Israeli-Palestinian Conflict

Survey research establishes a useful starting point for investigating how American Jews think about the Israeli-Palestinian conflict. According to the American Jewish Committee's 2010 Annual Survey, 48 percent of American Jews favor and 45 percent oppose establishment of a Palestinian state in the current situation.[9] In general, Orthodox Jews express more hawkish views, with most opposing establishment of a Palestinian state and dismantling Jewish settlements on the West Bank. Reform, Conservative, and unaffiliated Jews tend to express more dovish views, with most favoring the establishment of a Palestinian state and dismantling some or all settlements in the West Bank.[10] Regarding the future of Jerusalem, the dividing line is somewhat different, with Orthodox and Conservative Jews opposing and Reform and unaffiliated Jews supporting future compromises on the territorial unity of the capital city.[11] Analysis of survey data shows that general political orientation (e.g., conservative, liberal) as well as political party affiliation are also strong predictors of views on the Palestinian-Israeli conflict, with self-defined conservatives and Republicans favoring more hawkish positions. Age is not an important factor in views on the Palestinian-Israeli conflict.[12]

Participants in the Boston-area focus groups described earlier in this chapter were asked questions about the Israeli-Palestinian conflict (as well as the issues of religion and state, and civil rights, discussed below), and their responses provide the basis for a significant deepening of the analysis. Reflecting and giving voice to the public discourse, the focus group participants expressed the perspectives of the political right, left, and center.[13] Their comments provide a foundation for understanding not merely the distribution of opinions across the Jewish population but also the taken-for-granted assumptions, knowledge, and values that animate the various positions.

Zero-Sum Conflict: The View from the Right

In the public discourse, the political right frames its opposition to the establishment of a Palestinian state in the West Bank and Gaza in terms of security, history, and religious belief. The security argument contends that holding territory is necessary because the Palestinians cannot be trusted to uphold their side of a peace bargain. The historical argument underscores the importance of the West Bank as the cradle of Jewish civilization. The religious perspective describes the Land of Israel as divinely ordained for the Jewish people. Such themes were evident in several discussions—mainly but not exclusively among Orthodox discussion participants.

Skepticism regarding the intentions of the Palestinians—and their reliability as partners to a peace deal—was widespread in most of the discussions. However, in most discussions, the motivations of the Palestinians were treated as an obstacle that might be surmounted. The hallmark of right-wing discourse, in the focus groups, was its utter rejection of the possibility of reaching a secure, enforceable, and reliable settlement. In this discourse, the Palestinians are described as unwilling to accept Israel's existence under any terms. The following quote from Ephraim, a sixty-year-old lawyer in a modern Orthodox group, illustrates the theme:

> You have to take into account the reality of the situation and at the moment [it is] a life and death struggle. . . . Their covenant [Palestinian National Covenant] is for the destruction of Israel, they never repudiated that privately or publicly. . . . At the moment, I see very little difference between the Palestinians attitude towards Jews and Israel and Hitler's attitude towards Jews and Israel. . . . That's the reality of the situation and you deal accordingly. . . . The Palestinian Authority either doesn't have the will or the ability to control Hamas, so essentially they are the ones who are determining the process.

The conflict is thus depicted as zero-sum; either the Jews or the Palestinians will emerge victorious. In this context, peace talks are dangerous for Israel, insofar as Palestinians build on their strategic gains to pursue their actual goal of Israel's destruction. In the following extract, Pam, a forty-two-year-old physician, describes the peace process as a "Trojan horse." The discussants are members of a modern Orthodox group:

> JERRY: To them it's a matter of, look, we'll make an agreement now, but eventually, long term, we will get Israel.
>
> PAM: Well [former Palestinian leader Yasser] Arafat said it from the very beginning—it's a Trojan horse. We're gonna enter into a pact with our enemy just like the Prophet Mohammed . . . so that we may eventually overthrow him.
>
> JENNIFER: The Koran has that in it. You make agreements for when you're on the bottom and when you're on the top you don't need to honor them.

Perhaps surprisingly, relatively few participants discussed the importance of Israel keeping the West Bank for specifically historical or religious reasons. Speakers in all of the Orthodox and some of the Conservative discussions referred to the territories Israel occupied in 1967 by their biblical names, Judea and Samaria, and a few pointed out their historical significance. "That is where most of our history took place," one remarked. However, the historical themes were muted in comparison to the security arguments. Even rarer were arguments that struck specifically religious themes. In only one case did a speaker describe the Bible as a kind of property deed that established the Jewish people's right to the Land of Israel. By embracing security arguments, or, secondarily, arguments from history, the Orthodox Jews in the discussion groups challenged a media-driven caricature that attributes their political viewpoints to religious fundamentalism.

Saving Israel's Democracy: The View from the Left

The themes of the political left were especially prevalent in discussions among members of postdenominational and Reconstructionist synagogues, college students, and members of a Jewish peace organization. They were also occasionally expressed in Reform discussion groups. Participants in these groups emphasized that to protect the state's Jewish majority and democratic character, Israel must immediately withdraw from the territories conquered in 1967. Several speakers contended that, as a consequence of the occupation, Israel does not presently qualify as a democratic country. Consider the following, from Janet, a member of a Jewish peace organization:

> It puzzles me—demographically they know it is not going to work. . . . In a few years they will be outnumbered. And this whole issue of, you know, a Jewish state—what is a Jewish state and how do you keep the character of a Jewish state? And that is connected, in so many ways, to the Holocaust and Jewish identity. How do you keep that and then at the same time really make a democratic state, which it is not? I mean it is for the Jews in the state more or less.

Also characteristic of the discourse of the left is the claim that Israeli and Palestinian officials are equally to blame for the lack of progress in peace negotiations. Louise, a fifty-seven-year-old clinical social worker and participant in a Reconstructionist group, put it this way:

> I think that many people like to point to Oslo [peace process] and say it failed because of the Palestinian side, but my limited knowledge says, in fact, Oslo didn't really offer the Palestinians a true settlement that met their needs for a homeland. . . . I think all the efforts are failing because there isn't good leadership on either side. . . . There really has been a lack of leadership that truly wants peace and truly is willing to offer the security that one side wants and the freedom and independence the other side wants.

In these left-leaning conversations, Jewish West Bank settlers were often singled out for harsh criticism. The settlers were depicted as extremists and "crazies," and the broader settlement enterprise was described as a major obstacle to a peace agreement. The following statement by Bruce, a fifty-two-year-old participant in a Reform discussion group, illustrates this line of argument:

> The Israelis have made a mess of it with the settlements [that have] exacerbated the situation to no end. . . . Had they pulled out of the settlements

ten years ago and done what they should do in terms of keeping those crazy religious settlers out of those lands, then they would be in a much better situation now. They would be able to protect their people . . . but they're not willing to make the step. The Israelis don't have the backbone to do what's right. . . . You can't rely on the Palestinians, but you can't rely on the Israelis either.

Peace with Security: The View from the Center

The themes of the center were clearly dominant in the Reform, Conservative, and unaffiliated groups. A key theme in this discourse blames poor leadership, typically on the Palestinian side, as well as "extremists" on both sides, for the failure of previous peace deals. In the view of many discussion participants, ordinary Palestinians desire peace, but their leaders have failed to take the courageous steps necessary to confront the rejectionist groups in the Palestinian camp. Shelly, a fifty-one-year-old teacher and member of a Reform discussion group, expressed the theme in this way:

> I think . . . there certainly must be Palestinians who want to make peace and want to live side-by-side in two states. Unfortunately, there's no leader of the Palestinian people that has come forward and who lived long enough to try to make that happen. . . . I'm sure that there is a faction of the populace that feels that way [but] there's no leadership able to guide them.

A similar theme, expressed in relation to the Israeli side, depicts Israelis as desiring peace but realistic about the difficulty of achieving a reliable and secure deal with the Palestinians. David, a fifty-one-year-old investment banker and participant in a Conservative discussion group, put it this way:

> I think they operate on two totally different planes, and I think the number of Israelis who don't genuinely want peace is a truly, truly small minority. . . . But it has to be a legitimate peace, not just "We'll give up land and then see if we get peace." Israel has given up land for peace before, and will do it again. . . . I think there [are] more Palestinian

people who want peace, but Palestinian leadership and the Arab leadership do not.

As noted, skepticism regarding Palestinian intentions and capacity to honor a peace agreement was widespread in most of the discussions. In the discourse of the political center, however, Palestinian intransigence is not treated as inevitable or intractable. Rather, Palestinians are described as still unready for a peace deal. Consider the comments of the following three women, all members of a Conservative synagogue:

> BONNIE (STAY-AT-HOME MOTHER, FORTY-EIGHT): For me, it's a gut reaction that the Palestinians are simply not ready. I mean, they are raising their children to hate Jews and to kill Jews. They're raising their children like that. And we all know how Jews are raised to do mitzvahs. I mean it is two totally opposing things.
>
> MARCI (SOFTWARE ENGINEER, FORTY-FOUR): I agree with Bonnie. I think that's something I've been thinking that I haven't really found the words to express. There's a mindset . . . that's so deeply ingrained that needs to be changed on the Palestinian side. I don't feel that they feel that Israel has the right to exist . . . and so unless you believe that, you're not ready to negotiate.
>
> SHERI (BUSINESS MANAGER, FORTY-FOUR): Well, I really think that there are three groups. I don't think that the Palestinians really want peace. I think they just want Israel out of there. I think Israel proper does want peace. And I think that the settlements behind the Green Line do not want peace—or what peace would involve, giving away their territory.

The claim that the Palestinian side is unready to make peace was often linked to the claim that Palestinians teach their children to hate Jews. In many discussions, participants reported having heard about Palestinian textbooks that depict Jews in anti-Semitic terms and school maps that do not show the Jewish state. Paul, a sixty-seven-year-old clinical psychologist, commented, "What I find most discouraging is what I've heard about what the Muslim youth are taught in the schools there. They're shown maps that don't even have Israel on the maps."

Also common in this centrist discourse is the claim that the Palestinians were "offered everything" during the Camp David peace talks in 2000, but "walked away" from the deal. The following statement by David, a forty-seven-year-old lawyer and member of a Reform congregation, is typical of this kind of discourse:

> My instinct is not to lay all the blame on the Palestinians because it takes two to tango and to make peace. But I have a very difficult time laying any blame at the feet of the Israelis. . . . [Former prime minister Ehud] Barak came to the table [at Camp David], giving the Palestinians virtually everything that had been asked for, and even [former prime minister Ariel] Sharon, who was the great warrior, the great conservative, was willing to give virtually everything. . . . There is a complete lack of leadership on the Palestinian side.

Nevertheless, the centrist groups shared a broad consensus that Israel should pursue a peace deal and be willing to make the necessary compromises—but only for a deal that promises to stick. In most conversations, the details regarding territorial concessions—whether Israel should agree to withdraw from all or some of the West Bank and the final status of Jerusalem—were of secondary importance. The main issue in these conversations was whether the Palestinian side was prepared to accept and honor a peace deal. In the comment that follows, Len, a fifty-three-year-old writer and participant in a Conservative discussion group, displays the ambivalence of the political center:

> I think there should be a withdrawal to the '67 borders if that would buy peace. . . . But I don't know if even that would buy it, given so-called partners who take it as an item of faith that Israel ought to be annihilated. So it just depends if you feel that your partners are legitimate in wanting peace themselves and depending on what morning you wake up and ask the question, I guess you're going to answer it differently.

Religious and Minority Rights

Alongside the conflict with the Palestinians, Israelis have long struggled over the role of religion in the public arena and the rights of the

Palestinian Arab minority. In the domain of religion and state, Israeli secularists charge that Orthodox political leaders employ their swing votes to gain unjustifiable benefits for the religious sector of society and to impose religious regulations—especially regarding commerce and transportation on the Sabbath—upon society as a whole. The secularists oppose such "religious coercion"; they also demand civil wedding ceremonies and recognition of non-Orthodox Jewish movements. The Orthodox, for their part, view Orthodox rabbinic supervision of conversion and divorce as the minimum necessary framework for ensuring the Jewish character of the state and the future unity of the Jewish people.

In the domain of civil rights, Israelis increasingly debate whether the state can deliver on its promise of equality for all citizens while also preserving its Jewish character. In recent years, members of Israel's Arab minority, with the support of a number of academics, have charged that Israel cannot be both a Jewish and a democratic state. To qualify as a democratic state, these critics argue, Israel must cease de facto discrimination against the Arab minority, eliminate legal preferences for Jews in land rights and immigration, and alter the symbols of the state (including the flag and national anthem) to make them more inclusive.[14] Other scholars and public officials have defended the prevailing institutional arrangements by comparing Israel to European nation-states that privilege the language, culture, and immigration of their founding groups.[15]

American Jews find themselves in a paradoxical position regarding these struggles. On the one hand, American Jewish political culture is deeply committed to liberal values including separation of religion and state and minority rights.[16] These value commitments reflect the experience and structural situation of American Jews as a minority in an open democratic society.[17] On the other hand, American Jews are linked to Israel largely via their Jewish identities, and their status as a diaspora presupposes the Jewishness of the state of Israel. To oppose the extension of maximum equality to Palestinian citizens of the state would contradict their liberal commitments. To support full equality, however, might undermine the Jewish character of the state and hence their connection to it. How then do American Jews resolve the dilemmas associated with religious and civil rights in Israel?

Religion and State

There is less survey data on American Jewish opinion on issues of religion and state than concerning the Palestinian-Israeli conflict. Questions regarding the status of non-Orthodox religious movements in Israel have not been consistently asked in surveys of American Jewish opinion. The most recent instance of such a question appeared in the AJC's 1998 Annual Survey. Of respondents, 89 percent agreed with the statement, "Conversions performed in Israel by Reform and Conservative rabbis should be recognized as much as Orthodox conversions"; 9 percent disagreed. In the same survey, 92 percent agreed with the statement, "Conservative and Reform representatives should be permitted to serve on community religious councils in Israel alongside Orthodox representatives." Just 7 percent disagreed. The lopsided results likely explain why the questions were not repeated.

In the 2000 AJC survey, respondents were asked to comment on increasing tensions in Israel over the role of religion in the Jewish state. Respondents were asked to agree or disagree with the following statement: "Tension between secular and ultra-Orthodox in Israel is becoming sharper. In your view, who is principally responsible for this increase in tension?" Of respondents, 7 percent held secular Israelis to be mainly responsible for the conflict; 72 percent blamed the ultra-Orthodox.

The focus group participants were also asked about the role of religion in the Jewish state, and, in particular, about the standing of non-Orthodox Jewish movements.[18] The Orthodox respondents typically described the imposition of Orthodox standards for weddings, conversions, and divorce as necessary to ensure the unity of the Jewish people. In their discourse, Orthodox standards of religious law, or *halakha*, should be embraced for pragmatic reasons, as the lowest common denominator that would satisfy the needs of Orthodox and non-Orthodox Jews alike. For example, consider the following, from Dan, a forty-five-year-old engineer and participant in an Orthodox group.

> I think both religious and nonreligious have to develop more of a tolerance for each other on an individual level, but your question was more on a leadership level, a rabbinical level. In that regard, I think that [authority] should be kept in the reins of the Orthodox, simply because they are

the most stringent of the three opinions so . . . no one would have the complaint as far as their legitimacy or what it is that they're doing.

Notwithstanding their insistence on preserving Orthodox authority, the Orthodox discussion participants often claimed that the Reform and Conservative movements serve useful purposes, such as providing opportunities for Jewish observance for those who would not adopt an Orthodox lifestyle. In several discussions, participants stressed the need for Israel to support the non-Orthodox movements, albeit in ways short of full recognition. In their general openness to the non-Orthodox movements, the Orthodox Jews in our study sample distinguished themselves from their Israeli counterparts.[19]

The non-Orthodox Jews—who composed the vast majority of focus group participants—were fairly uniform in their opposition to Israel's religious status quo, in particular to the institutional control exercised by the state's official Orthodox rabbinate over personal status issues including marriage, conversion, divorce, and burial. Many denounced the Orthodox monopoly; some analogized it to the kind of religious fundamentalism they associate with Muslim countries such as Saudi Arabia. Consider this exchange from a Reform discussion group:

> BOB (RETIRED, AGE SEVENTY): Well, it's a very serious problem for Israel because if the state doesn't recognize other branches of Judaism, it's becoming a religious theocracy controlled by the Orthodox and you already see the effects—a lot of the secular Jews are beginning to leave Jerusalem because of the Orthodox. So, in many ways they will become the Jewish Saudi Arabia, unless they can open their religious establishment to all of the branches. . . .
> JONATHAN (PUBLISHER, AGE SIXTY-SEVEN): It's a huge issue for me personally because I do not want Israel to turn into the country—a fundamentalist nation that I'm forced to support in the diaspora out of a feeling of duty without any kind of feeling of affection.

Discussion participants also criticized the political power and influence of the ultra-Orthodox political parties. Many warned that the power of the religious parties threatened Israeli democracy and called for a U.S.-style separation of church and state. The following exchange is from the discussion of a mostly Conservative discussion group:

> SUSAN (ART HISTORIAN, AGE FORTY-FOUR): If Israel is going to try to be a democracy and Jewish—you know, you can be both, but you can't limit—if you're going to be a democracy, you can't limit how people practice certain things. I just think it's awful. It's a terrible precedent. . . .
>
> MARK (BUSINESS CONSULTANT, AGE FORTY-NINE): It's a secular country. I think that's what we'd all prefer for it. A secular democracy where Jews are safe to go there regardless of whether they wear "black hats" or don't.
>
> JEFF (LAWYER, AGE FIFTY-FOUR): And it's for that reason I think it is a serious problem. . . . To the extent the Orthodox within the community do not accept the idea of a pluralistic democracy, it . . . runs counter to the interests of observant American Jews. . . . That's a foreign issue to us! I mean [you would never hear that] in the United States. . . . It's a threat to democracy, because if the Orthodox view prevails, then you have a country in which the state is driven by religious scriptures. And that's not good.
>
> ALEX (SELF-EMPLOYED, WITH MBA, AGE SIXTY-ONE): Taking the comment one step further, I'll go ahead and assert that if Israel devolves to the point of maybe not being a theocratic body, but nevertheless behaving as one, then the conversation about "What to do about the Palestinians?" is moot. Israel will cease to exist as a modern state. And the assertion comes from the recognition that if we've accomplished anything in the last three hundred years of history, it is the separation of the religious push for dominance of a particular religion from the governance of a people, such that people can govern themselves and they can resolve their conflicts without resorting to jihad, without resorting to extremism, without resorting to crusades, and if the religious Orthodoxy within Israel surmounts the state, and the ability of the state to run itself and resolve its own conflicts, then surely we will drive ourselves into the ocean.

Members of Susan and Alex's discussion group strike themes that are common to most of the non-Orthodox groups: The state of Israel was meant to be a "modern, secular democracy" rather than a theocracy. The essence of a modern state is the "separation of . . . a particular religion from the governance of a people, such that the people can govern themselves." The Jewish character of the state derives from its demographic (rather than religious) character. The majority status of the Jewish people makes the democratic state of Israel a Jewish state. As a democracy, moreover, Israel ought to guarantee the religious freedom of all of its citizens, including its non-Orthodox Jewish citizens.

Several discussion participants also commented that Israel's binary religious/secular framework left them feeling out of place as liberal Jews. In the following quotation, Becca, a twenty-eight-year-old graduate student, explains that her recent visit to Israel made her feel closer to the country, but not to its people.

> Being in Israel last summer for a significant period of time . . . I didn't necessarily feel closer to Israeli people. I actually got more distant. . . . I feel like there's no place for someone whose Jewish identity is like mine, or like a lot of American Jews that I know, because Israelis don't really have this . . . Reform, Conservative, Reconstructionist idea. It's just all or nothing, and I feel like I met a lot of people who said, "Yeah, I'm Israeli, but big deal that I'm Jewish, I'm Israeli," and that made me uncomfortable.

Finally, respondents in several groups cited the ambiguous legal status of non-Orthodox movements in Israel as a reason for feeling personally alienated. In the following quotation, Liz describes the religious-secular divide in Israel and explains that, as a liberal Jew who cares deeply about her religion, she has no place in Israel religiously. Several of her conversation partners then pick up the general theme, charging that their own personal standing as Jews would be questioned in Israel. The following exchange is from a Reform discussion group:

> LIZ (PROFESSOR OF LAW, FORTY-FOUR): I think it's the biggest threat to American support of Israel. I think my cousins in Israel are all extremely Orthodox and have left America to be in Israel, and they are the kind of people who believe in the literal interpretation of everything in the Bible and all the rules of Judaism, and it makes

me have this vision of Israel as either completely nonreligious or my cousins. . . . I don't know where I would go there, where I would fit in because I feel very connected to my religion and feel very much a part of it, but feel I would be devalued completely in Israel in terms of the way I practice my religion and am involved in Judaism. It is alienating.

DEB (COLLEGE ADMISSIONS DIRECTOR, FORTY-THREE): As a Jew by choice, I certainly know that I'm not welcome. You know that the policies just don't—

JON (REAL ESTATE DEVELOPER, FIFTY-ONE): As a husband of a non-Jewish wife, with two children raised in a Jewish household, you could imagine how we feel.

DEB: Right.

DAVID (TEACHER, REFORM DAY SCHOOL, FORTY-SIX): Right, as the son of a woman who went through Reform conversion . . . I would need to convert were I to want to return to Israel under the Law of Return . . . so it's personal.

These comments were hardly exceptional. In several additional discussion groups, participants similarly claimed that their status as Jews (or their marriages, or conversions) would not be recognized as valid in Israel and described this state of affairs as profoundly alienating.[20]

Minority Civil Rights

Surveys have not asked American Jews their views regarding the issue of civil rights for Israel's Arab minority—but we did ask a relevant question of the focus groups. Specifically, we asked the groups whether as a Jewish and democratic state Israel should confer exactly the same rights on its Arab minority as its Jewish majority.[21] In their responses, as in the case of the Palestinian-Israeli conflict, participants in the discussion groups divided into right, left, and centrist factions. Participants in several groups (especially the right-leaning and left-leaning groups) dismissed the question as too obvious to warrant deliberation. Members of the right-leaning groups (mostly but not exclusively the Orthodox groups) stressed the priority of Israel's Jewish over its democratic character. Many also denied the existence of any contradiction between minority rights and the Jewishness of the state. In the following quote, Janet, a forty-two-year-old dermatologist, stresses the primacy of the Jewish character of the state:

> It's a Jewish state and that's it. The Arabs . . . enjoy lots of freedom. You know, you can be here if you want to or if you want to try and sabotage and kill us, you can leave. I think we have to have laws that limit their amount, their ability to become a majority in Parliament. And I think we have to have laws to protect ourselves, because there's one Jewish state [and] there are twenty-two Arab states. That's it. We're the little David; they're the Goliath. And if you pan out and you look at the whole region, that's it. We have to protect ourselves.

For Janet, equality is not as important a value as the Jewishness of the state. Other speakers on the right describe Arab Israelis as enjoying greater freedom and opportunity than Arabs elsewhere in the world and characterize discrimination as trivial or nonexistent.

The question regarding minority civil rights also proved easy for a small number of speakers in the left-leaning groups. Such speakers regard Israel's Jewish character as anachronistic. In the contemporary world, they contend, states should not declare an affiliation with a particular religious or national community. The following exchange, between members of a Jewish peace advocacy organization, illustrates this theme.

> KAREN (PEDIATRICIAN, AGE FIFTY-THREE): As an American I always find it so hard to understand how American Jews so staunchly are into American democracy and the principles of the Constitution, and yet for the state of Israel are so very willing to suspend those principles and say there I want to have a state that is Jewish, that is religiously Jewish, that is ethnically Jewish, whatever it is and that I am willing to sort of forego some of these basic constitutional principles because we need it to survive.
>
> NAOMI (RETIRED, AGE SIXTY-NINE): I don't like to use the term brainwash, but they have this sentimental concept of Israel which does not take into account the fact that it is a theocracy and the fact that the Arabs are second-class citizens and so on. There is kind of this veil that comes over our heads, which is why you get this kind of

havoc with, you know, we want democracy here, but we don't want to hear about what is going on there.

For Karen, a state that is religiously or ethnically Jewish contradicts "constitutional principles" that American Jews hold dear. She and her conversation partner express mystification that fellow American Jews fail to appreciate the contradiction between their embrace of democratic principles in the United States but not in Israel.

In sum, for discussion participants highly committed to partisan positions on the right and left, reconciling Israel's Jewish and democratic aspects would appear to be relatively simple: for those on the political right, the number one priority is the state's Jewish character; for those on the left, democracy takes precedence.

However, at the political center, where most American Jews reside, matters are far less clear. For most of the discussion participants, especially those in centrist Reform and Conservative groups, the question proved quite difficult to answer. On the one hand, for many discussion participants, the state's Jewishness implies a strong commitment to democracy and human rights. Consider the following comment by Jody, and twenty-two-year-old teacher:

Like all of the Jewish teachings, like *ve'ahavta le'reacha kamocha* [Love your neighbor as yourself], *b'tselem elohim* [Created in the image of God]. And it was just Passover: "You were once a stranger in Egypt, so don't be mean to people" [laughter]. To me, the Jewish thing is to extend rights and that will maintain the Jewish character of the state.

For Jody, and many of the other discussion participants (especially in the Reform and postdenominational groups), Judaism entails a commitment to human rights. Therefore, the democratic character of the state of Israel derives in part from its Jewishness.

On the other hand, among many of the self-described liberal Jews in the discussion groups, democracy is less a matter of absolutes than degree, and no one size fits every type of society. Only a small number of discussion participants argued that the state's Jewishness must ultimately accommodate its democratic character. Much more common was the claim that Israel should seek ways to balance the values of civic equality and the state's Jewish identity. The speaker in the following extract is Joel, a marketing executive in a high-tech company, age forty-five:

> If my kids went to social studies class in school and learned that the United States was a Christian country, and people who were not Christian were not allowed to vote, and they were encouraged to leave, that would just be wrong. And so I think it would violate Jewish values, I think it would violate human values. I recognize that there's a dichotomy between being a Jewish state and being a pure democracy, and I don't know what the balance would be, but there's got to be some way that you can have a balance and a country that protects the Jewish population.[22]

Moreover, to the extent one aspect of the state must accommodate the other, many discussion participants argued that it is the state's Jewish character that must be given priority. In this view, the Jewish character of the state does not imply that the state should embrace halakha (Jewish religious law), but rather that it should embrace policies that seek to ensure the continued existence of a Jewish majority. Thus, Israel must balance the democratic value of equal treatment for all its citizens against the need to encourage Jewish immigration and preserve the Law of Return that grants immediate citizenship to Jews and their relatives. Such views are evident in the following comment by Bill, a fifty-one-year-old financial consultant and participant in a mixed Reform and Conservative discussion group:

> I think it is a tough issue. To me, Israel can look like a democracy in most regards, but it can't offer all the same rights to non-Jewish citizens as it does to Jewish citizens. In order for it to be a "Jewish state," it has to do at least one thing: It has to offer the "right of return" to Jews and not offer it to non-Jews. Because if it offers it to non-Jews, then it soon loses its character as a Jewish state. And if it stops offering it to Jews, then it loses its capacity to protect Jewish communities that are in danger around the world, which is, I think, why diaspora Jews need Israel in order to survive in the long run. So, let's admit: It can't really be a true democracy, because a true democracy offers the same rights to all of its citizens, regardless of their religion. Israel can't do that.

The importance participants attach to maintaining Israel's Jewish majority and special role as a safe haven and refuge is also evident in the following exchange between Daniel, a forty-seven-year-old law professor, and Dick, a sixty-two-year-old patent attorney. The discussion participants, both members of a Reform synagogue, are discussing whether Israel can be both democratic and Jewish.

> DANIEL: In order to be a democracy, all citizens—all the individuals living within that democracy—have to have a feeling of equality. . . . If there's a group that is in power and a group that's not in power, and that out-of-power [situation] is perpetual and implemented now as law, then it's not a democracy.
> DICK: I think it's a difficult question to answer. If it weren't for the fact that the state was organized by the Zionists as a Zionist and Jewish state, then I would be in favor of democracy, because I happen to think that the U.S. [system is the] best form of government, and I would like to see that in Israel. However, I agree that I don't see it happening. It is a Jewish state. There's a lot of emotion involved, both with the formation of the Jewish state, what happened during the Second World War, ultimately with that immigration that occurred into Israel. . . . Thus, I can't see it as being democratic in that sense.
> DANIEL: The question was whether Israel *is* a democracy. You're asking me whether it *should* be a democracy, [and that's a different question] because I think there is something important about having a Jewish state. And I want to recognize that, by accepting that definition, I'm also accepting that you have a nondemocratic Jewish state or not-fully democratic Jewish state.

Daniel's qualification, at the end of his statement, implies that embracing the state's Jewish character does not entail rejecting democracy. Rather, in centrist discourse of this type, democracy is construed as existing on a continuum, with secular, democratic universalism of the sort practiced in the United States described as "full democracy," and European nation-states with their established churches and strong national cultures viewed as democratic, but less so. The centrist discussion participants are thus unwilling to totally discount the value of democracy; rather, they indicate that Israel can embrace a model of democracy that falls short of their democratic ideal. According to such a model, notwithstanding equal rights for all citizens of the state, Israel should continue to extend priority to Jewish immigration and absorption and embrace symbols (including the flag and national anthem) that represent the Jewish majority. Israel can adopt such policies in the interest of ensuring its Jewish character, which they also value highly.

Looking Ahead

Over the past quarter century, American Jews have increasingly swapped their idealistic conceptions for more realistic and critical perspectives on many aspects of Israeli society and public policy. At the same time, they also have retained their characteristic level of emotional attachment. Will this pattern hold in the future?

In most surveys of American Jews, younger respondents express a lower level of emotional connection to Israel than older respondents. The tendency is illustrated by responses to a national survey of American Jews administered in 2010 that asked, "To what extent do you feel a connection to Israel?" (Figure 5.1). Younger respondents as a whole were somewhat less attached than older respondents. This pattern, evident in most surveys, has prompted several researchers to claim that American Jews' attachment to Israel is declining across the generations.[23] The relatively greater level of attachment expressed by older Jews, in this view, reflects their experience coming of age in an era when Israel faced existential threats, as well as stronger memories of the Holocaust and founding of the state. In contrast, the relative disengagement of younger Jews reflects their experience coming of age in a context of greater moral ambiguity regarding Israel.

The difficulty with this interpretation is that it fails to account for the long-term trend data that are now available for analysis. The American Jewish Committee conducts an annual telephone survey of a panel of American Jews and has done so in a fairly consistent manner since 1986. The survey asks two questions, almost every year, using the same wording and response categories. One question asks respondents simply, "How close do you feel to Israel?" Another asks whether respondents agree or disagree with the statement, "Caring about Israel is a very important part of my being a Jew." Analysis of the AJC surveys

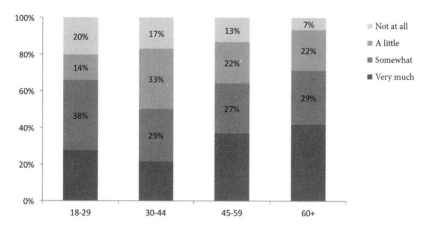

Figure 5.1. Connection to Israel by Age
Question: "To what extent do you feel a connection to Israel?"
Source: Sasson et al. *Still Connected.*

over time reveals that age-cohort differences in attachment to Israel are not a new phenomenon. Rather, in almost all surveys administered since 1986, younger respondents reported less attachment to Israel than older respondents.[24] Moreover, as discussed above, the overall level of attachment to Israel has been remarkably stable, fluctuating within a rather narrow band of about 15 percentage points for the "closeness" question and 10 percentage points for the "caring" question (Figure 5.2). It is difficult to reconcile these patterns with the notion that age-cohort differences are indicative of declining attachment across the genera-tions. If younger Jews were less attached to Israel in 1986—and if they maintained their characteristic level of attachment over the next two decades—then the overall level of attachment would necessarily have declined. But it did not.

The fact that that younger respondents have consistently reported lower levels of attachment to Israel for more than two decades, cou-pled with the observation that overall the level of attachment has remained stable, suggests an alternative explanation. Rather than declining across the generations, attachment to Israel has tended to increase over the life course. In other words, the age differences in attachment to Israel are not a generational phenomenon but rather a lifecycle phenomenon.

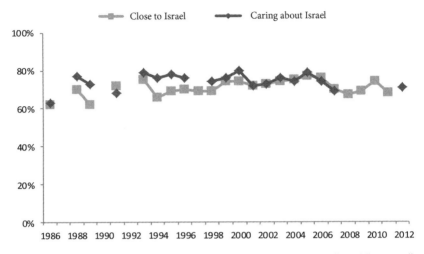

Figure 5.2. Trends in Attachment to Israel: "Feeling Close" and "Caring"
Questions: "Do you agree or disagree with the statement: 'Caring about Israel is a very important part of my being a Jew'?" (figure shows *agree*). "How close do you feel to Israel?" (figure shows *very close/fairly close*).
Data: Annual surveys of the American Jewish Committee.

In a recent study with my Cohen Center colleagues, we tested the lifecycle hypothesis by examining pairs of surveys conducted with identical populations at ten-year intervals. The pairs of surveys included the National Jewish Population Survey (1990 and 2000–2001) and the Jewish community surveys of Boston (1995 and 2005), Miami (1994 and 2004), and South Palm Beach (1995 and 2005). We found that as each birth cohort (e.g., respondents born between 1960 and 1970) aged by ten years, its average level of emotional attachment to Israel tended to increase, with the largest and most consistent increases occurring as respondents who were in their thirties at Time 1 (the first survey, administered in the 1990s) matured into their forties at Time 2 (the second survey, administered in the 2000s).[25]

The tendency of attachment to Israel to increase during the transition to adulthood may be related to more general lifecycle processes. It may express a subtle shift in worldview from universal to parochial that occurs when some people settle down and establish families. Alternatively, it may reflect the tendency for maturing Jews to become more embedded in Jewish communal life. But whatever the underlying explanation, the lifecycle interpretation suggests that—all things being equal—today's younger Jews will become more connected to Israel as they mature. For those who fret about the future of the diaspora's connection to Israel, this would appear to be good news—except for the fact that all other things are not equal.

First, there is the intermarriage trend. American Jews who were raised in intermarried households report lower levels of attachment to Israel. This is largely because such individuals tend to receive less Jewish education and therefore identify less with all aspects of Jewish life.[26] It may also be due to a lesser inclination of Jews from intermarried backgrounds to identify with Jewish "familism" or "peoplehood."[27] Among today's college students, as many as half of self-identifying Jews grew up in intermarried households. Whether this population will follow the established pattern and become more attached to Israel as it ages—or whether it will follow a different trajectory due to the high rate of parental intermarriage—is unknown. Viewed in isolation from other factors, however, today's high rate of intermarriage certainly puts downward pressure on the overall level of attachment to Israel.

Second, there is the related matter of trends in denominational affiliation and the qualities of religiosity they reflect. Orthodox Jews report the highest level of attachment to Israel, and they are followed, in rank order, by Conservative, Reform, and unaffiliated Jews.[28] Although the trends in emotional attachment to Israel within each denomination have held steady over the past several decades, the shifting pattern of denominational affiliation may herald important changes. Specifically, the Conservative movement, whose members have been among the most attached to Israel, has been losing population to the Reform movement over the past decade, a process that reflects, in part, the Reform movement's greater willingness to embrace intermarried households.[29] If the trend continues—and if Reform Jews maintain their characteristic levels of Israel attachment—the result will be downward pressure on the overall level of American Jewish attachment to Israel.

Third, there is the question of political alienation. Many observers of the American Jewish scene have discerned substantial political alienation from Israel among liberal American Jews.[30] In this view, Israel's oppressive policies toward Palestinians in the Occupied Territories and discriminatory behavior toward Arab citizens and non-Orthodox

Jews have caused liberal American Jews to turn away. As Peter Bein-art put it in a 2010 article in the *New York Review of Books*, "[A]mong the younger generation, fewer and fewer American Jewish liberals are Zionists; fewer and fewer American Jewish Zionists are liberals."[31] In the focus group discussions, we heard evidence of such alienation in the discourse on the Palestinian-Israeli conflict and—to a greater extent— the legal standing of non-Orthodox movements.

A different theme in the focus groups, however, contradicts the claim that liberal Jews are increasingly alienated from Israel: discussion participants frequently distinguished their personal political judgments about Israeli policies from their overall feelings of emotional connec-tion to the Jewish state. Moreover, as discussed above, analysis of sur-veys conducted in the 1990s and 2000s finds no statistically significant association between emotional attachment to Israel and political orien-tation (measured either on a liberal-to-conservative continuum or in terms of party affiliation).[32] Among Jews, liberals and Democrats were no less likely than conservatives and Republicans to report feeling emo-tionally attached to Israel.

The possibility of substantial political alienation in the future, how-ever, cannot be discounted. In the larger U.S. population, support for Israel is fairly strongly correlated with party identification: Republicans are the most pro-Israel, followed by Independents, and then Democrats. Although pro-Israel sentiment has increased in recent years among Republicans and Independents, it has remained stable among Demo-crats.[33] Given that political ideology influences the views of Americans as a whole, the possibility that it will eventually influence the views of American Jews cannot be dismissed.[34] Additionally, in the domain of religion and state, if ongoing conflicts, for example, over non-Orthodox conversions, wedding ceremonies, and religious rituals at the Western Wall, are resolved on terms favored by Israel's Orthodox rabbinical establishment, substantial alienation among liberal American Jews is likely.[35]

Finally, there is increased participation of young adults in educa-tional programs in Israel. Whereas the specters of intermarriage, Con-servative movement decline, and political alienation threaten to depress emotional attachment to Israel, the dramatic expansion of Israel travel among young adults will push it upward. For American Jews of all ages and backgrounds, visiting Israel is associated with much higher levels of subsequent emotional connection.[36] Since the introduction of Birthright Israel in 2000 and Masa in 2003 (see Chapter 4) the proportion of Jewish young adults who have been to Israel has increased significantly. As Israel tourism and education programs continue to expand and reach further into the population of Jews from intermarried families, the likely effect will be to counter trends that threaten to depress Israel attachment. Indeed, surveys conducted since 2010 suggest that a "Birthright Bump" may already be evident, with the youngest age group more likely to have visited Israel and more likely to feel emotionally attached than the adjacent older cohorts (see Figure 5.1, above).[37]

Conclusion

American Jews remain strongly connected to Israel and often explain their feelings in terms of anti-Semitism and the historical role of Israel as a refuge for persecuted Jews. More idealistic conceptions of Israel, of the sort reported by social scientists in the 1970s and 1980s, however, have increasingly yielded to realism. The "new realism" entails viewing Israel as a fallible nation, much like any other, including the United States. The ascendance of this view reflects, perhaps, a maturation of American Jewry beyond a mythic relationship to Israel to one more reflective of the complex realities of contemporary political choices and compromises. Today, many American Jews view Israel as an ordinary country, confronting difficult policy choices, and divided politically and socially. However, by their own account—and in terms of the objective record established by survey research—the advent of more critical views has not depressed American Jewish attachment to Israel.

Finally, recent trends, however reassuring to those who value a strong diaspora connection Israel, cannot be simply extrapolated into the future. New dynamics associated with intermarriage, assimilation, and political realignment will likely put downward pressure on attachment to Israel, even as new forms of direct engagement with Israel—including expanded educational programs for young adults and the new online sources of news and information—push upward.

6

Direct Engagement

The preceding chapters have argued that, contrary to conventional scholarly and political opinion, American Jewish engagement with Israel is not in any meaningful sense diminishing. On the contrary, across the diverse fields of the diaspora-homeland relationship, American Jewish engagement with Israel is at least as intensive as it was a quarter century ago, if not more so. To summarize very briefly the key evidence:

- In the field of advocacy, the number of organizations has increased and revenue to the top organizations has either surged (as in the case of AIPAC and J Street) or remained stable (as in the case of the AJC and ADL). In several categories of advocacy and activism, the number of grassroots participants has also increased.
- In the field of philanthropy, the amount donated by American Jews to causes in Israel sharply increased until the great recession and remains higher today than a quarter century ago. The size of the donor pool cannot be accurately measured but has likely increased or stabilized.
- In the field of Israel tourism, the overall number of American Jews traveling to Israel has increased. The number of young adults participating in educational tours of Israel has increased by more than 400 percent. For American

Jewish young adults, an "Israel experience" has become a normative rite of passage.

- In the domain of public opinion, the level of emotional attachment to Israel expressed by American Jews of all ages has remained more or less stable. There is no evidence of decline, and in fact the most recent surveys have shown increased attachment in the youngest cohort—the group that, because of the surge in Israel experience programs for teenagers and young adults, is also most likely to have visited Israel.

Based on the available evidence, scholars, organizational leaders, public officials, and journalists who depict American Jews as distancing from Israel appear to be mistaken. The modes of American Jewish engagement with Israel, however, are clearly changing: the organizational vehicles through which American Jews relate to Israel are multiplying and diversifying; political advocacy is becoming more contentious, partisan, and polarized; and the connection to Israel is becoming more personal and experiential.

As a consequence of these developments, this book has argued that the *mobilization* model of centralized, consensus-oriented advocacy and philanthropy is weakening. Increasingly, American Jews directly connect to Israel by expressing their own political views, targeting donations to favored causes, touring, studying, and volunteering in the country, consuming Israeli news and culture, and embracing the orientation of sober realists rather than wide-eyed idealists. Taken together, these changes represent the emergence of a new *direct engagement* paradigm for the diaspora-homeland relationship.

Mobilization to Engagement

It is useful to analyze in greater detail the distinguishing characteristics of the mobilization and direct engagement paradigms. The typical practices and signature organizations associated with each model are summarized schematically in Figure 6.1. In the domain of political action, although centrist, consensus-oriented organizations (e.g., AIPAC, AJC) that take their cues from Israel continue to dominate the field of Israel advocacy, today these organizations are flanked by an increasing number of groups on their right (e.g., ZOA) and left (e.g., J Street) advocating their own partisan positions, often in concert with Israeli counterparts. In the field of philanthropy, although the centralized fundraising apparatus of the federations continues to deliver the largest single package of funding to Israeli causes, the field as a whole has expanded, with hundreds of Israeli organizations now raising funds from American Jews. The field of educational tourism has similarly exploded with dozens of new companies offering an ever widening variety of educational, volunteer, and study programs, many operating under the auspices of Birthright Israel.[1] Finally, in the domain of communications and public opinion, the sources of information about Israel have proliferated, and American Jews are much more likely than ever before to consume news of Israel directly from Israeli sources.

Analytically, it is possible to further distinguish key structuring characteristics of the organizations and practices of each paradigm. At the organizational level (Figure 6.2), the waning paradigm features large umbrella or federated organizations pursuing centrist policies. The typical sphere of action is national, meaning that advocacy and fundraising are confined to the United States (i.e., the government of Israel is *not* a target of political advocacy), and the locus of organizational authority is quasi-public—the core lobbying and fundraising organizations belong to the Jewish polity as a whole. Under the emerging direct engagement paradigm, organizations tend to be single-purpose and independent, and to pursue partisan political projects aimed at bringing to life a particular vision of what Israel ought to be. In such pursuits, organizations increasingly engage in advocacy targeted not only at the U.S. government but also at the Israeli government, and they do so in transnational Jewish alliances with Israeli counterparts. The authority such organizations invoke tends to be private rather than public; they claim to represent their supporters rather than American Jewry as a whole.[2]

The two paradigms can also be distinguished by the distinctive practices of individuals relative to the Jewish state (Figure 6.3). Under the mobilization paradigm, the relationship between individuals and the state tends to be highly mediated (by organizations, rabbis) and their orientation tends to be idealistic. In addition, under the mobilization paradigm American Jews tend to identify as *American* Jews, which is to say, as U.S. political subjects who happen to have sentimental, ethnic, and religious ties to a foreign country. Under the emerging direct

Paradigm		Political action	Philanthropy	Tourism/immigration	Mass media	Public opinion
Mobilization 1967 —present	Practices	Consensus-oriented political advocacy, focused on gaining U.S. diplomatic and financial support for Israel.	Centralized fundraising by federated charities. Funds transferred to Jewish Agency for Israel.	Educational tourism sponsored by major denominations, coordinated by Jewish Agency. Immigration managed by Jewish Agency.	News of Israel filtered through U.S. media, Jewish press, and Jewish opinion leaders.	Idealism: "Israelolotry"
	Signature organizations	AIPAC American Jewish Committee Jewish Council of Public Affairs Conference of Presidents	United Jewish Appeal United Israel Appeal Jewish Agency for Israel	National Federation of Temple Youth United Synagogue Youth Jewish Agency	New York Times The Jewish Week	
Direct engagement 1993 —present	Practices	Partisan political advocacy, focused on influencing both U.S. and Israeli government policy.	Decentralized fundraising by Israeli NGOs. Donations made directly to Israeli organizations.	Educational tourism sponsored by private organizations and featuring mifgashim with Israeli peers. Immigration managed by private organizations.	News of Israel received directly from websites of major Israeli newspapers.	Realism
	Signature organizations	Zionist Organization of America Stand With Us J Street	"American Friends" organizations New Israel Fund One Israel Fund	Birthright Israel BRI Trip Providers Nefesh B'Nefesh	Haaretz.com JPost.com Timesofisrael.com	

Figure 6.1. Mobilization and
Direct Engagement Paradigms

	Mobilization	Direct engagement
Structure	Umbrella/federated	Independent/single purpose
Ideology	Centrist	Partisan
Sphere of action	National	Transnational
Authority	Public	Private

Figure 6.2. Characteristics of Organizations

engagement paradigm, the relationship of individuals to Israel tends to be more personal and experiential; moreover, their ideological orientation tends to mix idealism with a heavy dose of realism. Finally, under direct engagement, political subjectivity becomes more complex and fluid; individuals practicing according to the emerging paradigm are more likely to identify and behave as if they were dual citizens of both the United States and Israel.

Direct engagement practices are most characteristic of highly engaged, affiliated Jews, but there are entry points for the less engaged, including, for example, participating in a Birthright Israel trip, reading the Israeli press in English translation, and signing an online petition of a partisan advocacy organization. Indeed, individuals can and do engage in practices associated with both paradigms, for example, by giving money to their local federation as well as donating directly to an Israeli nonprofit organization, or by volunteering for the American Jewish Committee as well as their local chapter of J Street. Although less common, organizations can also cross over, as when several mobilization-type advocacy organizations joined together to establish the Inter-Agency Task Force on Israeli Arab Issues—a quintessentially direct engagement practice (see Chapter 2).

Direct engagement practices and organizations do not fully replace but develop alongside mobilization-type practices and organizations. Large, bureaucratic organizations, such as the federations, and national advocacy organizations of the center, such as AIPAC and the American Jewish Committee, continue to play a prominent role in the communal affairs of American Jewry. In addition, most moderately affiliated Jews

	Mobilization	Direct engagement
Experience	Mediated	Personal
Orientation	Idealistic	Realistic
Identity	Bounded	Fluid

Figure 6.3. Characteristics of Practices

continue to relate to Israel mostly through mobilization-type practices and organizations and to identify with Israel mainly as a symbol—and often in mythic terms.[3] However, the mobilization paradigm is no longer the locus of growth and creativity, and it does not appear to be the direction of future development.

Explaining the Paradigm Shift

How can we explain the rise of direct engagement practices and organizations? In part, the new model expresses the broader forces of globalization. As a consequence of the declining cost and increased wealth, international travel has increased throughout the developed world. Similarly, as a consequence of technological innovation, especially the advent of the Internet and digital technology, information flows across national boundaries more freely than ever. Increased travel to Israel and consumption of Israeli news, film, and culture thus reflect and express a much broader pattern: the shrinking of the globe and increased permeability of national boundaries.[4]

Increased travel to Israel and consumption of Israeli news contribute to increasing partisanship. The more American Jews know about Israel—and the more Israelis they know personally—the more likely they are to exercise individual judgment in the domains of political advocacy and philanthropy. The typically partisan nature of Israeli news media amplifies this tendency by reinforcing the preexisting political inclinations of American Jewish readers. Readers of the left-leaning *Haaretz* are reinforced in their critical views of Israel's treatment of ethnic and religious minorities. Readers of the right-leaning *Jerusalem Post* are reinforced in their favorable views of West Bank settlements.

Globalization's new electronic communications platform has also contributed to organizational diversification. In the information-rich environment created by the Internet, the need for organizations that mediate between diaspora and homeland—for example, the United Jewish Appeal—is much diminished. American Jews who wish to donate to a cause in Israel have easy access to information about an increasingly wide range of philanthropic choices that express their particular interests, values, and commitments. Conversely, the new information environment has made it cost-effective for start-up organizations in the fields of advocacy, philanthropy, tourism, and communications reach out directly to potential supporters. The diversification of organizations that mediate the diaspora-homeland relationship is thus also best perceived as an expression of broader social trends.

Beyond the forces of globalization, there are two additional explanations for the rise of direct engagement. First, political polarization in Israel created a context for polarization in the diaspora. Beginning in the late 1970s with the election of the first Likud government and becoming more pronounced during the 1990s as a result of the Oslo process, the Israeli public divided over how aggressively to pursue peace with the Palestinians. As the Israeli center hollowed out, Israeli parties on the right and left looked to the diaspora for contributions and political support. Moreover, as political debate over the conflict with the Palestinians deepened in Israel—and as Israeli governments shifted from right to left and back again—many American Jews found it difficult to keep track of the shifting positions, let alone adopt them as their own.[5] In this context, the conventional principle that diaspora Jews should support the policies of the elected government of Israel became increasingly difficult to honor.

Second, American Jews are less anxious today about the charge of dual loyalty and hence more willing to engage in citizenship-like behavior in relation to their ethno-religious homeland. High-ranking public officials, including Rahm Emanuel, Dennis Ross, Martin Indyk, and Daniel Kurtzer, have not been disqualified from working in Israel or on Middle East issues by virtue of their strong ties to the Jewish state. Indeed, in elite policy-making circles, diaspora ties to homelands are often viewed as a foreign policy asset. The *New York Times* recently editorialized that the "Israeli government needs the public support of

American Jews and moderate Israelis" to effectively confront the Israeli settler movement.[6] Increased comfort with direct involvement in homeland affairs reflects maturation in the political standing of American Jews and a growing tolerance throughout the developed world for diaspora political activity. It also provides a supportive context for direct-engagement-type activities.

Mainstream Responses to Change

The rise of direct engagement practices, in particular the new contentiousness in Israel advocacy, has been widely misinterpreted by the leadership of large Jewish organizations and philanthropies as indicative of the distancing of American Jewry from Israel. Ironically, these new practices reflect increased interest in and engagement with Israel— not alienation. Nonetheless, motivated by a desire to contain or defuse political contentiousness and promote strengthening American Jewish connection to Israel, Jewish organizations and philanthropies are promoting three kinds of initiatives. These initiatives are indicative of the response of the organized Jewish community to the paradigm shift that has been the topic of this book.

1. Initiatives Aimed at Shoring Up the Center, Setting the Boundaries of Legitimate Debate, and Encouraging Civility

In the run-up to the 2012 presidential election, the Anti-Defamation League and the American Jewish Committee jointly called upon Israel advocacy organizations to sign a National Pledge for Unity on Israel. The pledge declared that "for the past six decades, every American President and Congressional leaders in both parties have championed the shared values and outlook that bind the two nations." Signatories to the pledge were asked to affirm that "U.S.-Israel friendship should never be used as a wedge issue."

Reading between the lines, the apparent aim of the initiative was to discourage groups on the right from charging that President Obama and the Democratic Party were unsupportive of Israel and thereby prevent Israel from becoming a partisan issue. "The Jewish community has had a strong interest in ensuring that American support for Israel is one of the critical strategic issues that unites rather than divides parties and officials," wrote the sponsors of the initiative. Matt Brooks, director of the Republican Jewish Coalition, promptly rejected the pledge, describing it as an effort to "stifle debate." In Brooks's words, "The Republican Jewish Committee will not be silenced on this or any issue." Similarly, the Emergency Committee for Israel responded that "Directors Harris [of the AJC] and Foxman [of the ADL] need a refresher course on the virtues of free speech and robust debate in a democracy. Their effort to stifle discussion and debate is unworthy of the best traditions of America, and of Israel."[7] Nonetheless, the pledge remains significant as one among several new initiatives aimed at shoring up the political center and promoting unity in response to the sense of growing fragmentation.

In the same vein, federations and the national Hillel association have struggled to formulate guidelines for the community and campus-based organizations they support. The San Francisco federation, for example, established such guidelines in the wake of a firestorm of protest over the screening in 2010 of the film *Rachel* as part of a federation-supported Jewish Film Festival. The film tells the story of Rachel Corrie, an American killed in 2003 while intervening to prevent the demolition of a Palestinian house in Gaza. The event was cosponsored by Jewish Voice for Peace and featured remarks by Rachel's mother, Cindy Corrie, a Boycott, Divestment and Sanctions (BDS) advocate.

The federation's new policy, announced a few months after the controversial film and lecture, affirmed the federation's support for "pluralistic expressions and wide ranging perspectives that affirm a broad and inclusive tent vital to a strong and dynamic Jewish community." The guidelines then specified the kinds of organizations and activities the federation would in the future refrain from supporting, including "organizations that through their mission, activities or partnerships . . . advocate for, or endorse, undermining the legitimacy of Israel as a secure, independent, democratic Jewish state, including through participation in the BDS movement." The federation further specified that the new policy would cover organizations that engage in "co-sponsorship or co-presentations of public programs on Middle East issues with supporters of the BDS movement or others who undermine the legitimacy of the State of Israel."[8]

Similarly, the national association of campus Hillel groups issued guidelines for local chapters, declaring the organization's "support of Israel as a Jewish and democratic state with secure and recognized borders as a member of the family of nations." According to the guidelines, Hillel "welcomes a diversity of student perspectives on Israel and strives to create an inclusive, pluralistic community where students can discuss matters of interest and/or concern about Israel and the Jewish people in a civil manner." However, the guidelines further specify clear limits to the pluralism Hillel groups are permitted to tolerate. According to the guidelines, Hillel will not partner with, house, or host organizations, groups, or speakers that as a matter of policy or practice:

> Deny the right of Israel to exist as a Jewish and democratic state with secure and recognized borders;
> Delegitimize, demonize, or apply a double standard to Israel;
> Support boycott of, divestment from, or sanctions against the state of Israel;
> Exhibit a pattern of disruptive behavior toward campus events or guest speakers or foster an atmosphere of incivility.[9]

Cutting across these efforts at defining the outer limits of legitimate public discourse is an effort to forge consensus around support for Israel as a Jewish and democratic state. Although developed in response to leftist initiatives, in particular the BDS movement, the federation and Hillel guidelines would also seem to preclude funding or providing a forum to some groups on the political right. Specifically, although not yet tested in practice, the new guidelines would seem to ban funding or cooperating with groups that do not support full democratic rights for Israel's non-Jewish minorities or that oppose the establishment of recognized borders.

2. Initiatives That Promote Education about Israel on University Campuses and in Secondary Schools

During the 2000s, responding in part to the perception that American campuses had become hotbeds of anti-Israel activism, donors funded a number of initiatives to strengthen scholarship and teaching about Israel. These new initiatives included training seminars for university faculty to develop Israel-focused courses, new programs and chairs in Israel studies, and grants to support visiting Israeli professors. The result, according to researchers Annette Koren and Janet Aronson, has been a substantial increase in the number of Israel-focused courses. In a sample of 246 universities and colleges that were included in their study, the number of Israel-focused courses increased from 325 in 2005–6, to 548 in 2008–9, and to 570 in 2011–12.[10]

The new Israel studies initiatives typically recruit well-credentialed scholars and operate according to conventional academic rules. Donors, administrators, and participating faculty reject the charge that Israel studies has a political agenda. Such programs are predicated on the view, they contend, that solid scholarship and teaching rather than superficial propaganda is the correct way to restore balance on university campuses. "The truth out" best captures their viewpoint. Nonetheless, Israel studies courses tend to emphasize Israel's complexity and highlight aspects of Israeli history and society "beyond the conflict." While this approach has much scholarly merit, it also tends to render Israel as a more elusive target for political action. It is simply harder for activists to rally their forces to confront a country that is "multicultural," "complicated," and saturated with competing historical narratives. Thus, building up the field of Israel studies may serve, intentionally or otherwise, the political interests of funders who wish to defuse agitation against Israel.

Donors and educators have also launched initiatives in "Israel education" for younger students. The iCenter, a new organization, is designing curricula for teaching about Israel in Jewish day schools and supplementary schools. The Jewish Community Centers Association and the Foundation for Jewish Camp have similar projects in curriculum development for summer camps. At a 2012 symposium that included representatives from the largest Jewish foundations, the iCenter announced the goal of recruiting one thousand new Israel educators over the next several years.[11]

Like Israel studies at the university level, the goal of the new curricular initiatives for Jewish schools and camps is to teach about Israel in all of its aspects—i.e., not merely about the conflict with the Palestinians. It is also to forge a consensus narrative about Israel's importance and legitimacy as a nation-state of the Jewish people while bracketing or setting aside the occupation of the West Bank. This dimension of the teaching of Israel is an effort to strengthen the political center while simultaneously addressing the perceived weakening of emotional connection. Like the effort to prevent Israel from being used as a wedge issue in the presidential election, it is a kind of "boundary work" meant at least tacitly to manage contentiousness and contain, limit, and defuse dissent.

Some of the new Israel education initiatives, especially those geared to Jewish secondary schools, emphasize developing a critical voice. In one formulation, the desired critical stance is described as "hugging and wrestling."[12] Similarly, in a book on the new Israel education, Lisa Grant and Ezra Kopelowitz contrast Israel advocacy training, which they associate with the declining mobilization paradigm, with the new emphasis on Israel education. In contrast to advocacy training, education promotes "mature love":

> The Israel advocacy curriculum tends to continue a tradition of viewing Israel in mythical terms, an ideal society with which to express solidarity and defend. In contrast, in a situation of mature love, the individual is able to grapple with a deep understanding and complex relationship that includes an understanding that the other (in this case Israel) is not perfect. Nevertheless, the other is an important part of one's life, so important in fact that successful Israel education enables the student to develop critical opinions and political positions about how Israel's state and society can better reflect the values in which they believe. As in life, critical engagement breeds a mature, stable love which understands that life is not perfect, the other will not always be like me, nevertheless we are tied to each other based on the bonds of common history, perceptions of shared fate and mutual interests and desire to build a future together.[13]

The new Israel education curriculum developed by Hebrew University's Melton Center for Jewish Education similarly aims to cultivate students' critical capacities. The curriculum "introduces a host of social challenges including the divide between Orthodox and secular Jews, the status of Arabs with Israeli citizenship, problems of poverty, the plight of foreign workers in Israel, the Palestinian conflict and tensions between Orthodox and non-Orthodox religious Jews." As the author of the curriculum commented, "We are in trouble if people can't love the real Israel."[14]

3. Initiatives That Promote Israel Educational Travel and Structured Encounters between Israeli and American Jews

As we have seen, Jewish organizations and philanthropists have invested massively in the development of Israel educational tourism. Although the original impetus for the largest of these initiatives, Birthright Israel, was to promote Jewish identity rather than connection to Israel, today, Israel educational tourism is championed both as a vehicle for solidifying Jewish identity and as a strategy for promoting lifelong attachment to the Jewish state. Perhaps because of its well-documented capacity to deliver on both of these goals, donors increased support during the first decade of the twenty-first century and participation has sharply increased.[15]

Meanwhile, the mifgash, which serves as the centerpiece of many Israel education tours, has been exported to a broad range of educational settings. Mifgashim are becoming nearly ubiquitous as day and supplementary schools establish exchanges between their students and Israeli counterparts. In 2009–10, school twinning programs organized by the Jewish Agency's Partnership 2000 (P2K) sister city program included 159 Israeli schools and 211 diaspora schools (an estimated additional 100 schools were engaged in exchanges outside of the P2K framework).[16] School twinning programs typically include in-person exchanges, with American student groups traveling to Israel and reciprocal visits by Israeli groups to the United States. They also include virtual encounters through Skype, Facebook, and other communication technologies. Donors and educators increasingly embrace such mifgashim because they believe person-to-person contacts can promote emotional attachment, transcend political differences, and stabilize the contentious politics of Israel in the American Jewish community.

In addition to Israel experience and school twinning programs, summer camps are increasingly important sites for staging encounters between Israeli and American Jews. For decades, the Jewish Agency has supplied shlichim or emissaries to serve as counselors at North American Jewish summer camps. The scale of the endeavor has, however, increased from 1,200 Israeli staff at U.S. summer camps in 2003 to 1,700 in 2011. The role assigned to the young Israeli staff has also changed. Rather than merely representing Israel to diasporans, the Israeli counselors are now viewed as full participants in two-way encounters meant to enrich their own Jewish identities as well as those of campers and fellow counselors.[17]

By setting red lines and promoting Israel education, travel, and mifgashim, Jewish organizations hope to restore consensus on basic principles and foster ongoing attachment of American Jews to Israel. But, we might ask, why *should* American Jews care about Israel today?

New Vision

In comparison to the significant organizational responses to the new contentiousness about Israel, described above, there has been surprisingly little theoretical discussion of the nature of the diaspora-homeland relationship. The classic ideological models do not provide as convincing a justification for diaspora engagement with Israel as they once did. Political Zionism that construes Israel as a refuge for persecuted Jews no longer has the same visceral meaning for diaspora Jews who today mostly reside in stable, highly developed countries that reject anti-Semitism. Religious Zionism that highlights the biblical promise of the Land of Israel and anticipates messianic redemption does not resonate with the vast majority of American Jews who are not Orthodox or religiously traditional. Cultural Zionism that envisions Israel as the center of Jewish creativity, innovation, and renewal does not adequately recognize the contributions of the diaspora to Jewish civilization. Finally, Labor Zionism that seeks redemption in agricultural work and the creation of a socialist society seems anachronistic in the prevailing knowledge-intensive and unapologetically capitalist environment.[18]

Yet notwithstanding the lack of clear ideological guideposts, American Jews, especially young adults, report deriving a great deal of personal meaning from their encounters with Israel. This is especially true of their mifgashim with Israeli peers. Why are such encounters apparently so intellectually stimulating and personally meaningful? What lessons might we derive with respect to the contemporary bonds that link diaspora and homeland?

I believe the mifgash generates such excitement, at least in part, because it is an encounter with "the other" who is at once similar and different. As the political scientist Daniel Elazar observed, although sharing common roots, American Jewish and Israeli cultures have developed in opposite directions. Fighting for inclusion, American Jews emphasized equality, social justice, separation of church and state, and other universal values. Struggling against external enemies, Israeli Jews emphasized national solidarity, religious traditionalism, and caring for one's own. "If the consequences of the Jews existing as a minority seeking integration into the larger society are excessive universalism and individualism," wrote Elazar, "the consequences of the Jews existing as a majority seeking to preserve that majority status in every respect have led to new kinds of parochialism."[19]

Although muted somewhat by the forces of globalization, the deep cultural differences Elazar described make diasporans and homelanders mirror images of one another.[20] The mifgash thus enables the two sides to grapple emotionally and intellectually with alternative cultural possibilities. For American Jews, this means taking seriously the national, historical, and territorial dimensions of Jewish life, and engaging in a realistic way with security threats to Israel's survival. For Israelis, it means taking seriously versions of Judaism that stress civic equality, social justice, and feminism—all core features of American Jewish identity. It also means grappling with Judaism as a source of personal meaning as well as national culture. In a word, because the Jews of Israel and the United States embody diverse strands of Jewishness, their exchange opens up possibilities for personal growth and cultural expression that might not otherwise exist.

In an essay on Jewish peoplehood, Daniel Pekarsky, a philosopher of education, makes a similar observation albeit with an emphasis on the broader cultural significance of the diaspora-homeland exchange:

> As rich as are the opportunities for advancement of Jewish civilization in Israel and the diaspora respectively, the vitality of Jewish life and the potential for the emergence of profound ideas, insights, and ways of thinking are greatly enhanced when there is significant communicative interplay between the cultural representatives of these two very different sites of Jewish life. . . . Precisely because the perspectives of the two

groups and their beliefs are sometimes in tension with one another, there is the potential for serious and fruitful dialogue that encompasses the arts as well as social, political and religious matters. Such a dialogue may give rise to cultural products that neither community could produce on its own.[21]

The mifgash may thus prove to be a viable normative model for the future of the diaspora-homeland relationship, one that emphasizes mutual enrichment and cultural coproduction. This new focus need not stand alone. Shared fate, religious covenant, and a modicum of social utopianism will continue to undergird the relationship as well.

The Future

As Peter Beinart and others have warned, the differences that make the mifgash so fascinating may also threaten the solidarity of diaspora and homeland Jews.[22] In recent years, in the wake of demographic changes and the violence of the Second Intifada and the wars in Lebanon and Gaza, the center of gravity in Israel has moved in a nationalist and religious direction. In the United States, by embracing candidate and then president Barack Obama with enormous enthusiasm, American Jews affirmed their deep commitment to a vision of the good society that champions egalitarianism and social justice. The sense that the two global centers of Jewish life are moving in opposite directions is palpable. The resulting tensions will continue to feature prominently in the homeland-diaspora exchange. But will they lead to rupture?

I doubt it. If external threats to Israel intensify—today, the main focus of concern is Iran—then we can expect American Jews to rally in a fairly unified way in support of the Jewish state. If Israel's borders remain quiet and the occupation of the West Bank persists, then we should expect further polarization in the American Jewish community. In the end, however, the centrifugal tendencies explored in this book will likely be moderated by American Jews' growing firsthand knowledge of Israel, by personal relationships between Israelis and American Jews, and by the policy choices of Israeli and diaspora leaders seeking to contain conflict within reasonable bounds.

At a personal level, Israel's meaning for the hundreds of thousands of American Jews who visit the country, participate in Israel-related cultural events in the United States, consume Israeli news, and contribute to Israeli causes will likely deepen—a salutary development for those who favor a strong relationship between the world's two largest Jewish communities.

Paradoxically, however, the increasing tendency of American Jews to align with disparate Israeli political factions may translate into diminished political influence.[23] In the United States, the capacity of the Israel lobby to mobilize a united front of American Jewish organizations on Israel's behalf will likely weaken. In Israel, as well, the diffusion of American Jewish political demands—for and against West Bank settlements, in support of and against a division of Jerusalem, in favor of and opposed to Orthodox religious hegemony—may have the effect of canceling each other out and therefore translate into reduced diaspora influence. At the same time, Israel, once a source of Jewish unity, will continue to divide, as American Jews increasingly debate the limits of legitimate dissent and who can and should speak authoritatively on behalf of the American Jewish community.

Comparative Perspective

The mobilization by American Jewish organizations of near-consensus support for Israeli governments during the state's first four decades was atypical. There are just a few cases of diaspora communities that achieved comparable levels of consensus and unity. After Turkey invaded Cyprus in 1974, Greek American organizations—which had been divided in their attitudes toward the homeland's ruling military junta—closed ranks to demand that the United States halt military assistance to Turkey. According to Kathleen Newland, a migration policy expert, "Turkish aggression in Cyprus . . . and the displacement of more than 200,000 Greek Cypriots by the Turks' division of the island brought unprecedented unity and activism to the diaspora."[24] Similarly, in the 1980s, the Cuban American National Foundation (CANF), an organization that lobbied the U.S. government to unseat the Castro regime, "became the principal vehicle through which the diaspora was represented and organized." According to scholars Jean Grugel and

Henry Kippin, the organization achieved "near-hegemonic control over Cuban American politics."[25] (In the 1990s, new organizations that advocated slightly more conciliatory policies were established, dividing the Cuban diaspora.)

If consensus mobilization is rare, the more common pattern for diaspora groups is to support competing political objectives and rival homeland parties. As a result, "emigrants often replay the conflicts of their homelands in diaspora and try to enlist the governments and civil society institutions of the settlement country in their cause."[26] In the United States, the Dominican, Brazilian, and Mexican diaspora communities are divided in support of rival homeland political parties.[27] In the United Kingdom, the South Asian and Nigerian diaspora communities support diverse and often competing homeland religious and political causes.[28] In Germany, the large Turkish diaspora supports rival secular, Islamist, and ultra-nationalist homeland political parties. According to the political scientist Jacob M. Landau, Turkish diaspora political organizations "have been set up on the same ideological patterns as in Turkey and, indeed, have imported some Turkish domestic politics into their new environment. . . . Many, perhaps most, political groups mobilize their members on an agenda of support for, or opposition to the government, or a political party, in Turkey."[29]

More generally, the sizeable literature on "transnationalism" describes immigrants as heavily engaged with their countries of origin, sending home remittances, reproducing homeland cultural practices, participating in homeland political parties, and returning for frequent visits.[30] Ethnographic studies describe the dense web of connections linking diasporans to their homeland communities.[31] Studies of philanthropic behavior report a few instances of broad-based diaspora support for national homeland causes, such as economic development or disaster relief, but mostly stress donations for narrower religious, ethnic, political, and hometown causes.[32]

Today, highly engaged American Jews increasingly relate to Israel in the fashion of other contemporary diasporans: they consume Israeli news and information through the Internet and social media, they direct philanthropic contributions to the causes they care about most, and they advocate on behalf of their personal political views. In a sense, they are relating to Israel less as an ancient diaspora to its mythic homeland and more in the fashion of contemporary emigrants to their countries of origin. Thus, for the more highly engaged segment of American Jewry, Israel has become, in effect, a real country, in addition to serving as a symbol and source of identity.

The case of the Armenian American diaspora bears special mention as one that includes key features of the mobilization-to-engagement trajectory described in this book. Although not a major player in the creation of the independent state of Armenia in 1991, the Armenian American diaspora subsequently provided substantial diplomatic and philanthropic support.[33] Armenian American advocacy organizations, including the Armenian National Committee of America and the Armenian Assembly, lobbied the U.S. government to assist Armenia's transition to democratic governance and supply foreign aid. The Armenia Fund USA collected contributions to support the new state's economic development.

However, in relation to two homeland political issues—the disputed region of Nagorno-Karabakh (an Armenian enclave in Azerbaijan) and normalization of ties with Turkey—the positions adopted by the diaspora organizations diverged from those of the Armenian government. For the diaspora groups, promoting self-determination for Armenians in Nagorno-Karabakh and keeping alive the memory of the Turkish-perpetrated Armenian genocide took precedence over the more mundane state interests in security and development.[34] Analysts attribute the Armenian American diaspora's political orientation to its distance from homeland realities and tendency to think idealistically rather than realistically. "For most of them, Armenia is more of an idea than a real country."[35] In sum, in the years following independence, the Armenian American diaspora operated in the "mobilization" mold, albeit not consistently in support of the policies of the Armenian government.[36]

According to diaspora studies scholar Khachig Tölölyan, however, attitudes among Armenian Americans have since become more complex. "In recent years, some elements of the diaspora have become insistent that Armenians should attempt to retain all territories occupied by Armenian forces in the Karabagh conflict while other elements have become interested in conceptualizing an equitable form of conflict resolution. . . . Debate about how to attain the latter has often been muted but sometimes contentious."[37] Thus, like the case examined in this book, the Armenian American diaspora appears to be shifting from consensus mobilization (albeit in *opposition* to certain homeland policies) to contentiousness. As in the Jewish case, the shift may reflect the development of a more nuanced understanding of homeland realities.

Conclusion

This book has argued that the increasingly critical orientation of diverse sets of American Jews toward Israel and their disengagement from centralized fundraising do not indicate alienation but rather something closer to the opposite: more American Jews care sufficiently about Israel to seek to influence its future. The trend reflects primarily the actions of a minority of American Jews, but includes large sections of elite and organized segments of the community. For such individuals and the organizations they establish and support, mere support for Israel no longer reflects and expresses their deepest passions. Rather, they seek to mold, direct, shape, and influence Israel's future development. Moreover, they also seek to connect to Israel in a personal, direct, and experiential fashion. In these ways, they express tendencies that are widespread among contemporary diaspora groups. In a word, they have gone from passive fans sitting in the bleachers to active players on the field of contentious Israeli politics.

List of Organizations

Agudat Yisrael of America. Founded in Europe in 1912, the American branch serves as an advocacy organization for ultra-Orthodox Jews.

American Israel Public Affairs Committee (AIPAC). Founded in 1951, AIPAC is the flagship organization of the Israel lobby. The organization advocates a close relationship between the United States and Israel and generally follows Israel's line on major diplomatic issues.

American Council for Judaism. Founded in 1942 by a group of Reform rabbis, the organization opposed the Zionist movement in the 1940s and 1950s.

American Jewish Committee (AJC). Founded in 1906, the AJC is a centrist, multi-issue advocacy organization that emphasizes combating anti-Semitism, supporting Israel, promoting energy independence, and strengthening Jewish life.

American Jewish Joint Distribution Committee (JDC). Founded in 1914, the JDC is the world's largest Jewish humanitarian assistance organization. A founding partner in the United Jewish Appeal, the JDC remains one of the federation movement's primary vehicles for overseas activities, especially in the countries of the former Soviet Union and Israel.

American Zionist Committee for Public Affairs (AZCPA). AZCPA is a precursor of AIPAC.

Americans for a Safe Israel (AFSI). Founded in 1971, AFSI is a right-wing advocacy organization that supports Jewish settlement in the West Bank.

Anti-Defamation League (ADL). Founded in 1913, the ADL is the largest Jewish civil rights organization with a primary focus on combating anti-Semitism.

B'nai B'rith International. Founded in 1843 as a Jewish fraternal association, B'nai B'rith is a service and advocacy organization focused primarily on humanitarian assistance, senior citizens, anti-Semitism, and Israel.

Brit Tzedek V'Shalom. Founded in 2003 to advocate for a two-state solution to the Palestinian-Israeli conflict, Brit Tzedek merged with J Street in 2010.

Conference of Presidents of Major American Jewish Organizations (Presidents Conference). Founded in 1955 and comprising more than fifty national Jewish agencies, the Presidents Conference represents the unified voice of the organized Jewish community, especially on issues relating to Israel.

Conservative movement. The Conservative movement is the centrist religious denomination of American Judaism.

Council of Jewish Federations and Welfare Funds (CJF). Founded in 1932, CJF was the national umbrella group for local federations of Jewish charitable organizations. In 1999, CJF merged with the United Jewish Appeal (UJA) and the United Israel Appeal (UIA) to form United Jewish Communities (UJC). In 2009, the UJC changed its name to Jewish Federations of North America (JFNA).

David Project. Founded in 2002, the David Project is a right-leaning advocacy organization focused primarily on college campuses.

Emergency Committee for Israel (ECI). Founded in 2010 by prominent neoconservatives, the ECI is a right-leaning advocacy organization that seeks to shape the public discussion of Israel and the Middle East.

Hadassah. Founded in 1912, Hadassah is a women's Zionist organization with more than 330,000 members worldwide. Hadassah's primary activity is fundraising in support of Hadassah medical centers in Israel.

Hasbara Fellowships. Founded in 2001, Hasbara Fellowships is a right-leaning organization that trains Jewish students for pro-Israel advocacy on their college campuses.

Israel Project. Founded in 2002, the Israel Project is a centrist advocacy organization that supplies news outlets with information about Israel and the Middle East.

Jewish Agency for Israel (JAFI). Founded in 1929 as the de facto government of the *Yishuv* (Jewish community in Palestine), JAFI was reconstituted after the establishment of Israel as a partnership of diaspora organizations and the Jewish state. Throughout its history, JAFI has been funded primarily through the annual campaigns of the United Jewish Appeal. Today, the organization's primary foci are immigration, absorption, and Jewish Zionist education.

Jewish Council for Public Affairs (JCPA). Founded in 1944 as the National Jewish Community Relations Advisory Council (NJCRAC), the organization adopted its new name in 1997. As the advocacy arm of the federation movement, the JCPA seeks to express a unified Jewish voice on a variety of national and global policy issues.

Jewish Federations of North America (JFNA). JFNA is the national association of local federations. See Council of Jewish Federations and Welfare Funds, above.

Jewish National Fund (JNF). Founded in 1901 to purchase lands for Jewish settlement in Palestine, JNF has been one of American Jewry's primary vehicles for contributing to Israel's development. Today, JNF functions as Israel's largest environmental organization, managing forests, water reservoirs, and national parks, as well as building infrastructure for new Jewish communities.

J Street. Founded in 2008, J Street is a left-leaning advocacy organization that promotes a two-state solution to the Israel-Palestine conflict.

Jewish Voice for Peace (JVP). Founded in 1996, JVP is a left-wing organization that seeks an end to the Israeli occupation of the West Bank, Gaza, and East Jerusalem, a just solution to the Palestinian refugee crisis, and an end to violence against civilians.

National Council of Young Israel. Founded in 1912, Young Israel is an association of Orthodox synagogues.

Nefesh B'Nefesh. Founded in 2003, Nefesh B'Nefesh is a private organization that promotes and facilitates the immigration of Jews from the United States, Canada, and England to Israel.

New Israel Fund (NIF). Founded in 1980, the NIF raises funds for progressive causes in Israel, including human rights, women's rights, and Arab-Jewish coexistence.

Orthodox Union. Orthodox Union is a professional association of Orthodox rabbis.

Reform movement. The Reform movement is a liberal denomination of American Judaism.

Taglit-Birthright Israel. Founded in 1999, Birthright Israel provides free ten-day educational tours of Israel to diaspora Jewish young adults.

United Israel Appeal (UIA). Founded in 1925 as the United Palestine Appeal, the UIA is responsible for oversight of funds raised by the Jewish Federations of North America for the support of the Jewish Agency for Israel. A founding partner of the United Jewish Appeal (UJA), the UIA merged with UJA and the Council of Jewish Federations in 1999 to form the United Jewish Communities (later renamed Jewish Federations of North America).

United Jewish Appeal (UJA). Founded in 1939, the UJA was American Jewry's primary vehicle for fundraising for "overseas" causes, especially the American Jewish Joint Distribution Committee (JDC) and the United Israel Appeal (UIA). In 1999, the UJA merged with the Council of Jewish Federations (CJF) and the United Israel Appeal (UIA) to form the United Jewish Communities (UJC). In 2009, the UJC changed its name to the Jewish Federations of North America (JFNA).

United Palestine Appeal (UPA). See United Israel Appeal, above.

Zionist Organization of America (ZOA). Founded in 1896, the ZOA was the flagship organization of American Zionists until the establishment of the state of Israel. After a period of steep decline, the ZOA was revived in the 1990s as a right-leaning advocacy organization.

aliyah. Literally, "ascent," the term for Jewish immigration to Israel.

halakha. Jewish religious law.

hasbara. Literally, "explanation," but used to denote propaganda.

kibbutz. A farming collective.

Likud. A center-right Israeli political party.

mifgash (pl. mifgashim). A structured encounter between Israeli Jews and diaspora Jews.

oleh (pl. olim). New immigrant.

shaliach (pl. shlichim). Emissary, especially employed by the Jewish Agency for Israel (JAFI) to work in diaspora Jewish communities.

yeshiva. An academy for religious studies.

Yishuv. The Jewish community in pre-state Palestine.

Notes to the Introduction

1. Rabbi Leonard Gordon, personal communication with the author, November 29, 2012, emphasis in the original.

2. Jennifer M. Brinkerhoff, *Digital Diasporas: Identity and Transnational Engagement* (New York: Cambridge University Press, 2012); Yossi Shain, *Kinship and Diasporas in International Affairs* (Ann Arbor: University of Michigan Press, 2007); Kathleen Newland, *Voice after Exit: Diaspora Advocacy* (Washington, DC: Migration Policy Institute, 2010).

3. Linda Basch, Nina Glick Schiller, and Cristina Szanton-Blanc, *Nations Unbound: Transnational Projects, Postcolonial Predicaments and Deterritorialized Nation-States* (Amsterdam: Gordon and Breach, 1994); Peggy Levitt, *Transnational Villagers* (Berkeley: University of California Press, 2001); Milton J. Esman, *Diasporas in the Contemporary World* (Malden, MA: Polity, 2009).

4. Newland, *Voice after Exit*; Yossi Shain, *Marketing the American Creed Abroad: Diasporas in the U.S. and Their Homelands* (New York: Cambridge University Press, 1999); Gabriel Sheffer, *Diaspora Politics: At Home Abroad* (New York: Cambridge University Press, 2003).

5. Judith Brown, *Global South Asians: Introducing the Modern Diaspora* (Cambridge, UK: Cambridge University Press, 2006); Davesh Kapur, *Diaspora, Development and Democracy: The Domestic Impact of International Migration from India* (Princeton, NJ: Princeton University Press, 2010).

6. Jacob M. Landau, "Diaspora Nationalism: The Turkish Case," in *The Call of the Homeland: Diaspora Nationalisms, Past and Present*, ed. Allon Gal, Athena S. Leoussi, and Anthony D. Smith (Leiden, Netherlands: Brill, 2010); Newland, *Voice after Exit*.

7. British organizations created on the basis of subnational ethnic identities include Young Ibgos, the Oboziobodo Club, the Edo Association, the Oodua People's Congress, Bakassi Boys, Niger Delta People's Volunteer Force, and the Movement for the Actualization of the Sovereign State of Biafra. See Ben Lampert, "Diaspora and Development? Nigerian Organizations in London and the Transnational Politics of Belonging," *Global Networks* 9, no. 2 (2009).

8. Robin Cohen, *Global Diasporas* (Seattle: University of Washington Press, 1997); William Safran, "Jewish Diaspora in Comparative and Theoretical Perspective," *Israel Studies* 10 (2005); Stephane Dufoix, *Diasporas* (Berkeley: University of California Press, 2003).

9. Caryn Aviv and David Shneer, *New Jews: The End of the Jewish Diaspora* (New York: New York University Press, 2005); Karen Brodkin, *How Jews Became White Folks and What That Says about Race in America* (New Brunswick, NJ: Rutgers University Press, 2000); Sylvia Barack Fishman, *Jewish Life and American Culture* (Binghamton: State University of New York Press, 2000).

10. Daniel Elazar, *Community and Polity: The Organizational Dynamics of American Jewry* (Philadelphia: Jewish Publications Society, 1995).

11. Steven M. Cohen and Charles S. Liebman, "Israel and American Jewry in the Twenty-First Century: A Search for New Relationships," in *Beyond Survival and Philanthropy: American Jewry and Israel*, ed. Allon Gal and Alfred Gottschalk (Cincinnati, OH: Hebrew Union College, 2000).

12. For example, see Steven M. Cohen and Ari Y. Kelman, *Beyond Distancing: Young Adult American Jews and Their Alienation from Israel* (New York: Andrea and Charles Bronfman Philanthropies, 2007); Peter Beinart, "The Failure of the American Jewish Establishment," *New York Review of Books*, June 24, 2010.

13. The term "discourse on distancing" is from Shmuel Rosner and Inbal Hakman, *The Challenge of Peoplehood: Strengthening the Attachment of Young American Jews to Israel in the Time of the Distancing Discourse* (Jerusalem: Jewish People Policy Institute, 2012).

14. Gabriel Sheffer, "Loyalty and Criticism in the Relations between World Jewry and Israel," *Israel Studies* 17, no. 2 (Summer 2012); Cohen and Liebman, "Israel and American Jewry."

15. Cohen and Kelman, *Beyond Distancing*, 11.

16. The tendency to incorrectly attribute age cohort differences in Israel attachment to generation rather than stage of life is widespread. See also Robert Wexler, "Israel and the Identity of American Jews," in *Israel, the Diaspora and Jewish Identity*, ed. Danny Ben-Moshe and Zohar Segev (Brighton, UK: Sussex Academic Press, 2007); Jack B. Ukeles, Ron Miller, and Pearl Beck, *Young Jewish Adults in the United States Today* (New York: American Jewish Committee, 2006); Daniel Gordis, "No Jewish People without Israel," *Tablet Magazine*, August 20, 2012.

17. Beinart, "Failure of the American Jewish Establishment"; Peter Beinart, *The Crisis of Zionism* (New York: Times Books, 2012).

18. Beinart, "Failure of the American Jewish Establishment." The evidence regarding the political views of young adult American Jews is more ambiguous than Beinart allows. See Chapter 5 and Theodore Sasson and Leonard Saxe, "Wrong Numbers," *Tablet Magazine*, May 38, 2010.

19. My own coauthored piece on trends in American Jewish attachment to Israel was one of the lead articles in the special issue. See Theodore Sasson, Charles Kadushin, and Leonard Saxe, "Trends in American Jewish Attachment to Israel: An Assessment of the "Distancing" Hypothesis," *Contemporary Jewry* 30, nos. 2–3 (2010).

20. Rosner and Hakman, *Challenge of Peoplehood*.

21. For example, Gordis, "No Jewish People without Israel"; "Second Thoughts about the Promised Land," *The Economist*, January 11, 2007.

22. On the concept of field, see Pierre Bourdieu, *Distinction: A Social Critique of the Judgement of Taste* (Cambridge, MA: Harvard University Press, 1984).

Notes to Chapter 1

1. Quoted in Edward Tivnan, *The Lobby: Jewish Political Power and American Foreign Policy* (New York: Simon & Schuster, 1987), 258–59.

2. Zvi Ganin, *An Uneasy Relationship: American Jewish Leadership and Israel, 1948–1957* (Syracuse, NY: Syracuse University Press, 2005), 3–25.

3. Naomi W. Cohen, *The Americanization of Zionism, 1897–1948* (Hanover, NH: Brandeis University Press/University Press of New England, 2003).

4. Beginning in Boston in 1895, American Jewish communities established confederations of local Jewish human services agencies and welfare funds to coordinate fundraising; by the 1930s, Jewish federations were active in most Jewish population centers.

5. The umbrella organization was called the Council of Jewish Federations and Welfare Funds. Marc Lee Raphael, *A History of the United Jewish Appeal 1939–1982* (Providence, RI: Scholars Press, 1982), 13.

6. Ibid., 6–7.

7. Ibid., 17.

8. Business divisions included "industry and trade," "real estate," "publishers and news dealers," and "women's apparel." Divisions were further subdivided. Women's apparel, for example, included "department stores, dry goods, furs, millinery, retail stores, women's wear, coats and belts, contractors, dresses, garment salesmen, sportswear, trimmings, and wholesale dresses." Ibid., 24, 40.

9. Melvin I. Urofsky, *American Zionism from Herzl to the Holocaust* (Garden City, NY: Anchor Press, 1975), 125.

10. Melvin I. Urofsky, *We Are One! American Jewry and Israel* (Garden City, NY: Anchor Press, 1978), 33.Three years later, the membership rolls would reach nearly one million, approximately one-fifth of the U.S. Jewish population.

11. On the AJC's ambivalent support for the Jewish state after 1947, see Ganin, *Uneasy Relationship*, 5. On the American Council for Judaism's anti-Zionist campaign, see ibid., 11–16.

12. Tivnan, *The Lobby*, 24.

13. Urofsky, *We Are One!*, 97, 279. See also Mitchell Geoffrey Bard, *The Water's Edge and Beyond: Defining the Limits to Domestic Influence on United States Middle East Policy* (New Brunswick, NJ: Transaction, 1991), 129–55.

14. Ganin, *Uneasy Relationship*, 58.

15. Tivnan, *The Lobby*, 31; Raphael, *History of the United Jewish Appeal*, 37.

16. Tivnan, *The Lobby*, 34.

17. J. J. Goldberg, *Jewish Power: Inside the American Jewish Establishment* (New York: Addison-Wesley, 1996), 153.

18. Urofsky, *We Are One!*, 302.

19. Estimated from Raphael, *History of the United Jewish Appeal*, 142–43.

20. Ibid., 69.

21. The reform was accomplished in stages over a period of several years, and there were several additional legal entities involved along the way. For a full account, see Raphael, *History of the United Jewish Appeal*.

22. Urofsky, *We Are One!*, 351.

23. Raphael, *History of the United Jewish Appeal*, 79.

24. Ibid., 80.

25. Ibid., 80.

26. Ibid., 83.

27. The UJA was not the only vehicle for American Jewish philanthropic support for Israel during the post–World War II period. American Jews also provided financial support to the state of Israel through their investments, in particular, the purchase of Israel Bonds. By 1993, they had purchased over $13 billion in bonds, and over $1 billion in that year alone. Jack Wertheimer, "American Jews and Israel: A 60-Year Retrospective," in *American Jewish Yearbook 2008*, ed. David Singer and Lawrence Grossman (New York: American Jewish Committee, 2008), 50.

28. Goldberg, *Jewish Power*, 355. The U.S. government also provided loan guarantees.

29. Gershom Gorenberg, *The Accidental Empire: Israel and the Birth of the Settlements, 1967–1977* (New York: Holt, 2007).

30. Goldberg, *Jewish Power*, 203.

31. Bard, *Water's Edge and Beyond*, 91–117; Goldberg, *Jewish Power*, 179–80.

32. Tivnan, *The Lobby*, 88. Seventy-six U.S. senators signed a letter to President Ford declaring their support for Israel and discouraging any further "reassessment" of U.S. policy in the region.

33. Bard, *Water's Edge and Beyond*, 229–34.

34. Tivnan, *The Lobby*, 96.

35. Jack Wertheimer, "Breaking the Taboo: Critics of Israel and the American Jewish Establishment," in *Envisioning Israel: The Changing Images and Ideals of North American Jews*, ed. Allon Gal (Detroit, MI: Wayne State University Press, 1996), 397–419.

36. Tivnan, *The Lobby*, 129–30.

37. Goldberg, *Jewish Power*, 208.

38. Ibid., 208.

39. Tivnan, *The Lobby*, 61.

40. Steven T. Rosenthal, *Irreconcilable Differences* (Hanover, NH: Brandeis University Press/University Press of New England, 2001), 26–27. See also Tivnan, *The Lobby*, 60.

41. Goldberg, *Jewish Power*, 211.

42. Sol Stern, "Menachem Begin vs. the Jewish Lobby," *New York Magazine*, April 24, 1978.

43. Rosenthal, *Irreconcilable Differences*, 59.

44. Tivnan, *The Lobby*, 78.

45. According to one estimate, Jews were responsible for 30 to 50 percent of the Democratic Party's campaign fund. Ibid., 84.

46. Ibid., 248.

47. Goldberg, *Jewish Power*, 201.

48. Daniel J. Elazar, "Changing Places, Changing Cultures: Divergent Jewish Political Cultures," in *Divergent Jewish Cultures: Israel and America*, ed. Deborah Dash Moore and S. Ilan Troen (New Haven, CT: Yale University Press, 2001), 107.

49. For example, in a 1981 survey, 84 percent of respondents agreed with the statement. Steven M. Cohen, *The 1981–1982 National Survey of American Jews* (New York: American Jewish Committee, 1983).

50. Rosenthal, *Irreconcilable Differences*, 36.

51. Ibid., 29.

52. Jonathan Woocher, *Sacred Survival: The Civil Religion of American Jews* (Bloomington: Indiana University Press, 1986).

53. Urofsky, *We Are One!*, 444.

54. Wertheimer, "American Jews and Israel," 24.

55. Quoted in Goldberg, *Jewish Power*, 147.

56. Ibid., 147.

57. Wertheimer, "American Jews and Israel," 46.

58. Shalom Z. Berger, Daniel Jacobson, and Chaim I. Waxman, *Flipping Out? Myth or Fact: The Impact of the "Year in Israel"* (New York: Yashar Books, 2007).

59. Wertheimer, "American Jews and Israel," 35.

60. On the Jonathan Pollard spy affair, see Rosenthal, *Irreconcilable Differences*, 76–92.

61. On political struggles over conversion, see ibid., 134–55.

62. Ibid., 99.

63. Ibid., 104.

64. Goldberg, *Jewish Power*, 99.

Notes to Chapter 2

1. John Mearsheimer and Stephen Walt, "The Israel Lobby," *London Review of Books* 28, no. 6 (2006).

2. Dan Fleshler, *Transforming America's Israel Lobby: The Limits of Power and the Potential for Change* (Dulles, VA: Potomac Books, 2009), 136.

3. Rosenthal, *Irreconcilable Differences*, 120; see also Fleshler, *Transforming America's Israel Lobby*, 135–36. The federations' lobbying arm, NJCRAC, similarly reached an impasse over a resolution on the settlement freeze, with the UHAC (Reform movement) and American Jewish Congress supporting and the Orthodox Union opposing it; see Ofira Seliktar, *Divided We Stand: America Jews, Israel, and the Peace Process* (Westport, CT: Praeger, 2002), 104.

4. Seliktar, *Divided We Stand*, 136–37.

5. Mitchell Bard, interview, July 11, 2012.

6. Rosenthal, *Irreconcilable Differences*, 128.

7. Seliktar, *Divided We Stand*, 137; Rosenthal, *Irreconcilable Differences*, 129.

8. Seliktar, *Divided We Stand*, 137.

9. Ibid., 135.

10. Ibid., 137.

11. Quoted in ibid., 141.

12. Rosenthal, *Irreconcilable Differences*, 129.

13. Seliktar, *Divided We Stand*, 158; Fleshler, *Transforming America's Israel Lobby*, 109.

14. Rosenthal, *Irreconcilable Differences*, 161.

15. Michael J. Jordan, "U.S. Jews Launch Offensive over Mount," *Jerusalem Post*, December 28, 2000.

16. Rosenthal, *Irreconcilable Differences*, 197.

17. Ibid., 211; Yossi Shain and Neil Rogachevsky, "Between Jdate and J Street: U.S. Foreign Policy and the Liberal Jewish Dilemma in America," *Israel Journal of Foreign Affairs* 3 (2011).

18. Ori Nir, "Pressing Peace in Era of GOP," *The Forward*, June 3, 2005.

19. Ron Kampeas, "In Major Policy Shift, AIPAC Offers Strong Backing for With-drawal Plan," *Jewish Telegraphic Agency*, May 24, 2005. On AIPAC's support for disengagement, see also Fleshler, *Transforming America's Israel Lobby*, 68.

20. Stewart Ain, "Leaders Here Debate Backing Gaza Pullout," *The Jewish Week*, October 22, 2004.

21. Ibid.

22. Jennifer Siegel, "Pullout Critics in U.S. Draw Few Backers," *The Forward*, August 19, 2005.

23. Adam Dickter, "Evangelicals Joining Gaza Pullout Protest," *The Jewish Week*, May 27, 2005.

24. Siegel, "Pullout Critics."

25. Ori Nir, "Israel Targets U.S. Foes of Gaza Plan," *The Forward*, July 15, 2005.

26. Ori Nir, "Orthodox Group Ups Criticism of Israel," *The Forward*, September 9, 2005.

27. Stewart Ain, "Israel Criticism Gets an O-U," *The Jewish Week*, December 1, 2006.

28. Gregory Levey, "The Right Wing's Jerusalem Gambit," *Salon*, December 13, 2007.

29. James Taub, "The New Israel Lobby," *New York Times*, September 13, 2009.

30. Jeremy Ben-Ami interviewed by Jeffrey Goldberg, New York Society for Ethical Culture, June 16.

31. Isi Liebler, "Candidly Speaking: Marginalize the Renegades," *Jerusalem Post*, October 5, 2009.

32. "There are organizations that have been created to take single elements of what the American Jewish organizations have been doing all along. . . . The pie hasn't gotten bigger, but the slicing has increased." Abraham Foxman, explaining declining ADL revenue. Nathan Guttman, "ADL and AJC Suffer Big Drop in Donations," *The Forward*, December 9, 2011.

33. The professionals and activists who lead these organizations recognize these divisions. When I asked a number of such individuals who is "inside" and who is "outside" their camp, they readily reproduced categories very close to those

that appear in Table 2.1. For example, the spokesperson for the Emergency Committee mentioned JINSA and AIPAC as "inside" and J Street and the Israel Policy Forum as "outside." Similarly, the spokesperson for Ameinu mentioned Partners for Progressive Israel and J Street as "inside" and Jewish Voice for Peace and the ZOA as "outside."

34. "Poll: 54% of Israelis Would Have Favored Continuing Gaza Operation." Press release, Zionist Organization of America, 2009.

35. Nathan Guttman, "Peace Groups Lose First Major Gaza Challenge on Capitol Hill," *The Forward*, January 16, 2009.

36. Eric Fingerhut, "Reform Rabbis Back Obama on Settlements," *Jewish Telegraphic Agency*, June 10, 2009.

37. Natasha Mozgovaya, "U.S. Congress Urges Obama to Impose 'Crippling Sanctions' on Iran," *Haaretz*, April 4, 2010.

38. Mark Landler, "U.S. Backers of Israel Pressure Obama over Policy on Iran," *New York Times*, March 3, 2012.

39. Eric Lichtblau and Mark Landler, "Hawks Steering Debate on How to Take on Iran," *New York Times*, March 19, 2012.

40. The organizations on the political right, including the ZOA, do not host large policy conferences or seek to substantially influence the flow of campaign funding.

41. Mandy Katz, "The Man on J Street: The Story of Jeremy Ben-Ami," *Moment Magazine*, March/April 2010. See also Dov Waxman, "The Israel Lobbies: A Survey of the Pro-Israel Community in the United States," *Israel Studies Forum* 25, no. 1 (March/April 2010).

42. Josh Nathan-Kazis, "Critics Counter J Street at U Penn Hillel," *The Forward*, February 10, 2010.

43. Simone Zimmerman, Jeremy Elster, Isaiah Kirshner-Breen, and Alon Mazor, "J Street U Bounced by Berkeley Group," *The Forward*, December 16, 2011.

44. Peter Schworm, "Brandeis Groups Clash on Israel Stance," *Boston Globe*, March 11, 2011.

45. Nathan Guttman, "JCCs Are the New Front Line in the Culture War on Israel," *The Forward*, March 23, 2011.

46. Caroline Glick, "American Jewry's Fight," *Jerusalem Post*, January 4, 2011.

47. Further to the left, the Jewish Voice for Peace has chapters at twenty-six universities.

48. The survey was administered in 2012. Leonard Saxe, Michelle Shain, Shahar Hecht, Graham Wright, and Shira Fishman, *Jewish Futures Study: 2012 Update* (Waltham, MA: Cohen Center for Modern Jewish Studies, Brandeis University, 2012).

49. Steven M. Cohen, *JTS Rabbis and Israel, Then and Now: The 2011 Survey of JTS Ordained Rabbis and Current Students* (New York: Jewish Theological Seminary, 2011), 30.

50. Rosenthal, *Irreconcilable Differences*, 147.

51. According to prevailing practice, Israeli Orthodox authorities have de facto authority over all conversions conducted inside Israel but not conversions conducted abroad. Israeli Supreme Court decisions, however, have steadily liberalized conversion law. The struggle over the Rotem Bill was in part an effort by Orthodox authorities to preempt further court-ordered liberalization, and by Reform and Conservative leaders to enable it. See Gal Beckerman, "Conversion Bill Sparks Unusual Push Back from Diaspora Jews," *The Forward*, March 26, 2010; Shain and Rogachevsky, "Between Jdate and J Street."

52. Mike Prashker, "Teaming up for Equality in Israel," *The Forward*, December 5, 2008; see also Ron Kampeas, "Defending Israel, Mainstream U.S. Groups Critique It," *Jewish Telegraphic Agency*, January 11, 2011; and Jeffrey Solomon, interview, April 12, 2011.

53. James D. Besser, "New Coalition to Fight Any Division of Jerusalem," *The Jewish Week*, October 18, 2007; Shlomo Shamir, "Reform Head: U.S. Jews Must Not Oppose Compromise on Jerusalem," *Haaretz*, December 23, 2007.

54. Seliktar, *Divided We Stand*.

55. Kampeas, "Defending Israel, Mainstream U.S. Groups Critique It."

56. "U.S. Jewish Groups Slam Rabbis Anti-Migrant Decrees," *Jewish Telegraphic Agency*, June 11, 2010.

57. Ron Friedman, "Do Not Send These Children Away, Foxman Pleads," *Jerusalem Post*, October 20, 2010.

Notes to Chapter 3

1. The federations raised an additional $1 billion to $2.5 billion annually for endowments and donor-advised funds. Data supplied by the Jewish Federations of North America. See also Chaim I. Waxman, "American Jewish Philanthropy, Direct Giving, and the Unity of the Jewish Community," in *Toward a Renewed Ethic of Jewish Philanthropy*, ed. Yossi Prager (New York: Yeshiva University Press, 2010); Jack Wertheimer, "Current Trends in American Jewish Philanthropy," in *American Jewish Year Book*, ed. David Singer and Ruth R. Seldin (New York: American Jewish Committee, 1997).

2. United Jewish Communities Leadership Briefing, February 9, 2009. An alternative source reports a drop from 630,486 in 1999 to 564,343 in 2005; see Jacob Berkman, "UJC to Make Major Changes," Jewish Telegraphic Association, April 17, 2007.

3. Steven M. Cohen, Jack B. Ukeles, and Ron Miller, *Jewish Community Study of New York: 2011* (New York: UJA Federation, 2012), 193.

4. Helen Roberts, "American Jewish Donations to Israel," *Contemporary Jewry* 20 (1999).

5. Mark Hrywna, "United Way Drives to Diversify Income," *NonProfit Times*, October 15, 2011.

6. In the 2000s, the portion individual federations allocated for overseas varied from 17 to 43 percent. Mark I. Rosen, *Mission, Meaning and Money* (Waltham, MA: Brandeis University Press, 2010).

7. Yossi Beilin, *"Taglit" Hayai: Sipuro Shel Maavak Bamimsad Ha-Yehudi* (ha-Kibuts hame'uhad, 2009).

8. Wertheimer, "Current Trends in American Jewish Philanthropy," 20.

9. Ibid., 34.

10. http://www.jewishvirtuallibrary.org/jsource/US-Israel/ujatab.html (accessed August 7, 2012).

11. Misha Galperin, interview, May 2011. See also Rosen, *Mission, Meaning and Money*; Gerald B. Bubis and Steven F. Windmueller, *From Predictability to Chaos: How Jewish Leaders Reinvented Their National Communal System* (Baltimore: Center for Jewish Community Studies, 2005).

12. Morton B. Plant, *ONAD Review Report* (New York: Jewish Federations of North America, 2005).

13. Eric Fleisch, *Israeli NGOs and Their Overseas Partners: The Real and Perceived Boundaries of Influence and Legitimacy* (Waltham, MA: Brandeis University, 2014).

14. Wertheimer, "Current Trends in American Jewish Philanthropy," 39.

15. To track the number of American Friends organizations raising funds for Israeli affiliates, we examined the Guidestar database of U.S.-registered nonprofit organizations. The database includes information on the year established as well as a description of philanthropic activities. See Eric Fleisch and Theodore Sasson, *The New Philanthropy: American Jewish Giving to Israeli Organizations* (Waltham, MA: Cohen Center for Modern Jewish Studies, 2012).

16. Today, Israel's nonprofit sector consists of more than 30,000 organizations employing 360,000 people, or 18 percent of the workforce. Dvora Blum, "The Ambivalent Emergence of Philanthropy in Israel," *Journal of Jewish Communal Service* 84, no. 1/2 (2009): 96.

17. For a discussion of the legal framework for donations to foreign charities, see Fleisch, *Israeli NGOs and Their Overseas Partners*.

18. Wertheimer, "Current Trends in American Jewish Philanthropy," 14.

19. As tax-exempt organizations, foundations and federations can operate in Israel and/or donate directly to Israeli charities under the same favorable tax laws as the American Friends organizations and pass-through and ideological umbrella funds.

20. S. P. Goldberg, "Jewish Communal Services: Programs and Finances," in *American Jewish Yearbook*, ed. Morris Fine and Milton Himmelfarb (New York: American Jewish Committee, 1978), 191.

21. Data attributed to Barry Kosmin and Jack Wertheimer, cited in Wertheimer, "Current Trends in American Jewish Philanthropy."

22. For a more thorough discussion of our methodology and list of American Friends groups, see Fleisch and Sasson, *New Philanthropy*. Although the sums we report almost certainly represent more than the proverbial "tip of the iceberg," they are not comprehensive. Donations through synagogues and donations made directly, without the benefit of tax deductibility, are not included in these data. It is also possible that we failed to identify all of the relevant organizations, as well as all of

the private foundations that engage in direct giving to Israeli organizations. The actual total of American Jewish giving in Israel is therefore certainly greater than we have reported—exactly how much greater we cannot know.

23. For the American Friends organizations, umbrella funds, and pass-through funds, we report the dollar amount received in direct donations. For federations and foundations, we report the dollar amount granted to Israeli organizations.

24. We included only organizations that fundraise primarily in the Jewish community. Donations by non-Jews, including Christian Zionists, typically flow through different organizations.

25. Fleisch and Sasson also document the upward trend by tabulating donations to the largest American Friends organizations for the period 1998–2009. See *New Philanthropy*.

26. Donations to causes in Israel seem to have been more adversely affected by the recession than has general charitable giving. According to the organization Giving USA, overall charitable donations by Americans dropped 13.4 percent in the wake of the recession and in 2011 still remained 11 percent below the 2007 peak. Holly Hall, "Charitable Donations Barely Grew Last Year, 'Giving USA' Finds," *Chronicle of Higher Education*, June 19, 2012.

27. Jim Gerstein, *J Street: National Survey of American Jews* (Washington, DC: J Street, 2008).

28. Cohen, Ukeles, and Miller, *Jewish Community Study of New York: 2011*.

29. For a full description of methodology and related considerations, see Fleisch and Sasson, *New Philanthropy*.

30. PEF is a very low-overhead organization with administrative costs of less than 2 percent of donated funds. The organization channels donations to 1,200 approved Israeli NGOs. "Areas of support include, but are not limited to: primary and secondary education; supporting scientific research; promoting greater tolerance and understanding between religious and secular communities and between Arabs and Jews; the special needs of women, children and families in distress; special education and education for the gifted; veterans programs; drug abuse; promotion of the arts; and relief for the handicapped" (www.pefisrael.org).

31. Josh Nathan-Kazis, "JNF Challenged on Discrimination," *The Forward*, April 20, 2011.

32. Russell Robinson, interview, September 2011. The JNF includes anyone who has given within a three-year period as part of its active donor base.

33. Rosen, *Mission, Meaning and Money*.

34. The JDC's programs typically receive matching grant support from the government of Israel, enlarging their scope. The JDC contributes about $60 million of its own funds annually. Steven Schwager, interview, August 2011.

35. One of the largest poverty relief organizations in 2010, raising nearly $11 million, ostensibly for a network of soup kitchens in Jerusalem, was Hazon Yeshayahu ("Isaiah's Vision"). In 2012 the organization's chief executive and members of his staff were charged with embezzlement and fraud. The crimes were uncovered by

the "Canadian Friends" organization. Alarmed by apparent financial irregularities, the Canadian group hired a private investigator to infiltrate the Israeli organization. See Mordechai Twersky, "Israeli Charity Executive Arrested on Suspicion of Embezzling Millions of Shekels from Donors," *Haaretz*, April 12, 2012.

36. Tova Kantrowitz, interview, Technion Society, April 14, 2011. The term "start-up nation" references the recent book by the same name; see Dan Senor and Saul Singer, *Start-Up Nation: The Story of Israel's Economic Miracle* (Twelve, 2009).

37. Gal Beckerman, "Hadassah Changing the Way It Does Business," *The Forward*, December 11, 2009.

38. Nathan Guttman, "Hadassah Cuts Staff, Closes Offices, Spins Off Young Judea to Plug Madoff Hole," *The Forward*, July 8, 2011.

39. Judy Siegel-Itzkovich, "AFMDA Kindness Is in the Blood," *Jerusalem Post*, November 27, 2010.

40. Arnold Gerson, interview, August 12, 2011.

41. Siegel-Itzkovich, "AFMDA Kindness Is in the Blood."

42. "Israel Museum Inaugurates Its Renewed Campus and Reinstalled Collection Wings" (Press release, Israel Museum, Jerusalem, July 26, 2010).

43. Daniel Luria, interview, April 2011.

44. In 2003, the most recent year in which the Central Fund listed its beneficiary organizations, most were West Bank charities. On the basis of the limited information at our disposal, we assigned half of the Central Fund's revenue to the settlements category and half to miscellaneous.

45. Jim Rutenberg, Mike McIntire, and Ethan Bronner, "Tax-Exempt Funds Aid Settlements in West Bank," *New York Times*, July 5, 2010. See also Yitzhak Ben-Chorin, "M'america L'hitnachaluyot: Kach Zormim Hamilionim" [From America to the settlements: How the millions flow], *Haaretz*, March 23, 2009.

46. Beinart, *Crisis of Zionism*, 192.

47. Chaim Levinson, "Settlements Have Cost Israel $17 Billion, Study Finds," *Haaretz*, March 23, 2010.

48. Rutenberg, McIntire, and Bronner, "Tax-Exempt Funds Aid Settlements."

49. Varda Shiffer, interview, April 2011.

50. Itzik Shanan, interview, April 2011.

51. Additional civil rights and human rights advocacy organizations supported by the New Israel Fund include Yesh Din, Physicians for Human Rights, Machsom Watch, and Gisha: Legal Center for Freedom of Movement.

52. Gerald M. Steinberg, "The Politics of NGOs, Human Rights and the Arab-Israel Conflict," *Israel Studies* 16 (2011).

53. The organization's name derives from Theodor Herzl's phrase: "If you will it [a Jewish state] then it is no dream."

54. An additional feature of the ferment over the New Israel Fund was the announcement, in 2008, of the formation of the Israel Independence Fund. The new charity seeks to raise money among American Jews for Israeli organizations that "strengthen the Jewish and Zionist core of Israel." See www.fundisrael.org.

55. Rebecca Caspi, interview, April 2011.

56. The goals of the new initiative are strikingly similar to those of the ill-fated Overseas Needs Assessment and Distribution (ONAD) process discussed previously in this chapter.

57. Jacob Berkman, "UJC May End Exclusive Partnership with Jewish Agency and JDC," *Jewish Telegraphic Agency*, January 28, 2009.

58. Jewish Agency for Israel, *Securing the Future: The Jewish Agency's New Strategic Directions* (Jerusalem: Jewish Agency for Israel, 2010).

59. Alan Hoffman, interview, April 2011.

60. Abe Selig, "New Israel Fund Comes Out Swinging Against Im Tirtzu Report," *Jerusalem Post*, February 2, 2010.

61. Fundraising costs run similarly high for Jewish organizations that raise small contributions, including the Jewish National Fund. The International Fellowship's fundraising steadily increased from nearly $50 million in 2005 to nearly $96 million in 2010.

62. Senor and Singer, *Start-Up Nation*.

63. Tjai M. Nielsen and Liesl Riddle, "Why Diasporas Invest in the Homeland: A Conceptual Model of Motivation" (Working paper series, George Washington University, 2007).

64. Morton Mandel, *It's All About Who* (San Francisco: Jossey-Bass, 2013).

Notes to Chapter 4

1. From the 1970s to the 1990s, JAFI and the WZO functioned as quasi–state agencies with nominally discrete functions. JAFI was primarily responsible for immigration and resettlement; the WZO was primarily responsible for diaspora education. In practice, the two organizations shared staff and were under the direction of overlapping boards of directors. The boards of directors represented a broad and shifting constellation of Israeli political parties and diaspora Jewish organizations and philanthropies. Helen Chapin Metz, ed., *Israel: A Country Study* (Washington, DC: Government Printing Office for the Library of Congress, 1988).

2. These rough estimates are based on data reported by Cohen for worldwide participation in Israel experience programs. Erik H. Cohen, *Youth Tourism in Israel: Educational Experiences of the Diaspora* (Clevedon, UK: Channel View, 2008), 28. My calculations assume that North American Jews composed 60 to 70 percent of all participants in such programs during the period in question, as they do today.

3. Cohen, *Youth Tourism in Israel*.

4. Elan Ezrachi, interview, April 2011.

5. Ibid. See also Ezra Kopelowitz, Minna Wolf, and Stephen Markowitz, *High School Israel Experience Programs: A Policy-Oriented Analysis of the Field* (Jerusalem: Makom/JAFI, 2009).

6. Chaim I. Waxman, *The Impact of Aliyah on the American Jewish Community* (Jersey City, NJ: Ktav, 1989), 179–99.

7. Waxman, *Impact of Aliyah on the American Jewish Community*.

8. The intermarriage estimate for 1990 was later revised downward to 43 percent. Nacha Cattan, "New Population Survey Retracts Intermarriage Figure," *The Forward*, September 12, 2003.

9. Yossi Beilin, *'Taglit' Hayai: Sipuro Shel Ma'avak Ba-mimsad Ha-Yehudi* (Tel Aviv, Israel: ha-kibuts hame'uhad, 2009).

10. See, for example, Barry Chazan, *Does the Israel Teen Experience Make a Difference?* (New York: Israel Experience, Inc., 1997); David Mittelberg, *The Israel Connection and American Jews* (London: Praeger, 1999).

11. Beilin, *'Taglit' Hayai*.

12. Barry Chazan, "The Israel Trip: A New Form of Jewish Education," in *Youth Trips to Israel: Rationale and Realization* (New York: CRB Foundation and the Mandell L. Berman Jewish Heritage Center at JESNA, 1994).

13. Barry Chazan, *Birthright Israel: A Five Year Education Report* (Jerusalem: Taglit-Birthright Israel, June 1, 2004). See also Leonard Saxe and Barry Chazan, *Ten Days of Birthright Israel: A Journey in Young Adult Identity* (Lebanon, NH: Brandeis University Press/University Press of New England, 2008).

14. Theodore Sasson, field notes, July 2005.

15. In 2011 Taglit canceled a tour that J Street had announced, explaining that Taglit no longer supported trips with overt political orientations.

16. These ethnographic field notes derive from research I conducted with colleagues Charles Kadushin and Leonard Saxe on the narrative components of the Taglit trips. The notes were taken by a team of trained observers during the 2005 summer trips and are published here for the first time.

17. In 2012, the Birthright organization established a training program for tour guides who lead Birthright trips. One aim of the new program is to encourage guides to expand the focus on contemporary Israel, in particular the environment, business, science, arts, and culture. According to Birthright's director of education, Zohar Raviv, "[I]t's important for participants to go back to their roots, but it's also important for them to connect to Israel's future." Judy Maltz, "To Masada or Not to Masada, That Is the Question," *Haaretz*, January 5, 2013.

18. Yael Zerubavel, *Recovered Roots: Collective Memory and the Making of Israeli National Tradition* (Chicago: University of Chicago Press, 1997); Nachman Ben-Yehuda, *Masada Myth: Collective Memory and Mythmaking in Israel* (Madison: University of Wisconsin Press, 1995).

19. Theodore Sasson and Shaul Kelner, "From Shrine to Forum: Masada and the Politics of Jewish Extremism," *Israel Studies* 13, no. 12 (2008): 152.

20. Ibid., 154–55.

21. Shaul Kelner, *Tours That Bind: Diaspora, Pilgrimage and Israeli Birthright Tourism* (New York: New York University Press, 2010). For other views on Birthright's politics, see Jasmin Habib, *Israel, Diaspora and the Routes of National Belonging* (Toronto: University of Toronto Press, 2004); Aviv and Shneer, *New Jews*.

22. The survey was conducted in July–September 2012 and targeted all eligible North American applicants to the Winter 2010–11, Summer 2011, and Winter

2011–12 Taglit trips. Participants were therefore six to eighteen months post-trip at the time of the survey. See Theodore Sasson, "The Impact of Taglit-Birthright Israel on the Political Attitudes of Trip Participants." Unpublished paper presented at Taglit-Birthright Israel: An Academic Symposium, Hebrew University, Jerusalem, 2013.

23. "Peter Beinart and Boston Federation Head Spar over Birthright," *The Jewish Week*, April 5, 2012.

24. David Landau, "Judaism and the Jews," *The Economist*, July 27, 2012. See also Kiera Feldman, "The Romance of Birthright Israel," *The Nation*, June 15, 2011.

25. The research project on Birthright Israel mifgashim was conducted in 2007 by Brandeis University's Cohen Center and Oranim Academic College of Education. See Theodore Sasson, David Mittelberg, Shahar Hecht, and Leonard Saxe, "Guest-Host Encounters in Diaspora-Heritage Tourism: The Taglit-Birthright Israel Mifgash (Encounter)," *Diaspora, Indigenous, and Minority Education* 5, no. 3 (2011); Theodore Sasson, David Mittelberg, Shahar Hecht, and Leonard Saxe, *Encountering the Other, Finding Oneself: The Birthright Israel Mifgash* (Waltham, MA: Cohen Center for Modern Jewish Studies, Brandeis University, 2008).

26. Of respondents, 75 percent agreed "very much" that the trip made them feel "proud to be an Israeli"; 80 percent agreed "very much" that the trip made them feel proud of their military service. Sasson et al., "Guest-Host Encounters," 91.

27. Of respondents, 85 percent indicated that the participation of Israelis "contributed to the trip's success"; 77 percent indicated that the participation of Israelis "taught me about my Jewish identity." Unpublished data collected by the Henrietta Szold Institute, Jerusalem, from North American participants during 2011–12 Birthright Israel trips.

28. Unpublished data collected from July to October 2012 by the Cohen Center for Modern Jewish Studies, Brandeis University, from North American participants during 2011–12 Birthright Israel trips.

29. I served as co–principal investigator on several of these evaluation studies. See, for example, Leonard Saxe, Benjamin Phillips, Theodore Sasson, Shahar Hecht, Michelle Shain, Graham Wright, and Charles Kadushin, *Generation Birthright Israel: The Impact of an Israel Experience on Jewish Identity and Choices* (Waltham, MA: Cohen Center for Modern Jewish Studies, Brandeis University, 2009); Leonard Saxe, Benjamin Phillips, Matthew Boxer, Shahar Hecht, Graham Wright, and Theodore Sasson, *Taglit-Birthright Israel: Evaluation of the 2007–2008 North American Cohorts* (Waltham, MA: Cohen Center for Modern Jewish Studies, Brandeis University, 2008); Leonard Saxe, Theodore Sasson, and Shahar Hecht, *Israel at War: The Impact of Peer-Oriented Israel Programs on Responses of American Young Adults* (Waltham, MA: Steinhardt Social Research Institute, Brandeis University, 2006); Leonard Saxe, Charles Kadushin, Shahar Hecht, Mark I. Rosen, Benjamin Phillips, and Shaul Kelner, *Evaluating Birthright Israel: Long-Term Impact and Recent Findings* (Waltham, MA: Cohen Center for Modern Jewish Studies, Brandeis University, 2004).

30. Birthright runs trips for North Americans in the summer and winter; applications to the program continue to outstrip available places. Data on registration for 2012 summer trips were provided by the Cohen Center for Modern Jewish Studies, Brandeis University.

31. The best recent estimate of the size of each American Jewish birth cohort is 75,000; see Elizabeth Tighe, Leonard Saxe, Charles Kadushin, Raquel Magidin de Kramer, Begli Nursahedov, Janet Aronson, and Lynn Cherny, *Estimating the Jewish Population of the United States: 2000–2010* (Waltham, MA: Steinhardt Social Research Institute, Brandeis University, 2011). For half to participate in an Israel experience program, the annual number of participants must be maintained at greater than 37,500 annually. Together, Birthright, Masa, and programs for high school students have surpassed that number each year since 2007; see Figure 4.1.

32. In all, 8 percent had attended both a Jewish supplementary school and a Jewish day school. Data provided by Taglit-Birthright Israel.

33. Theodore Sasson, Benjamin Phillips, Charles Kadushin, and Leonard Saxe, *Still Connected: American Jewish Attitudes about Israel* (Waltham, MA: Cohen Center for Modern Jewish Studies, Brandeis University, 2010). Steven M. Cohen and Samuel J. Abrams report similar findings in a 2012 survey; see Simi Lampert, "Young Jews More Interested in Israel," *The Forward*, July 9, 2012.

34. See www.yearcourse.org/about/the-history-of-young-judaea/ (accessed February 12, 2011).

35. "Survey Statistics by Program Type, USA 2009/2010" (Unpublished document, Masa: The Israel Journey).

36. Data supplied by Masa. See also Steven M. Cohen and Ezra Kopelowitz, *Long-Term Trips to Israel: The Contribution to Jewish Commitment and Leadership* (Jerusalem: Research Success, October 2010).

37. "OTZMA to Close," *eJewish Philanthropy*, November 1, 2012.

38. A substantial experience in Israel is characteristic of young leaders of both "establishment" and "nonestablishment" types of organizations. See Steven M. Cohen, "From Jewish People to Jewish Purpose: Establishment Leaders and Their Nonestablishment Successors," in *The New Jewish Leaders: Reshaping the American Jewish Landscape*, ed. Jack Wertheimer (Lebanon, NH: Brandeis University Press, 2011).

39. Ibid.

40. Kopelowitz, Wolf, and Markowitz, *High School Israel Experience Programs*, 6.

41. Ibid., 22.

42. Ramie Arian, *Mapping the Field of Israel Travel* (Northbrook, IL: iCenter, 2011), 12, www.icenter.org; see also Kopelowitz, Wolf, and Markowitz, *High School Israel Experience Programs*. The average number of worldwide diaspora participants in high school programs in Israel in the 1990s was about 10,000 per year, a majority from the United States. See Cohen, *Youth Tourism in Israel*, 28.

43. Saxe et al., *Generation Birthright Israel*; Saxe and Sasson, *Impact of Taglit-Birthright Israel*; Saxe et al., *Taglit-Birthright Israel*. For another view on how the

programs influence participants, see Faydra Shapiro, *Building Jewish Roots: The Israel Experience* (Montreal: McGill-Queens University Press, 2006).

44. In most years, American Jews compose 35 to 55 percent of all American tourists. During the peak years of the Second Intifada (2002–4), however, American Jews composed 68 to 72 percent of all American tourists.

45. Sergio DellaPergola, *Jewish Demographic Policies: Population Trends and Options in Israel and in the Diaspora* (Jerusalem: Jewish People Policy Institute, 2011).

46. See www.Jewishtelegraph.com/prof_38.html (accessed March 22, 2011).

47. Whereas the Jewish Agency is precluded by Israeli law from settling immigrants in the West Bank, the prohibition does not extend to Nefesh, which provides information about West Bank Jewish communities alongside information about Jewish communities inside the Green Line on its website.

48. Chaim Levinson, Uri Blau, and Mordechai I. Twersky, "Nefesh B'nefesh an Ineffective Monopoly with Overpaid Executives, Say Critics," *Haaretz*, October 20, 2012. For historical data on immigration to Israel, see http://www.jafi.org.il/JewishAgency/English/About/Press+Room/Aliyah+Statistics/jul27.htm.

49. In a lengthy 2012 article in the Israeli newspaper *Haaretz*, reporters Levinson, Blau, and Twersky criticized the privatization of the Jewish Agency's immigration functions, charging that Nefesh pays excessive salaries to its executives and provides inadequate support to new immigrants. They also charged that the organization has not brought about "a strategic shift" in the overall level of immigration to Israel from the United States. Nefesh, the Jewish Agency, and the Immigrant Absorption Ministry sharply disputed the reporters' analysis. In 2011, Israel's Immigrant Absorption Ministry approved regulations to encourage additional private organizations to compete with Nefesh. See Levinson, Blau, and Twersky, "Nefesh B'nefesh an Ineffective Monopoly."

Notes to Chapter 5

1. Steven M. Cohen, *Ties and Tensions: The 1986 Survey of American Jewish Attitudes towards Israel and Israelis* (New York: American Jewish Committee, 1986); see also Charles S. Liebman, "The Religious Life of American Jewry," in *Understanding American Jewry*, ed. Marshall Sklare (New Brunswick, NJ: Transaction Books, 1982).

2. The study examined attitudes about Israel and Israeli political issues. Thirty focus group discussions were held in diverse Jewish settings, including Orthodox, Conservative, Reform, and postdenominational synagogues and schools, and 156 individuals participated. The discussions were held in 2005 and 2006. The names of speakers quoted in the text are pseudonyms. See Theodore Sasson, *The New Realism: American Jewish Views about Israel* (New York: American Jewish Committee, 2009).

3. Cohen and Kelman, *Beyond Distancing*; Sasson, Kadushin, and Saxe, "Trends in American Jewish Attachment to Israel." An unpublished analysis of the American Jewish Committee's 2012 survey finds a correlation between measures

of political orientation and measures of emotional attachment to Israel, with attachment increasing along the continuum from liberal to conservative respondents. See Chapter 5, note 34.

4. A similar shift from "idealistic" to "realistic" discourse about the homeland has been observed in the Armenian American community. See Khachig Tololyan, "Beyond the Homeland: From Exilic Nationalism to Diasporic Transnationalism," in Gal, Leoussi, and Smith, *Call of the Homeland*.

5. Noga Tamopolsky, "Adelson's Other Pet Project: The Israeli Right," *Salon*, February 9, 2012.

6. Cohen, *JTS Rabbis and Israel*.

7. Ari Y. Kelman, "The Reality of the Virtual: Looking for Jewish Leadership Online," in Wertheimer, *New Jewish Leaders*.

8. Saxe et al., *Generation Birthright Israel*.

9. The AJC survey asks, "In the current situation, do you favor or oppose the establishment of a Palestinian state?" Surveys that ask whether respondents support a two-state solution in principle (rather than a Palestinian state "in the current situation") report greater support. For example, a 2012 election-eve survey commissioned by J Street reports 79 percent in favor of "a two-state solution that declares an end to the Palestinian-Israeli conflict, resulting in all Arab countries establishing full diplomatic ties with Israel and creating an independent Palestinian state in the West Bank, Gaza, and East Jerusalem." See "J Street: National Post-Election Survey," November 6, 2012.

10. In the 2005 AJC survey—the most recent for which full data sets have been made available for secondary analysis—69 percent of Orthodox respondents opposed establishment of a Palestinian state, versus 38 percent Conservative, 39 percent Reform, and 34 percent unaffiliated. Similarly, 65 percent of Orthodox respondents opposed dismantling any West Bank settlements in a peace deal, versus 36 percent Conservative, 31 percent Reform, and 32 percent unaffiliated. See American Jewish Committee, *Annual Survey* (New York: American Jewish Committee, 2005).

11. In all, 84 percent of Orthodox and 70 percent of Conservative respondents oppose dividing Jerusalem in a peace deal, versus 50 percent of Reform and 51 percent of unaffiliated. American Jewish Committee, *Annual Survey*.

12. Joel Perlmann, "American Jewish Opinion about the Future of the West Bank" (Working Paper 526, Levy Economics Institute of Bard College, Annandale-on-Hudson, New York, 2007); Sasson, Kadushin, and Saxe, "Trends in American Jewish Attachment to Israel."

13. Drawing on survey data, we can estimate the proportions of the American Jewish population that subscribe to each of these perspectives as follows: The right-wing perspective is embraced by about 30 percent, a figure derived from the portion that opposes dismantling any settlements and that regards U.S. support for Israel as "too little." This population is disproportionately Orthodox but also includes Conservative Jews as well as those who define themselves politically as

conservative. The left-wing perspective is embraced by about 10 percent of the population, a figure derived from those who favor dismantling all settlements that view U.S. support for Israel as "too much." The left is disproportionately postdenominational and Reform, as well as very liberal and highly educated. Finally, the centrist perspective is embraced by about 50 to 60 percent of the population, including those who favor dismantling some settlements and who view U.S. support for Israel as "about right." See Sasson et al., *Still Connected*.

14. For example, see Baruch Kimmerling, *The Invention and Decline of Israeliness* (Berkeley: University of California Press, 2001); Asad Ganim, Nadim Rouhana, and Oren Yiftachel, "Questioning 'Ethnic Democracy': A Response to Sammy Smooha," *Israel Studies* 3, no. 2 (1998).

15. For example, see Alexander Yakobson, "Jewish Peoplehood and the Jewish State, How Unique?—A Comparative Study," *Israel Studies* 13 (2008).

16. Charles S. Liebman and Steven M. Cohen, *Two Worlds of Judaism* (New Haven, CT: Yale University Press, 1990).

17. Elazar, "Changing Places, Changing Cultures."

18. We asked a number of questions regarding religion and state, including this one: "Leaders in the Israeli Conservative and Reform movements complain that Israel's recognition of only Orthodox weddings, conversions, and divorces amounts to religious discrimination against non-Orthodox Jews. The country's Orthodox authorities counter that recognizing non-Orthodox weddings, conversions, and divorces will lead to a split in the Jewish people. In your view, how serious a problem is this, and what if anything should be done about it?"

19. For a comparison of the views of Israeli and American Jews, see Theodore Sasson and Ephraim Tabory, "Converging Political Cultures: How Globalization Is Shaping the Discourses of American and Israeli Jews," *Nationalism and Ethnic Politics* 16, no. 1 (2010).

20. Notably, some claims advanced by Reform and other discussion participants regarding recognition of their Jewish status in Israel appear predicated on misinformation. Given the complexity of Israeli law—which recognizes weddings and conversions conducted by non-Orthodox rabbis outside of Israel, but only those conducted by Orthodox rabbis inside of Israel—the confusion is certainly understandable. Nevertheless, it seems noteworthy that many of the discussion participants characterized the rejection of their religious movements and Jewish identities in more sweeping terms than might be justified by (an arguably complex) reality.

21. We asked the following question: "Today, Arab citizens of Israel comprise roughly one-fifth of Israel's citizenry. Advocates for equal rights for the Arab minority say that as a democracy Israel must treat all of its citizens exactly the same. Others disagree, arguing that Israel is first and foremost a state of the Jewish people and that too much emphasis on equality will undermine the Jewish character of the state. What do you think? Can Israel be both a democratic state of 'all of its citizens' and at the same time a 'Jewish state'?"

22. It is unclear whether Joel is referring to Palestinians under Israeli occupation, who do not vote in Israeli elections, or Palestinian citizens of the state, who do.

23. Jonathon Ament, *Israel Connections and American Jews* (New York: United Jewish Communities, 2005); Wexler, "Israel and the Identity of American Jews"; Cohen and Kelman, *Beyond Distancing*; Beinart, "Failure of the American Jewish Establishment."

24. Sasson, Kadushin, and Saxe, "Trends in American Jewish Attachment to Israel." For survey reports of age-cohort differences in the 1980s, see Cohen, *Ties and Tensions* and Steven M. Cohen, *Content or Continuity: Alternative Bases for Commitment (the 1989 National Survey of American Jews)* (New York: American Jewish Committee, 1989).

25. Theodore Sasson, Benjamin Phillips, Graham Wright, Charles Kadushin, and Leonard Saxe, "Understanding Young Adult Attachment to Israel: Period, Lifecycle, and Generational Dynamics," *Contemporary Jewry* 32, no. 1 (2012).

26. Fern Chertok, Benjamin Phillips, and Leonard Saxe, *"It's Not Just Who Stands under the Chuppah": Intermarriage and Engagement* (Waltham, MA: Cohen Center for Modern Jewish Studies, Brandeis University, 2008).

27. For a discussion of "Jewish familism" and its impact on connection to Israel, see Steven M. Cohen and Arnold M. Eisen, *The Jew Within: Self, Family, and Community in America* (Bloomington: Indiana University Press, 2000). For a discussion of the impact of intermarriage, see Steven M. Cohen and Jack Wertheimer, *Whatever Happened to the Jewish People?* (New York: American Jewish Committee, 2006); Cohen and Kelman, *Beyond Distancing*.

28. See Sasson, Kadushin, and Saxe, "Trends in American Jewish Attachment to Israel."

29. Cohen, "From Jewish People to Jewish Purpose."

30. See, for example, Rosenthal, *Irreconcilable Differences*; Frank Luntz, *Israel and American Jews in the Age of Eminem* (New York: Andrea and Charles Bronfman Philanthropies, 2003); Seliktar, *Divided We Stand*.

31. Beinart, "Failure of the American Jewish Establishment."

32. Cohen and Kelman, *Beyond Distancing*; Sasson, Kadushin, and Saxe, "Trends in American Jewish Attachment to Israel."

33. According to a Gallup (2010) survey, 85 percent of Republicans, 60 percent of Independents, and 48 percent of Democrats sympathize more with Israelis than with Palestinians in the current situation. Between 2001 and 2010, support for Israel among Republicans increased by 25 points and among Independents by 18 points. During this period, support for Israel among Democrats remained unchanged. Lydia Saad, "Support for Israel in U.S. at 63%, Near Record High," *Gallup News Service*, February 24, 2010, http://www.gallup.com/poll/126155/support-israel-near-record-high.aspx (accessed September 1, 2010).

34. Indeed, in an unpublished analysis of the American Jewish Committee's 2012 survey, Charles Kadushin finds (for the first time) a correlation between general political orientation and caring about Israel. In the new survey, politically

conservative and moderate respondents are more likely than liberal respondents to agree that "caring about Israel is a very important part of my being a Jew" (Charles Kadushin, personal communication with the author, November 2012). It is too early to tell whether this is a one-off finding or an indicator of a new development.

35. On the conflict over non-Orthodox religious rituals at the Western Wall, see Jodi Rudoren, "Israel to Review Curbs on Women's Prayer at Western Wall," *New York Times*, December 25, 2012.

36. Saxe et al., *Generation Birthright Israel*; Sasson, Kadushin, and Saxe, "Trends in American Jewish Attachment to Israel"; Cohen and Kelman, *Beyond Distancing*.

37. The term "Birthright Bump" is Steven M. Cohen's. Cohen reports a similar spike in both travel to Israel and emotional attachment in the young adult cohort in a 2012 survey conducted for the Workmen's Circle. See Lampert, "Young Jews More Interested in Israel."

Notes to Chapter 6

1. As a large organization with a centrist political reputation, Birthright Israel has an affinity with the mobilization paradigm. The organization fits better within the direct engagement paradigm, however, because it (a) operates mostly outside of the federation-JAFI system, (b) outsources its activities to dozens of trip providers, (c) expresses a commitment to ideological pluralism in its educational program, and (d) is a leading vehicle for promoting personal encounters of diaspora Jews with Israel and Israelis.

2. Steven Bayme, "On Gabriel Sheffer's 'Loyalty and Criticism in the Relations between World Jewry and Israel,'" *Israel Studies* 17, no. 2 (July 9, 2012).

3. On the attitudes toward Israel of moderately affiliated Jews, see Cohen and Eisen, *The Jew Within*.

4. Thomas Friedman, *Lexus and the Olive Tree: Understanding Globalization* (New York: Picador, 2012); Manfred Steger, *Globalization: A Very Short Introduction* (New York: Oxford University Press, 2009).

5. Jonathan Rynhold, "Israel's Foreign and Defense Policy and Diaspora Jewish Identity," in Ben-Moshe and Segev, *Israel, the Diaspora and Jewish Identity*. See also Ofira Seliktar, "The Changing Identity of American Jews," in Ben-Moshe and Segev, *Israel, the Diaspora and Jewish Identity*.

6. "The War Within," *New York Times*, November 5, 2008.

7. Natasha Mozgovaya, "ADL Bid for U.S. Bipartisan Support for Israel Faces Staunch Resistance," *Haaretz*, October 25, 2011.

8. Other federations have embraced guidelines that stopped short of the "guilt-by-association" approach that bans federation-supported groups from cosponsoring events with BDS advocates. John Ruskay, head of the New York Federation, rejects the more restrictive approach: "If we draw a tighter and tighter circle around those whose views and actions on Israel are considered kosher, we create a real danger that many Jews will simply

disengage—in effect declaring, 'a pox on both your houses.'" John Ruskay, "Combating Delegitimization Requires a Big Tent," *The Jewish Week*, February 15, 2011.

9. See http://www.hillel.org/israel/guidelines.htm (accessed August 23, 2012).

10. Annette Koren and Janet Krasner Aronson, "Israel in the Curriculum of Higher Education: Growth, Placement, and Future Prospects" (unpublished manuscript on file with the author, 2012).

11. Additional efforts to build the field of Israel education include the Shalom Hartman Institute's Engaging Israel initiative, the Jewish Agency's Makom: The Israel Engagement Network, and Emory University's Center for Israel Education.

12. Robbie Gingras, "Hugging and Wrestling: Alternative Paradigms for the Diaspora-Israel Relationship" (2004), makomisrael.org/blog/hugging-and-wrestling-2.

13. Lisa Grant and Ezra Kopelowitz, *Israel Education Matters: A 21st Century Paradigm for Jewish Education* (Jerusalem: Center for Peoplehood Education, 2012), 97.

14. Ibid., 100.

15. Saxe and Chazan, *Ten Days of Birthright Israel*. See also Saxe et al., *Generation Birthright Israel*.

16. Grant and Kopelowitz, *Israel Education Matters*, 87. Partnership 2000 (P2K) changed its name in 2011 to Partnership 2Gether (P2G).

17. Ibid., 94.

18. On the leading expressions of Zionism, see Ben Halpern and Jehuda Reinharz, *Zionism and the Creation of a New Society* (Waltham, MA: Brandeis University Press, 2000); Arthur Hertzberg, ed., *The Zionist Idea* (New York: Jewish Publications Society, 1997).

19. Elazar, "Changing Places, Changing Cultures." See also Liebman and Cohen, *Two Worlds of Judaism* and David Mittelberg, "Jewish Peoplehood Education," in *The International Handbook of Jewish Education*, ed. Helena Miller, Lisa D. Grant, and Alex Pomson (Amsterdam: Springer, 2011).

20. On the impact of globalization on diaspora and homeland cultures, see Sasson and Tabory, "Converging Political Cultures."

21. Daniel Pekarsky, personal communication with the author, January 2013. For a similar perspective, see Simon Rawidowicz, *State of Israel, Diaspora, and Jewish Continuity: Essays on the "Ever-Dying People,"* ed. Benjamin C. I. Ravid (Waltham, MA: Brandeis University Press/University Press of New England, 1988).

22. Beinart, *Crisis of Zionism*.

23. Yossi Shain and Aharon Barth, "Diasporas and International Relations Theory," *International Organizations* 57, no. 3 (2012).

24. Newland, *Voice after Exit*, 5.

25. Jean Grugel and Henry Kippin, "The Cuban Diaspora," in *Diasporas in Conflict: Peace-Makers or Peace Wreckers?*, ed. Hazel Smith and Paul Stares (Tokyo: United Nations University Press, 2007), 161.

26. Newland, *Voice after Exit*, 5.

27. Ibid., 5.

28. Brown, *Global South Asians*; Kapur, *Diaspora, Development and Democracy*; Lampert, "Diaspora and Development?"

29. Landau, "Diaspora Nationalism," 228–29.

30. Basch, Schiller, and Szanton-Blanc, *Nations Unbound*.

31. Levitt, *Transnational Villagers*; Brown, *Global South Asians*.

32. Kathleen Newland and Hiroyuki Tanaka, *Mobilizing Diaspora: Entrepreneurship for Development* (Washington, DC: Migration Policy Institute, 2010).

33. Simon Payaslian, "Imagining Armenia," in Gal, Leoussi, and Smith, *Call of the Homeland*.

34. Bahar Baser and Ashok Swain, "Diaspora Design versus Homeland Realities: Case Study of Armenian Diaspora," *Caucasian Review of International Affairs* 3, no. 1 (2009).

35. Ibid., 56.

36. See also Gabriel Sheffer, "Transnationalism and Ethno-National Diasporism," *Diasporas* 15, no. 1 (2006); Shain, *Kinship and Diasporas*, 147.

37. Quoted in Baser and Swain, "Diaspora Design versus Homeland Realities," 60.

Ain, Stewart. "Israel Criticism Gets an O-U." *The Jewish Week*, December 1, 2006.

———. "Leaders Here Debate Backing Gaza Pullout." *The Jewish Week*, October 22, 2004.

Ament, Jonathon. *Israel Connections and American Jews*. New York: United Jewish Communities, 2005.

American Jewish Committee. *Annual Survey*. New York: American Jewish Committee, 2005.

Arian, Ramie. *Mapping the Field of Israel Travel*. Northbrook, IL: iCenter, 2011. www.icenter.org.

Aviv, Caryn, and David Shneer. *New Jews: The End of the Jewish Diaspora*. New York: New York University Press, 2005.

Bard, Mitchell Geoffrey. *The Water's Edge and Beyond: Defining the Limits to Domestic Influence on United States Middle East Policy*. New Brunswick, NJ: Transaction, 1991.

Basch, Linda, Nina Glick Schiller, and Cristina Szanton-Blanc. *Nations Unbound: Transnational Projects, Postcolonial Predicaments and Deterritorialized Nation-States*. Amsterdam: Gordon and Breach, 1994.

Baser, Bahar, and Ashok Swain. "Diaspora Design versus Homeland Realities: Case Study of Armenian Diaspora." *Caucasian Review of International Affairs* 3, no. 1 (2009): 45–62.

Bayme, Steven. "On Gabriel Sheffer's 'Loyalty and Criticism in the Relations between World Jewry and Israel.'" *Israel Studies* 17, no. 2 (July 9, 2012): 111–19.

Beckerman, Gal. "Conversion Bill Sparks Unusual Push Back from Diaspora Jews." *The Forward*, March 26, 2010.

———. "Hadassah Changing the Way It Does Business." *The Forward*, December 11, 2009.

Beilin, Yossi. *'Taglit' Hayai: Sipuro Shel Ma'avak Ba-mimsad ha-Yehudi*. Tel Aviv, Israel: ha-Kibuts ha-me'uhad, 2009.

Beinart, Peter. *The Crisis of Zionism*. New York: Times Books, 2012.

———. "The Failure of the American Jewish Establishment." *New York Review of Books*, June 24, 2010.

Ben-Chorin, Yitzhak. "M'america L'hitnachaluyot: Kach Zormim Hamilionim" [From America to the settlements: How the millions flow]. *Haaretz*, March 23, 2009.

Ben-Moshe, Danny, and Zohar Segev, eds. *Israel, the Diaspora and Jewish Identity*. Brighton, UK: Sussex Academic Press, 2007.

Ben-Yehuda, Nachman. *Masada Myth: Collective Memory and Mythmaking in Israel.* Madison: University of Wisconsin Press, 1995.

Berger, Shalom Z., Daniel Jacobson, and Chaim I. Waxman. *Flipping Out? Myth or Fact: The Impact of the "Year in Israel."* New York: Yashar Books, 2007.

Berkman, Jacob. "UJC May End Exclusive Partnership with Jewish Agency and JDC." *Jewish Telegraphic Agency,* January 28, 2009.

Besser, James D. "New Coalition to Fight Any Division of Jerusalem." *The Jewish Week,* October 18, 2007.

Blum, Dvora. "The Ambivalent Emergence of Philanthropy in Israel." *Journal of Jewish Communal Service* 84, no. 1/2 (2009): 96–105.

Bourdieu, Pierre. *Distinction: A Social Critique of the Judgement of Taste.* Cambridge, MA: Harvard University Press, 1984.

Brinkerhoff, Jennifer M. *Digital Diasporas: Identity and Transnational Engagement.* New York: Cambridge University Press, 2012.

Brodkin, Karen. *How Jews Became White Folks and What That Says about Race in America.* New Brunswick, NJ: Rutgers University Press, 2000.

Brown, Judith. *Global South Asians: Introducing the Modern Diaspora.* Cambridge, UK: Cambridge University Press, 2006.

Bubis, Gerald B., and Steven F. Windmueller. *From Predictability to Chaos: How Jewish Leaders Reinvented Their National Communal System.* Baltimore: Center for Jewish Community Studies, 2005.

Cattan, Nacha. "New Population Survey Retracts Intermarriage Figure." *The Forward,* September 12, 2003.

Chazan, Barry. *Birthright Israel: A Five Year Education Report.* Jerusalem: Taglit-Birthright Israel, June 1, 2004.

———. *Does the Israel Teen Experience Make a Difference?* New York: Israel Experience, Inc., 1997.

Chazan, Barry. "The Israel Trip: A New Form of Jewish Education." In *Youth Trips to Israel: Rationale and Realization,* A1–A26. New York: CRB Foundation and the Mandell L. Berman Jewish Heritage Center at JESNA, 1994.

Chertok, Fern, Benjamin Phillips, and Leonard Saxe. *"It's Not Just Who Stands under the Chuppah": Intermarriage and Engagement.* Waltham, MA: Cohen Center for Modern Jewish Studies, Brandeis University, 2008.

Cohen, Erik H. *Youth Tourism in Israel: Educational Experiences of the Diaspora.* Clevedon, UK: Channel View, 2008.

Cohen, Naomi W. *The Americanization of Zionism, 1897–1948.* Hanover, NH: Brandeis University Press/University Press of New England, 2003.

Cohen, Robin. *Global Diasporas.* Seattle: University of Washington Press, 1997.

Cohen, Steven M. *Content or Continuity: Alternative Bases for Commitment (the 1989 National Survey of American Jews).* New York: American Jewish Committee, 1989.

———. "From Jewish People to Jewish Purpose." In *The New Jewish Leaders,* edited by Jack Wertheimer, 45–83, Lebanon, NH: Brandeis University Press, 2011.

———. *JTS Rabbis and Israel, Then and Now: The 2011 Survey of JTS Ordained Rabbis and Current Students*. New York: Jewish Theological Seminary, 2011.

———. *The 1981–1982 National Survey of American Jews*. New York: American Jewish Committee, 1983.

———. *Ties and Tensions: The 1986 Survey of American Jewish Attitudes towards Israel and Israelis*. New York: American Jewish Committee, 1986.

Cohen, Steven M., and Arnold M. Eisen. *The Jew Within: Self, Family, and Community in America*. Bloomington: Indiana University Press, 2000.

Cohen, Steven M., and Ari Y. Kelman. *Beyond Distancing: Young Adult American Jews and Their Alienation from Israel*. New York: Andrea and Charles Bronfman Philanthropies, 2007.

Cohen, Steven M., and Ezra Kopelowitz. *Long-Term Trips to Israel: The Contribution to Jewish Commitment and Leadership*. Jerusalem: Research Success, October 2010.

Cohen, Steven M., and Charles S. Liebman. "Israel and American Jewry in the Twenty-First Century: A Search for New Relationships." In *Beyond Survival and Philanthropy: American Jewry and Israel*, edited by Allon Gal and Alfred Gottschalk, 3–24. Cincinnati, OH: Hebrew Union College, 2000.

Cohen, Steven M., Jack B. Ukeles, and Ron Miller. *Jewish Community Study of New York: 2011*. New York: UJA Federation, 2012.

Cohen, Steven M., and Jack Wertheimer. *Whatever Happened to the Jewish People?* New York: American Jewish Committee, 2006.

DellaPergola, Sergio. *Jewish Demographic Policies: Population Trends and Options in Israel and in the Diaspora*. Jerusalem: Jewish People Policy Institute, 2011.

Dickter, Adam. "Evangelicals Joining Gaza Pullout Protest." *The Jewish Week*, May 27, 2005.

Dufoix, Stephane. *Diasporas*. Berkeley: University of California Press, 2003.

Elazar, Daniel J. "Changing Places, Changing Cultures: Divergent Jewish Political Cultures." In *Divergent Jewish Cultures: Israel and America*, edited by Deborah Dash Moore and S. Ilan Troen, 320–330. New Haven, CT: Yale University Press, 2001.

———. *Community and Polity: The Organizational Dynamics of American Jewry*. Philadelphia: Jewish Publications Society, 1995.

Esman, Milton J. *Diasporas in the Contemporary World*. Malden, MA: Polity, 2009.

Feldman, Kiera. "The Romance of Birthright Israel." *The Nation*, June 15, 2011.

Fingerhut, Eric. "Reform Rabbis Back Obama on Settlements." *Jewish Telegraphic Agency*, June 10, 2009.

Fishman, Sylvia Barack. *Jewish Life and American Culture*. Binghamton: State University of New York Press, 2000.

Fleisch, Eric. *Israeli NGOs and Their Overseas Partners: The Real and Perceived Boundaries of Influence and Legitimacy*. Doctoral dissertation. Waltham, MA: Brandeis University, 2014.

Fleisch, Eric, and Theodore Sasson. *The New Philanthropy: American Jewish Giving to Israeli Organizations*. Waltham, MA: Cohen Center for Modern Jewish Studies, 2012.

Fleshler, Dan. *Transforming America's Israel Lobby: The Limits of Power and the Potential for Change.* Dulles, VA: Potomac Books, 2009.

Friedman, Ron. "Do Not Send These Children Away, Foxman Pleads." *Jerusalem Post,* October 20, 2010.

Friedman, Thomas. *Lexus and the Olive Tree: Understanding Globalization.* New York: Picador, 2012.

Gal, Allon, Athena S. Leoussi, and Anthony D. Smith, eds. *The Call of the Homeland: Diaspora Nationalisms, Past and Present.* Leiden, Netherlands: Brill, 2010.

Ganim, Asad, Nadim Rouhana, and Oren Yiftachel. "Questioning 'Ethnic Democracy': A Response to Sammy Smooha." *Israel Studies* 3, no. 2 (1998): 253–67.

Ganin, Zvi. *An Uneasy Relationship: American Jewish Leadership and Israel, 1948–1957.* Syracuse, NY: Syracuse University Press, 2005.

Gerstein, Jim. *J Street: National Survey of American Jews.* Washington, DC: J Street, 2008.

Gingras, Robbie. "Hugging and Wrestling: Alternative Paradigms for the Diaspora-Israel Relationship." 2004. makomisrael.org/blog/hugging-and-wrestling-2.

Glick, Caroline. "American Jewry's Fight." *Jerusalem Post,* January 4, 2011.

Goldberg, J. J. *Jewish Power: Inside the American Jewish Establishment.* New York: Addison-Wesley, 1996.

Goldberg, S. P. "Jewish Communal Services: Programs and Finances." In *American Jewish Yearbook,* vol. 78, edited by Morris Fine and Milton Himmelfarb, 172–221. New York: American Jewish Committee, 1978.

Gordis, Daniel. "No Jewish People without Israel." *Tablet Magazine,* August 20, 2012.

Gorenberg, Gershom. *The Accidental Empire: Israel and the Birth of the Settlements, 1967–1977.* New York: Holt, 2007.

Grant, Lisa, and Ezra Kopelowitz. *Israel Education Matters: A 21st Century Paradigm for Jewish Education.* Jerusalem: Center for Peoplehood Education, 2012.

Grugel, Jean, and Henry Kippin. "The Cuban Diaspora." In *Diasporas in Conflict: Peace-Makers or Peace Wreckers?,* edited by Hazel Smith and Paul Stares, 153–171. Tokyo: United Nations University Press, 2007.

Guttman, Nathan. "ADL and AJC Suffer Big Drop in Donations." *The Forward,* December 9, 2011.

———. "Hadassah Cuts Staff, Closes Offices, Spins Off Young Judea to Plug Madoff Hole." *The Forward,* July 8, 2011.

———. "JCCs Are the New Front Line in the Culture War on Israel." *The Forward,* March 23, 2011.

———. "Peace Groups Lose First Major Gaza Challenge on Capitol Hill." *The Forward,* January 16, 2009.

Habib, Jasmin. *Israel, Diaspora and the Routes of National Belonging.* Toronto: University of Toronto Press, 2004.

Hall, Holly. "Charitable Donations Barely Grew Last Year, 'Giving USA' Finds." *Chronicle of Higher Education,* June 19, 2012.

Halpern, Ben, and Jehuda Reinharz. *Zionism and the Creation of a New Society.* Waltham, MA: Brandeis University Press, 2000.

Hertzberg, Arthur, ed. *The Zionist Idea*. New York: Jewish Publications Society, 1997.

Hrywna, Mark. "United Way Drives to Diversify Income." *NonProfit Times*, October 15, 2011.

"Israel Museum Inaugurates Its Renewed Campus and Reinstalled Collection Wings." Press release, Israel Museum, Jerusalem, July 26, 2010.

Jewish Agency for Israel. *Securing the Future: The Jewish Agency's New Strategic Directions*. Jerusalem: Jewish Agency for Israel, 2010.

Jordan, Michael J. "U.S. Jews Launch Offensive over Mount." *Jerusalem Post*, December 28, 2000.

Kampeas, Ron. "Defending Israel, Mainstream U.S. Groups Critique It." *Jewish Telegraphic Agency*, January 11, 2011.

———. "In Major Policy Shift, AIPAC Offers Strong Backing for Withdrawal Plan." *Jewish Telegraphic Agency*, May 24, 2005.

Kapur, Davesh. *Diaspora, Development and Democracy: The Domestic Impact of International Migration from India*. Princeton, NJ: Princeton University Press, 2010.

Katz, Mandy. "The Man on J Street: The Story of Jeremy Ben Ami." *Moment Magazine*, March/April 2010.

Kelman, Ari Y. "The Reality of the Virtual: Looking for Jewish Leadership Online." In *The New Jewish Leaders*, edited by Jack Wertheimer, 214–60, Lebanon, NH: Brandeis University Press, 2011.

Kelner, Shaul. *Tours That Bind: Diaspora, Pilgrimage and Israeli Birthright Tourism*. New York: New York University Press, 2010.

Kimmerling, Baruch. *The Invention and Decline of Israeliness*. Berkeley: University of California Press, 2001.

Kopelowitz, Ezra, Minna Wolf, and Stephen Markowitz. *High School Israel Experience Programs: A Policy-Oriented Analysis of the Field*. Jerusalem: Makom/JAFI, 2009.

Koren, Annette, and Janet Krasner Aronson. "Israel in the Curriculum of Higher Education: Growth, Placement, and Future Prospects." Unpublished manuscript on file with the author, 2012.

Lampert, Ben. "Diaspora and Development? Nigerian Organizations in London and the Transnational Politics of Belonging." *Global Networks* 9, no. 2 (2009): 162–84.

Lampert, Simi. "Young Jews More Interested in Israel." *The Forward*, July 9, 2012.

Landau, David. "Judaism and the Jews." *The Economist*, July 27, 2012.

Landau, Jacob M. "Diaspora Nationalism: The Turkish Case." In *The Call of the Homeland: Diaspora Nationalisms, Past and Present*, edited by Allon Gal, Athena S. Leoussi, and Anthony D. Smith, 219-40. Leiden, Netherlands: Brill, 2010.

Landler, Mark. "U.S. Backers of Israel Pressure Obama over Policy on Iran." *New York Times*, March 3, 2012.

Levey, Gregory. "The Right Wing's Jerusalem Gambit." *Salon*, December 13, 2007.

Levinson, Chaim. "Settlements Have Cost Israel $17 Billion, Study Finds." *Haaretz*, March 23, 2010.

Levinson, Chaim, Uri Blau, and Mordechai I. Twersky. "Nefesh B'nefesh an Ineffective Monopoly with Overpaid Executives, Say Critics." *Haaretz*, October 20, 2012.

Levitt, Peggy. *Transnational Villagers*. Berkeley: University of California Press, 2001.

Lichtblau, Eric, and Mark Landler. "Hawks Steering Debate on How to Take on Iran." *New York Times*, March 19, 2012.

Liebler, Isi. "Candidly Speaking: Marginalize the Renegades." *Jerusalem Post*, October 5, 2009.

Liebman, Charles S. "The Religious Life of American Jewry." In *Understanding American Jewry*, edited by Marshall Sklare, 96–124. New Brunswick, NJ: Transaction, 1982.

Liebman, Charles S., and Steven M. Cohen. *Two Worlds of Judaism*. New Haven, CT: Yale University Press, 1990.

Luntz, Frank. *Israel and American Jews in the Age of Eminem*. New York: Andrea and Charles Bronfman Philanthropies, 2003.

Maltz, Judy. "To Masada or Not to Masada, That Is the Question." *Haaretz*, January 5, 2013.

Mandel, Morton. *It's All About Who*. San Francisco: Jossey-Bass, 2013.

Mearsheimer, John, and Stephen Walt. "The Israel Lobby," *London Review of Books* 28, no. 6 (2006).

Metz, Helen Chapin, ed. *Israel: A Country Study*. Washington, DC: Government Printing Office for the Library of Congress, 1988.

Mittelberg, David. *The Israel Connection and American Jews*. London: Praeger, 1999.

———. "Jewish Peoplehood Education." In *The International Handbook of Jewish Education*, edited by Helena Miller, Lisa D. Grant, and Alex Pomson, 515–40. Amsterdam: Springer, 2011.

Mozgovaya, Natasha. "ADL Bid for U.S. Bipartisan Support for Israel Faces Staunch Resistance." *Haaretz*, October 25, 2011.

———. "U.S. Congress Urges Obama to Impose 'Crippling Sanctions' on Iran." *Haaretz*, April 4, 2010.

Nathan-Kazis, Josh. "Critics Counter J Street at U Penn Hillel." *The Forward*, February 10, 2010.

———. "JNF Challenged on Discrimination." *The Forward*, April 20, 2011.

Newland, Kathleen. *Voice after Exit: Diaspora Advocacy*. Washington, DC: Migration Policy Institute, 2010.

Newland, Kathleen, and Hiroyuki Tanaka. *Mobilizing Diaspora: Entrepreneurship for Development*. Washington, DC: Migration Policy Institute, 2010.

Nielsen, Tjai M., and Liesl Riddle. "Why Diasporas Invest in the Homeland: A Conceptual Model of Motivation." Working paper series, George Washington University, 2007.

Nir, Ori. "Israel Targets U.S. Foes of Gaza Plan." *The Forward*, July 15, 2005.

———. "Orthodox Group Ups Criticism of Israel." *The Forward*, September 9, 2005.

———. "Pressing Peace in Era of GOP." *The Forward*, June 3, 2005.

"OTZMA to Close." *eJewish Philanthropy*, November 1, 2012.

Payaslian, Simon. "Imagining Armenia." In *The Call of the Homeland: Diaspora Nationalisms, Past and Present*, edited by Allon Gal, Athena S. Leoussi, and Anthony D. Smith, 105–38. Leiden, Netherlands: Brill, 2010.

Perlmann, Joel. "American Jewish Opinion about the Future of the West Bank." Working Paper 526, Levy Economics Institute of Bard College, Annandale-on-Hudson, NY, 2007.

"Peter Beinart and Boston Federation Head Spar over Birthright." *The Jewish Week*, April 5, 2012.

Plant, Morton B. *ONAD Review Report*. New York: Jewish Federations of North America, 2005.

"Poll: 54% of Israelis Would Have Favored Continuing Gaza Operation." Press release, Zionist Organization of America, 2009.

Prashker, Mike. "Teaming Up for Equality in Israel." *The Forward*, December 5, 2008.

Raphael, Marc Lee. *A History of the United Jewish Appeal 1939–1982*. Providence, RI: Scholars Press, 1982.

Rawidowicz, Simon. *State of Israel, Diaspora, and Jewish Continuity: Essays on the "Ever-Dying People."* Edited by Benjamin C. I. Ravid. Waltham, MA: Brandeis University Press/University Press of New England, 1988.

Roberts, Helen. "American Jewish Donations to Israel." *Contemporary Jewry* 20 (1999): 201–13.

Rosen, Mark I. *Mission, Meaning and Money*. Waltham, MA: Brandeis University Press, 2010.

Rosenthal, Steven T. *Irreconcilable Differences*. Hanover, NH: Brandeis University Press/University Press of New England, 2001.

Rosner, Shmuel, and Inbal Hakman. *The Challenge of Peoplehood: Strengthening the Attachment of Young American Jews to Israel in the Time of the Distancing Discourse*. Jerusalem: Jewish People Policy Institute, 2012.

Rudoren, Jodi. "Israel to Review Curbs on Women's Prayer at Western Wall." *New York Times*, December 25, 2012.

Ruskay, John. "Combating Deligitimization Requires a Big Tent." *The Jewish Week*, February 15, 2011.

Rutenberg, Jim, Mike McIntire, and Ethan Bronner. "Tax-Exempt Funds Aid Settlements in West Bank." *New York Times*, July 5, 2010.

Rynhold, Jonathan. "Israel's Foreign and Defense Policy and Diaspora Jewish Identity." In *Israel, the Diaspora and Jewish Identity*, edited by Danny Ben-Moshe and Zohar Segev, 144–57. Brighton, UK: Sussex Academic Press, 2007.

Saad, Lydia. "Support for Israel in U.S. at 63%, Near Record High." *Gallup News Service*, February 24, 2010. http://www.gallup.com/poll/126155/support-israel-near-record-high.aspx.

Safran, William. "Jewish Diaspora in Comparative and Theoretical Perspective." *Israel Studies* 10 (2005): 36–60.

Sasson, Theodore. "The impact of Taglit-Birthright Israel on the Political Attitudes of Trip Participants." Unpublished paper presented at Taglit-Birthright Israel: An Academic Symposium. Hebrew University, Jerusalem, 2013.

———. *The New Realism: American Jewish Views about Israel*. New York: American Jewish Committee, 2009.

Sasson, Theodore, Charles Kadushin, and Leonard Saxe. "Trends in American Jewish Attachment to Israel: An Assessment of the 'Distancing' Hypothesis." *Contemporary Jewry* 30, nos. 2–3 (2010): 297–319.

Sasson, Theodore, and Shaul Kelner. "From Shrine to Forum: Masada and the Politics of Jewish Extremism." *Israel Studies* 13, no. 12 (2008): 146–63.

Sasson, Theodore, David Mittelberg, Shahar Hecht, and Leonard Saxe. *Encountering the Other, Finding Oneself: The Birthright Israel Mifgash.* Waltham, MA: Cohen Center for Modern Jewish Studies, Brandeis University, 2008.

———. "Guest-Host Encounters in Diaspora-Heritage Tourism: The Taglit-Birthright Israel Mifgash (Encounter)." *Diaspora, Indigenous, and Minority Education* 5, no. 3 (2011): 178–97.

Sasson, Theodore, Benjamin Phillips, Charles Kadushin, and Leonard Saxe. *Still Connected: American Jewish Attitudes about Israel.* Waltham, MA: Cohen Center for Modern Jewish Studies, Brandeis University, 2010.

Sasson, Theodore, Benjamin Phillips, Graham Wright, Charles Kadushin, and Leonard Saxe. "Understanding Young Adult Attachment to Israel: Period, Lifecycle, and Generational Dynamics." *Contemporary Jewry* 32, no. 1 (2012): 67–84.

Sasson, Theodore, and Leonard Saxe. "Wrong Numbers." *Tablet Magazine*, May 38, 2010.

Sasson, Theodore, and Ephraim Tabory. "Converging Political Cultures: How Globalization Is Shaping the Discourses of American and Israeli Jews." *Nationalism and Ethnic Politics* 16, no. 1 (2010): 22–41.

Saxe, Leonard, and Barry Chazan. *Ten Days of Birthright Israel: A Journey in Young Adult Identity.* Lebanon, NH: Brandeis University Press/University Press of New England, 2008.

Saxe, Leonard, Charles Kadushin, Shahar Hecht, Mark I. Rosen, Benjamin Phillips, and Shaul Kelner. *Evaluating Birthright Israel: Long-Term Impact and Recent Findings.* Waltham, MA: Cohen Center for Modern Jewish Studies, Brandeis University, 2004.

Saxe, Leonard, Benjamin Phillips, Matthew Boxer, Shahar Hecht, Graham Wright, and Theodore Sasson. *Taglit-Birthright Israel: Evaluation of the 2007–2008 North American Cohorts.* Waltham, MA: Cohen Center for Modern Jewish Studies, Brandeis University, 2008.

Saxe, Leonard, Benjamin Phillips, Theodore Sasson, Shahar Hecht, Michelle Shain, Graham Wright, and Charles Kadushin. *Generation Birthright Israel: The Impact of an Israel Experience on Jewish Identity and Choices.* Waltham, MA: Cohen Center for Modern Jewish Studies, Brandeis University, 2009.

Saxe, Leonard, Theodore Sasson, and Shahar Hecht. *Israel at War: The Impact of Peer-Oriented Israel Programs on Responses of American Young Adults.* Waltham, MA: Steinhardt Social Research Institute, Brandeis University, 2006.

Saxe, Leonard, Theodore Sasson, Shahar Hecht, Benjamin Phillips, Michelle Shain, and Charles Kadushin. *Jewish Futures Project: The Impact of Taglit-Birthright Israel, 2010 Update.* Waltham, MA: Cohen Center for Modern Jewish Studies, Brandeis University, 2011.

Saxe, Leonard, Michelle Shain, Shahar Hecht, Graham Wright, and Shira Fishman. *Jewish Futures Study: 2012 Update*. Waltham, MA: Cohen Center for Modern Jewish Studies, Brandeis University, 2012.

Schworm, Peter. "Brandeis Groups Clash on Israel Stance." *Boston Globe*, March 11, 2011.

"Second Thoughts about the Promised Land." *The Economist*, January 11, 2007.

Selig, Abe. "New Israel Fund Comes Out Swinging Against Im Tirtzu Report." *Jerusalem Post*, February 2, 2010.

Seliktar, Ofira. "The Changing Identity of American Jews." In *Israel, the Diaspora and Jewish Identity*, edited by Danny Ben-Moshe and Zohar Segev, 124–37. Brighton, UK: Sussex Academic Press, 2007.

———. *Divided We Stand: America Jews, Israel, and the Peace Process*. Westport, CT: Praeger, 2002.

Senor, Dan, and Saul Singer. *Start-Up Nation: The Story of Israel's Economic Miracle*. New York: Twelve, 2009.

Shain, Yossi. *Kinship and Diasporas in International Affairs*. Ann Arbor: University of Michigan Press, 2007.

———. *Marketing the American Creed Abroad: Diasporas in the U.S. and Their Homelands*. New York: Cambridge University Press, 1999.

Shain, Yossi, and Aharon Barth. "Diasporas and International Relations Theory." *International Organizations* 57, no. 3 (2012): 449–79.

Shain, Yossi, and Neil Rogachevsky. "Between Jdate and J Street: U.S. Foreign Policy and the Liberal Jewish Dilemma in America." *Israel Journal of Foreign Affairs* 3 (2011): 37–48.

Shamir, Shlomo. "Reform Head: U.S. Jews Must Not Oppose Compromise on Jerusalem." *Haaretz*, December 23, 2007.

Shapiro, Faydra. *Building Jewish Roots: The Israel Experience*. Montreal: McGill-Queens University Press, 2006.

Sheffer, Gabriel. *Diaspora Politics: At Home Abroad*. New York: Cambridge University Press, 2003.

———. "Loyalty and Criticism in the Relations between World Jewry and Israel." *Israel Studies* 17, no. 2 (Summer 2012): 111–19.

———. "Transnationalism and Ethno-National Diasporism." *Diasporas* 15, no. 1 (2006): 121–45.

Siegel, Jennifer. "Pullout Critics in U.S. Draw Few Backers." *The Forward*, August 19, 2005.

Siegel-Itzkovich, Judy. "AFMDA Kindness Is in the Blood." *Jerusalem Post*, November 27, 2010.

Steger, Manfred. *Globalization: A Very Short Introduction*. New York: Oxford University Press, 2009.

Steinberg, Gerald M. "The Politics of NGOs, Human Rights and the Arab-Israel Conflict." *Israel Studies* 16 (2011): 24–54.

Stern, Sol. "Menachem Begin vs. the Jewish Lobby." *New York Magazine*, April 24, 1978.

Tamopolsky, Noga. "Adelson's Other Pet Project: The Israeli Right." *Salon*, February 9, 2012.

Taub, James. "The New Israel Lobby." *New York Times*, September 13, 2009.

Tighe, Elizabeth, Leonard Saxe, Charles Kadushin, Raquel Magidin de Kramer, Begli Nursahedov, Janet Aronson, and Lynn Cherny. *Estimating the Jewish Population of the United States: 2000–2010*. Waltham, MA: Steinhardt Social Research Institute, Brandeis University, 2011.

Tivnan, Edward. *The Lobby: Jewish Political Power and American Foreign Policy*. New York: Simon & Schuster, 1987.

Tölölyan, Khachig. "Beyond the Homeland: From Exilic Nationalism to Diasporic Transnationalism." In *The Call of the Homeland: Diaspora Nationalisms, Past and Present*, edited by Allan Gal, Athena S. Leoussi, and Anthony D. Smith, 27–45. Leiden, Netherlands: Brill, 2010.

Twersky, Mordechai. "Israeli Charity Executive Arrested on Suspicion of Embezzling Millions of Shekels from Donors." *Haaretz*, April 12, 2012.

Ukeles, Jack B., Ron Miller, and Pearl Beck. *Young Jewish Adults in the United States Today*. New York: American Jewish Committee, 2006.

Urofsky, Melvin I. *American Zionism from Herzl to the Holocaust*. Garden City, NY: Anchor Press, 1975.

———. *We Are One! American Jewry and Israel*. Garden City, NY: Anchor Press, 1978.

"U.S. Jewish Groups Slam Rabbis' Anti-Migrant Decrees." *Jewish Telegraphic Agency*, June 11, 2010.

"The War Within." *New York Times*, November 5, 2008.

Waxman, Chaim I. "American Jewish Philanthropy, Direct Giving, and the Unity of the Jewish Community." In *Toward a Renewed Ethic of Jewish Philanthropy*, edited by Yossi Prager, 53–78. New York: Yeshiva University Press, 2010.

———. *The Impact of Aliyah on the American Jewish Community*. Jersey City, NJ: Ktav, 1989.

Waxman, Dov. "The Israel Lobbies: A Survey of the Pro-Israel Community in the United States." *Israel Studies Forum* 25, no. 1 (March/April 2010): 5–28.

Wertheimer, Jack. "American Jews and Israel: A 60-Year Retrospective." In *American Jewish Yearbook 2008*, edited by David Singer and Lawrence Grossman, 3–79. New York: American Jewish Committee, 2008.

———. "Breaking the Taboo: Critics of Israel and the American Jewish Establishment." In *Envisioning Israel: The Changing Images and Ideals of North American Jews*, edited by Allon Gal, 397–419. Detroit, MI: Wayne State University Press, 1996.

———. "Current Trends in American Jewish Philanthropy." In *American Jewish Year Book*, edited by David Singer and Ruth R. Seldin, 3–92. New York: American Jewish Committee, 1997.

———, ed. *The New Jewish Leaders: Reshaping the American Jewish Landscape*. Lebanon, NH: Brandeis University Press, 2011.

Wexler, Robert. "Israel and the Identity of American Jews." In *Israel, Diaspora and Jewish Identity*, edited by Danny Ben-Moshe and Zohar Segev, 268–78. Brighton, UK: Sussex Academic Press, 2007.

Woocher, Jonathan. *Sacred Survival: The Civil Religion of American Jews*. Bloomington: Indiana University Press, 1986.

Yakobson, Alexander. "Jewish Peoplehood and the Jewish State, How Unique?—A Comparative Study." *Israel Studies* 13 (2008): 1–27.

Zerubavel, Yael. *Recovered Roots: Collective Memory and the Making of Israeli National Tradition.* Chicago: University of Chicago Press, 1997.

Zimmerman, Simone, Jeremy Elster, Isaiah Kirshner-Breen, and Alon Mazor. "J Street U Bounced by Berkeley Group." *The Forward*, December 16, 2011.

ABOUT THE AUTHOR

Theodore Sasson is Professor of International and Global Studies at Middlebury College and Senior Research Scientist at the Cohen Center for Modern Jewish Studies. He is also Visiting Research Professor of Sociology at Brandeis University and a consultant to the Mandel Foundation.